Regulatory Reform in China and the EU

NEW HORIZONS IN LAW AND ECONOMICS

Series Editors: Gerrit De Geest, *Washington University in St. Louis, USA*, Roger Van den Bergh, *Erasmus University Rotterdam, The Netherlands* and Thomas S. Ulen, *University of Illinois at Urbana-Champaign, USA*

The application of economic ideas and theories to the law and the explanation of markets and public economics from a legal point of view is recognized as one of the most exciting developments in both economics and the law. This important series is designed to make a significant contribution to the development of law and economics.

The main emphasis is on the development and application of new ideas. The series provides a forum for original research in areas such as criminal law, civil law, labour law, corporate law, family law, regulation and privatization, tax, risk and insurance and competition law. International in its approach it includes some of the best theoretical and empirical work from both well-established researchers and the new generation of scholars.

Titles in the series include:

Law, Economics and Cyberspace
The Effects of Cyberspace on the Economic Analysis of Law
Niva Elkin-Koren and Eli M. Salzberger

Games and Public Administration
The Law and Economics of Regulation and Licensing
Georg von Wangenheim

Law and the State
A Political Economy Approach
Edited by Alain Marciano and Jean-Michel Josselin

Democracy, Freedom and Coercion
A Law and Economics Approach
Edited by Alain Marciano and Jean-Michel Josselin

The Economics of Courts and Litigation
Francisco Cabrillo and Sean Fitzpatrick

Transport, Welfare and Externalities
Replacing the Polluter Pays Principle with the Cheapest Cost Avoider Principle
Dieter Schmidtchen, Christian Koboldt, Jenny Helstroffer, Birgit Will, Georg Haas and Stefan Witte

New Trends in Financing Civil Litigation in Europe
A Legal, Empirical, and Economic Analysis
Mark Tuil and Louis Visscher

Comparative Contract Law and Economics
Mitja Kovač

The Law and Economics of Class Actions in Europe
Lessons from America
Edited by Jürgen G. Backhaus, Alberto Cassone and Giovanni B. Ramello

Corporate Compliance
New Approaches to Regulatory Enforcement
Sharon Oded

Regulatory Reform in China and the EU
A Law and Economics Perspective
Edited by Stefan E. Weishaar, Niels Philipsen and Wenming Xu

Regulatory Reform in China and the EU

A Law and Economics Perspective

Edited by

Stefan E. Weishaar

Associate Professor of Law and Economics, Faculty of Law, University of Groningen, the Netherlands

Niels Philipsen

Professor of Shifts in Private and Public Regulation, Erasmus School of Law – RILE, Erasmus University Rotterdam and Vice-Director, METRO, Faculty of Law, Maastricht University, the Netherlands

Wenming Xu

Assistant Professor, School of Law and Economics, China University of Political Science and Law, China

NEW HORIZONS IN LAW AND ECONOMICS

Edward Elgar PUBLISHING

Cheltenham, UK • Northampton, MA, USA

Published by
Edward Elgar Publishing Limited
The Lypiatts
15 Lansdown Road
Cheltenham
Glos GL50 2JA
UK

Edward Elgar Publishing, Inc.
William Pratt House
9 Dewey Court
Northampton
Massachusetts 01060
USA

A catalogue record for this book
is available from the British Library

Library of Congress Control Number: 2017936567

This book is available electronically in the **Elgar**online
Law subject collection
DOI 10.4337/9781785368547

MIX
Paper from
responsible sources
FSC® C013056

ISBN 978 1 78536 853 0 (cased)
ISBN 978 1 78536 854 7 (eBook)

Typeset by Servis Filmsetting Ltd, Stockport, Cheshire

Printed and bound in Great Britain by TJ International Ltd, Padstow, Cornwall

Contents

Contributors

Ruohong Chen, Associate Professor of Law, Beijing Foreign Studies University, China.

Yang Chen, Master candidate at the School of Law and Economics, China University of Political Science and Law.

Jiajia Dai, Lecturer at the School of Foreign Languages, China University of Political Science and Law.

Michael G. Faure, Professor of Comparative and International Environmental Law at Maastricht University and Professor of Comparative Private Law and Economics at Erasmus University Rotterdam, the Netherlands.

Shiting Feng, Ph.D. candidate at the School of Law and Economics, China University of Political Science and Law.

Binwei Gui, Associate Professor at the School of Law and Economics, China University of Political Science and Law.

Jiye Hu, Professor at the School of Law and Economics, China University of Political Science and Law.

Jonathan Klick, Professor of Law, University of Pennsylvania, USA and Erasmus Chair of Empirical Legal Studies, Erasmus University Rotterdam, the Netherlands.

Wenjing Li (Ph.D. in Law, Bologna), Assistant Professor at the School of Law and Economics, China University of Political Science and Law.

Roy A. Partain, Reader of Law and Director of Post-Graduate Research, School of Law, University of Aberdeen, Scotland.

Niels Philipsen, Professor of Shifts in Private and Public Regulation, Erasmus School of Law (Rotterdam, the Netherlands), Vice-Director of research institute METRO, Maastricht University (Maastricht, the Netherlands) and Adjunct Professor of the School of Law and Economics at CUPL (Beijing, China).

Stefan E. Weishaar, Associate Professor of Law and Economics,

University of Groningen (the Netherlands) and Research Affiliate at the Center for Energy and Environmental Policy Research at the Massachusetts Institute of Technology (MIT CEEPR), USA.

Tao Xi, Professor and the Dean of the School of Law and Economics, China University of Political Science and Law.

Guangdong Xu, Associate Professor at the School of Law and Economics, China University of Political Science and Law.

Wenming Xu, Assistant Professor at the School of Law and Economics, China University of Political Science and Law.

Qi Zhou, Associate Professor of Law, School of Law, University of Leeds, United Kingdom.

Tianshu Zhou (Ph.D. in Law, Edinburgh), Associate Professor at the School of Law and Economics, China University of Political Science and Law.

1. Introduction

Wenming Xu, Stefan E. Weishaar and Niels Philipsen

1. REGULATORY REFORM IN CHINA AND THE EU

China has achieved spectacular economic achievements since the 1990s with a GDP growth rate of around 10 per cent per year on average. It has rapidly changed from an agricultural to an industrialized country. A strategy of incremental reform has been adopted, rather than the 'shock therapy' applied by former Eastern European socialist economies. To stimulate incentives for regional executives, China has enforced a 'regionally decentralized authoritarian regime', which combines the political centralization of political appointment and promotion structures, and economic decentralization, whereby regional governments are deeply involved in economic development within their own jurisdiction.[1]

Consequently, both central and regional governments have maintained significant influence during the development and reform process. Public fixed investments and exports have always been two important engines leading economic growth at the expense of domestic consumption. To fuel the economic success, factor prices of, for example, land, labour and capital have been (and still are) distorted and repressed.[2] In some cases, inefficient state-owned enterprises have enjoyed the low-cost inputs and resources that could have been channelled to more efficient private firms. According to many commentators, this model is unsustainable.[3]

This volume proposes to analyse Chinese regulation from a comparative (mainly EU) and law and economics ('regulatory state' and economics of regulation) perspective to set out a reform agenda in selected legal areas including financial, administrative and environmental law and regulation

[1] Xu (2011), 1078. In the literature this is also referred to as 'governance structures'.

[2] Xu (2014), 141–68.

[3] Cull and Xu (2003).

of contracts. This is particularly important considering that the Chinese government recently launched a national project to comprehensively deepen its regulatory reform that only sets out general principles.[4] Many details of the reform plan need to be fleshed out, and the EU and US experience is likely to contribute to this process.

We will continue this introductory chapter by first providing a short overview of the relevant economic literature on the regulatory state and economics of regulation (section 2). After that, we will introduce the structure of the book (section 3), its origins (section 4) and contributors (section 5).

2. A LAW AND ECONOMICS PERSPECTIVE

This section provides a brief introduction to the literature on the regulatory state and economics of regulation and is not meant to be all-encompassing.[5] It is the object and purpose of this section to present the relevant conceptual framework that is employed in later chapters of this book.

The concept of the 'regulatory state' is used inter alia by Shleifer, who notes that different governance models can be chosen and ranked according to the degree of public involvement in the governance structures for attaining a multitude of objectives including the minimization of social harm from market activities.[6] Such models include 'laissez-faire' government, regulatory interventions by the state (the 'regulatory state') and (complete) state ownership. The laissez-faire government does very little besides offering an essential legal framework, and relies largely on private enforcement action (litigation) to solve conflicts. The regulatory state is characterized by independent regulatory agencies overseeing specific areas of the economy, ex ante designing of regulatory rules, and ex post public enforcement by public agencies and private enforcement via litigation. Not surprisingly, the concept of complete state ownership is characterized by full state control of industries.

---

[4] See Decision of the Central Committee of the Communist Party of China on Some Major Issues Concerning Comprehensively Deepening the Reform (Zhonggong Zhongyang Guanyu Quanmian Shenhua Gaige Ruogan Zhongda Wenti de Jueding, adopted at the Third Plenary Session of the 18th Central Committee of the Communist Party of China, 12 November 2013) (PRC).

[5] See Deller and Vantaggiato (2015) for a comprehensive survey of the legal and economic literature. It should be noticed that there is also an extensive political science literature on the regulatory state: see Majone (1994).

[6] Schleifer (2005).

Each of these governance models has its own comparative advantages in controlling society; the specific conditions in a given country are crucial determinants of the optimal strategies for social control of business.[7] For example, in a country with a highly efficient court system, the laissez-faire model, relying solely on private litigation, would generate the most efficient outcome.[8] However, both the American and European societies today are more regulated than before.[9] From an efficiency perspective, there are three potential justifications for the increasing reliance on regulations. First, regulators are specialized; second, regulators as central representatives could overcome free-rider problems; third, the ex ante regulatory rules could reduce the costs of identification of violations.[10]

These notions of the role of the regulatory state by Shleifer and his many co-authors are in line with the so-called 'public interest' theory of regulation. This theory puts forward market failure as the only (potential) justification for regulatory intervention when the goal of the legislator is to maximize efficiency.[11] Information asymmetry, market power, externalities and free-rider problems are the main causes of market failure that are discussed in the law and economics literature.[12] The term 'regulatory state' has also been used by others, including Susan Rose-Ackerman. In her book *Rethinking the Progressive Agenda* (1992), she discusses the possibilities of a progressive public agenda that combines active government and market competition.

However, the regulatory capture theories warn that government regulations run the risk of being sought by private interest groups in order to increase their own benefits.[13] The starting point of these theories, which are based on empirical findings from the United States, is that there is a market (supply and demand) for regulation, just as for other types of goods and services. Politicians, maximizing their own utility in terms of number of votes, size of bureaucracy or power, for example, may be tempted to respond to requests for regulatory favours from special interest

---

[7] Djankov et al. (2003).

[8] Glaeser and Shleifer (2003).

[9] Shleifer (2005). A growing literature also identifies China as a regulatory state: see Du et al. (2009).

[10] Glaeser and Shleifer (2003).

[11] Of course, public interest theory recognizes that there are many other policy goals besides efficiency, such as income distribution, fairness, non-discrimination, preventing climate change, and so on. On the discussion of different policy goals, see the chapter by Philipsen in this volume.

[12] For a more elaborate discussion see e.g. Ogus (1994), Philipsen (2009) and Cooter and Ulen (2012), 38–42.

[13] See Stigler (1971), Posner (1974), Peltzman (1976), Becker (1983).

groups that do not (necessarily) correspond to the public interest. Whether such interest groups are successful, according to Olson, will depend on both the transaction costs of organizing as an interest group and on information asymmetries between the 'insiders' and the public at large.[14] In the law and economics literature, this view on regulation has also been termed the 'private interest' approach to regulation.[15] There is obviously a strong overlap with the 'public choice' literature, in which topics such as corruption, voting behaviour and political decision-making are discussed by the likes of Buchanan, Tullock, Mueller and others.[16]

Sunstein argues that a centralized review of agency rule-making is necessary to minimize the adverse effect of rent-seeking behaviour.[17] It can be seen that cost–benefit analysis (CBA) and regulatory impact assessments are among the most popular instruments governing the process of rule-making. They are employed to control and monitor subordinate public agencies because they reduce the asymmetry of information between the principals and these agencies.[18]

In addition to the process of rule-making, it is crucial for the regulatory state to also have an enforcement strategy that transfers 'black letter law' to de facto deterrence.[19] Both public and private enforcement strategies have their comparative advantages. Public enforcement relies on public agencies, which have limited resources for enforcing the law.[20] Civil servants generally lack appropriate incentives and tend to shirk their responsibilities, which may result in an undersupply of law enforcement. However, public enforcement benefits from economies of scale and could overcome the collective action problem ('rational apathy'), which can be a major problem in discouraging private enforcement.[21]

In contrast, private enforcement relies on private parties, which usually enforce the rules through civil litigations. The law and economics analysis of private enforcement of law dates back to at least Becker and Stigler

---

[14] Olson (1965).

[15] See again Ogus (1994), Philipsen (2009), and the sources quoted therein.

[16] For references, see e.g. Boehm (2007) and Philipsen (2009).

[17] Sunstein (1990).

[18] Posner (2001).

[19] The seminal paper of Becker (1968) argues that the expected cost of crimes, which is determined by the size of the sanction and the enforcement intensity (probability of detection), determines criminals' choices. Building on his work, scholars have pointed out that the enforcement intensity also depends on the probability of being prosecuted and convicted. See Faure et al. (2009).

[20] See the survey article by Polinsky and Shavell (2000) on the literature of public enforcement.

[21] On rational apathy, see Schäfer (2000). See also Faure and Philipsen (2014).

and Landes and Posner.[22] Even if private parties have sufficient incentives to bring suits, private enforcement could lead to inefficient outcomes if the private and social payoffs are not identical. When the net social benefits of law enforcement are greater than the net private benefits, dispersed affected parties face severe problems in bringing collective actions, whereas if net private benefits are greater than net social benefits, private parties tend to bring frivolous suits.[23]

3. OUTLINE OF THE BOOK

After this introduction, which discusses the analytical framework and the relevant law and economics literature, subsequent chapters present case studies from diverse regulatory experiences in the EU and China, and assess these from a regulatory state/economics of regulation perspective. The concluding chapter reflects on the lessons learnt in those chapters.

The book has three parts addressing financial markets, social and administrative regulation and the environment. Each of these parts consists of independent but related chapters. In the fourth and final part of this book, we provide conclusions, as well as an essay by Jonathan Klick on the empirical analysis of regulation, with a particular focus on field experiments in China.

Part 1 consists of four chapters on regulatory reform in financial markets. The first chapter is devoted to a discussion of the reform in the banking sector, which is the major source of financing for undertakings. The saving and borrowing rates in China are regulated and repressed in order to direct cheap credits to the state sector, but private enterprises have difficulty in obtaining loans from the banking system and are hence driven to the informal financing market. Tao Xi analyses the commercial banking system from the perspective of asymmetric information and proposes a new framework for reforming the Law of the People's Republic of China on Commercial Banks.

The remaining three chapters in Part 1 address stock markets. Regulators scrutinize firms applying for public equities offerings, closely control the number of newly listed firms and monitor their conduct. This process thus merits close examination. The market is underdeveloped and compromised by securities fraud, such as misrepresentation, insider trading

---

22 Becker and Stigler (1974); Landes and Posner (1975).

23 Shavell (1993) points out that private parties in possession of information about the identity of those culpable should enforce regulations privately.

and market manipulation. Such practices harm the interests of investors significantly and undermine their confidence. A recent reform mandated deregulation of the stock markets and an increase in the proportion of direct financing to reduce leverages by domestic firms. Jiye Hu and Yang Chen use international panel data to show the importance of institutional investors in maintaining the development and stability of stock markets across China and OECD countries. In addition, it is widely accepted that enforcement of securities laws is crucial if the confidence of investors is to be restored. Tianshu Zhou and Wenjing Li collect cases and carry out an investigation of the insider trading rules in the stock market. Finally, Jiajia Dai, Shiting Feng and Wenming Xu provide an empirical analysis of the weakness of the private enforcement regime by addressing securities litigation.

Part 2 of this book addresses social and administrative regulation and contains two chapters. Qi Zhou analyses the potential benefits from collaborations between contract lawyers and law and economic scholars, and provides insights into improving contract law. Niels Philipsen critically assesses the changing goals of EU state aid policy, from market integration and equity to efficiency and fiscal discipline in the EU, and discusses the possibility of also including this type of control on local government spending in China's Anti-Monopoly Law.

In Part 3, three chapters are devoted to the environmental problems in China. Because of an emphasis on economic growth, regulators in China have until recently to some extent overlooked the problem of environmental pollution. Industrial firms have been able to externalize many of their environmental costs and water, air and land pollution has increased dramatically. Michael Faure and Roy Partain discuss the regulatory strategies for reducing carbon dioxide emissions via offshore carbon capture and storage. Binwei Gui, Michael Faure and Guangdong Xu empirically estimate the environmental Kuznets curve, that is the relationship between environmental pollution and economic growth in China. Stefan Weishaar and Ruohong Chen discuss environmental standards as possible regulatory strategies for reduction of greenhouse gas emissions in China and the EU under World Trade Organization rules.

In Part 4 Jonathan Klick sets a law and economics research agenda by outlining the challenges of empirical analysis and by underlining the great potential of field experiments, particularly in China. A conclusion by the editors highlights the main contributions of this book.

4. ORIGINS OF THIS BOOK

This book originates from a long-standing cooperation between various Chinese and European institutions. The editors have worked together for a long time through collaboration between the School of Law and Economics (SLE) at the China University of Political Science and Law (CUPL) in Beijing, to which Wenming Xu is connected, the Maastricht European Institute for Transnational Legal Research (METRO), where Niels Philipsen is Vice-Director, and the Department of Law and Economics at the University of Groningen, to which Stefan Weishaar is affiliated. Both Niels Philipsen and Stefan Weishaar are teaching or have taught courses at the China–EU School of Law (CESL) at CUPL. Moreover, Niels Philipsen was recently appointed Adjunct Professor of the School of Law and Economics at CUPL.

5. CONTRIBUTORS

The contributors to this book are from various universities in China, Europe and the United States. Many of the Chinese contributors, including Binwei Gui, Jiye Hu, Wenjing Li, Guangdong Xu, Wenming Xu and Tianshu Zhou, are connected to the SLE of CUPL. Ruohong Chen is affiliated to the Beijing Foreign Studies University (Beiwai). Qi Zhou, one of the Chinese contributors, has resided abroad for many years. He is associated with the University of Leeds (UK).

The European contributors have either Belgian, Dutch and/or German nationalities and include Stefan Weishaar from the University of Groningen (the Netherlands) as well as Michael Faure and Niels Philipsen, who are both associated with Maastricht University and the Erasmus University Rotterdam (the Netherlands). Jonathan Klick is affiliated to the University of Pennsylvania (USA) and Erasmus University Rotterdam (the Netherlands). Roy Partain is affiliated to the University of Aberdeen (UK).

6. ACKNOWLEDGEMENTS

As editors, we are grateful to the many people who made this book possible. We are especially grateful to all the contributors for their willingness to participate in this highly interesting and challenging project and for meeting the deadlines that we imposed upon them.

We are thankful for the financial support received from the Program for

Young Innovative Research Team in China University of Political Science and Law (16CXTD09).

BIBLIOGRAPHY

Bagley, N. and Revesz, R. (2006), 'Centralized Oversight of the Regulatory State', *Columbia Law Review*, 106(6), 1260–329.

Becker, G. (1968), 'Crime and Punishment: An Economic Approach', *Journal of Political Economy*, 76(2), 169–217.

Becker, G.S. (1983), 'A Theory of Competition among Pressure Groups for Political Influence', *Quarterly Journal of Economics*, 98(3), 371–400.

Becker, G. and Stigler, G. (1974), 'Law Enforcement, Malfeasance, and Compensation of Enforcers', *The Journal of Legal Studies*, 3(1), 1–18.

Boehm, F. (2007), 'Regulatory Capture Revisited – Lessons from Economics of Corruption', Working Paper. Available online at: http://www.icgg.org/downloads/Boehm%20-%20Regulatory%20Capture%20Revisited.pdf. Accessed 23 June 2016.

Buchanan, J.M. and Tullock, G. (1962), *The Calculus of Consent: Logical Foundations of Constitutional Democracy*, Ann Arbor: University of Michigan Press.

Cooter, R. and Ulen, T. (2012), *Law and Economics*, sixth edition, Boston, MA: Pearson Education International.

Cull, R. and Xu, L. (2003), 'Who Gets Credit? The Behavior of Bureaucrats and State Banks in Allocating Credit to Chinese State-Owned Enterprises', *Journal of Development Economics*, 71(2), 533–59.

Deller, D. and Vantaggiato, F. (2015), 'Revisiting the Regulatory State: A Multidisciplinary Review Establishing a New Research Agenda', CCP Working Papers, No. 14-9, University of East Anglia, UK: Centre for Competition Policy. Available at: http://competitionpolicy.ac.uk/documents/8158338/8368036/CCP+Working+Paper+14-9.pdf/6de9dcd3-0b0f-4c1c-a311-cc472f384653. Accessed 1 March 2017.

Djankov, S., Glaeser, E., La Porta, R., Lopez-de-Silanes, F. and Shleifer, A. (2003), 'The New Comparative Economics', *Journal of Comparative Economics*, 31(4), 595–619.

Du, J., Lu, Y. and Tao, Z. (2009), 'China as a Regulatory State', BOFIT Discussion Papers, No. 17/2009, Hong Kong. Available at SSRN: http://ssrn.com/abstract=1489412 or http://dx.doi.org/10.2139/ssrn.1489412. Accessed 1 March 2017.

Faure, M.G., Ogus, A.I. and Philipsen, N.J. (2009), 'Curbing Consumer Financial Losses', *Law & Policy*, 31(2), 161–91.

Faure, M.G. and Philipsen, N.J. (eds) (2014), *Access to Justice in Environmental Matters: A Socio-Economic Analysis*, The Hague, Netherlands: Eleven International Publishing.

Glaeser, E. and Shleifer, A. (2003), 'The Rise of the Regulatory State', *Journal of Economic Literature*, 41(2), 401–25. doi: 10.2307/3216964.

Landes, W. and Posner, R. (1975), 'The Private Enforcement of Law', *The Journal of Legal Studies*, 4(1), 1–46.

Majone, G. (1994), 'The Rise of the Regulatory State in Europe', *West European Politics*, 17(3), 77–101.

Ogus, A.I. (1994), *Regulation: Legal Form and Economic Theory*, Oxford: Clarendon Press.
Olson, M. (1965), *The Logic of Collective Action: Public Goods and the Theory of Groups*, Cambridge, MA: Harvard University Press.
Peltzman, S. (1976), 'Toward a More General Theory of Regulation', *Journal of Law and Economics*, 211–40.
Philipsen, N.J. (2009), 'Regulation and Competition in the Legal Profession: Developments in the EU and China', *Journal of Competition Law and Economics*, 6(2), 203–31.
Pildes, R. and Sunstein, C. (1995), 'Reinventing the Regulatory State', *University of Chicago Law Review*, 62(1), 1–129.
Polinsky, A. and Shavell, S. (2000), 'The Economic Theory of Public Enforcement of Law', *Journal of Economic Literature*, 38(1), 45–76.
Posner, E. (2001), 'Controlling Agencies with Cost-Benefit Analysis: A Positive Political Theory Perspective', *University of Chicago Law Review*, 68(4), 1137–99.
Posner, R. (1974), 'Theories of Economic Regulation', *Bell Journal of Economics*, 5(2), 335–58.
Rose-Ackerman, S. (1992), *Rethinking the Progressive Agenda: The Reform of the American Regulatory State*, New York: The Free Press.
Schäfer, H.B. (2000), 'The Bundling of Similar Interest in Litigation. The Incentives for Class Action and Legal Actions taken by Associations', *European Journal of Law and Economics*, 3, 183–213.
Shavell, S. (1993), 'The Optimal Structure of Law Enforcement', *Journal of Law and Economics*, 36(1), 255–87.
Shleifer, A. (2005), 'Understanding Regulation', *European Financial Management*, 11(4), 439–51.
Stigler, G. (1971), 'The Theory of Economic Regulation', *The Bell Journal of Economics*, 2(1), 3–21.
Sunstein, C. (1990), 'Paradoxes of the Regulatory State', *University of Chicago Law Review*, 57(2), 407–41.
Xu, C. (2011), 'The Fundamental Institutions of China's Reforms and Development', *Journal of Economic Literature*, 49(4), 1076–151.
Xu, G. (2014), *Does Law Matter for Economic Growth? A Re-Examination of the Legal Origin Hypothesis*, European Studies in Law and Economics No. 14, Antwerp–Groningen: Intersentia.

PART I

Financial markets

2. Money, banks, and the commercial banking law: a framework for law and economics analysis

Tao Xi*

1. INTRODUCTION

China has been relying heavily on the indirect financing provided by its banking sector to satisfy the needs of domestic firms.[1] By the end of 2011 total bank assets accounted for 189 per cent of GDP.[2] Around 70 per cent of these assets are owned by the State and hence the interests of incumbent banks are extensively protected,[3] which according to previous studies could obstruct financial development.[4] The high level of government ownership brings with it both costs and benefits. On the one hand, it results in significant costs in terms of a high level of non-performing loans due to governmental intervention in business practices; on the other, the implicit governmental insurance helps to prevent major bank failures during a financial crisis.[5] Recently, the central government launched a reform plan to liberalize its banking sector, which calls for a more efficient regulatory system to control the risks of the domestic banking market.[6]

However, the commercial banking law – in the form of the Law of the People's Republic of China on Commercial Banks of 2015 (henceforth

* This chapter is sponsored by the Beijing Municipal Key Interdisciplinary Project 'Law and Economics'.

1 Allen et al. (2005).

2 Barth et al. (2013).

3 Prasad and Rajan (2006).

4 La Porta et al. (2002).

5 Allen et al. (2012).

6 See Zhonggong Zhongyang Guanyu Quanmian Shenhua Gaige Ruogan Zhongda Wenti de Jueding, adopted at the Third Plenary Session of the 18th Central Committee of the Communist Party of China, 12 November 2013 (PRC).

Law of Commercial Banks)[7] – has lagged behind the development of the domestic banking sector, which has become more complex and interconnected. Commercial banks are credit intermediaries and engage in various activities including absorbing deposits, aggregating funds, extending loans, and engaging in indirect financing methods. The banks consequently form a debtor–creditor relationship with depositors and borrowers. But commercial banks in China have gradually launched comprehensive management services, including bank financing, bank asset securitization, bank derivatives, and so on, which tend to blur the traditional debtor–creditor relationship.

The banks' legal relationships have become complicated and confusing. These new banking products have resulted in the formation of buy–sell contractual relationships between banks and individual customers, fund companies, trust companies, and securities companies. The coexistence of indirect and direct financing services provided by Chinese banks is a recent developing trend. Because of the complexity of banking products and the diversification of transactions, banks experience a variety of hidden risks. This chapter reviews the theoretical explanations of how banking risks occur and analyses how they can be prevented by laws and regulations that ensure the security and efficiency of banking operations.

We employ the concepts of information asymmetry, adverse selection, and moral hazard to construct an analytical law and economics framework for the Law of Commercial Banks and related regulations, which is illustrated in Figure 2.1. This framework explores important systems in the commercial banking law, such as bank access, business scope, banks and borrowers, banks and comprehensive management companies, deposit insurance, and others. It also defines the various legal relationships and legal properties of bank credit services, bank service fees, and bank asset management services, which facilitate establishing the rules of conduct for market players among banks and individuals, enterprises, fund companies, securities companies, trust companies, and insurance companies, and which guard against the occurrence and spread of market risks, credit risks, and liquidity risks. The economic and social conditions that restrict amendment of the Law of Commercial Banks are empirically analysed. Finally, we propose a number of recommendations to improve the commercial banking law in order to ensure banking security and efficiency.

This chapter is arranged as follows. Section 2 reviews the theoretical

---

[7] See Zhonghua Renmin Gongheguo Shangye Yinhangfa, available at http://www.pkulaw.cn/fulltext_form.aspx?Db=chl&Gid=256594&keyword=%E5%95%86%E4%B8%9A%E9%93%B6%E8%A1%8C%E6%B3%95&EncodingName=&Search_Mode=accurate.

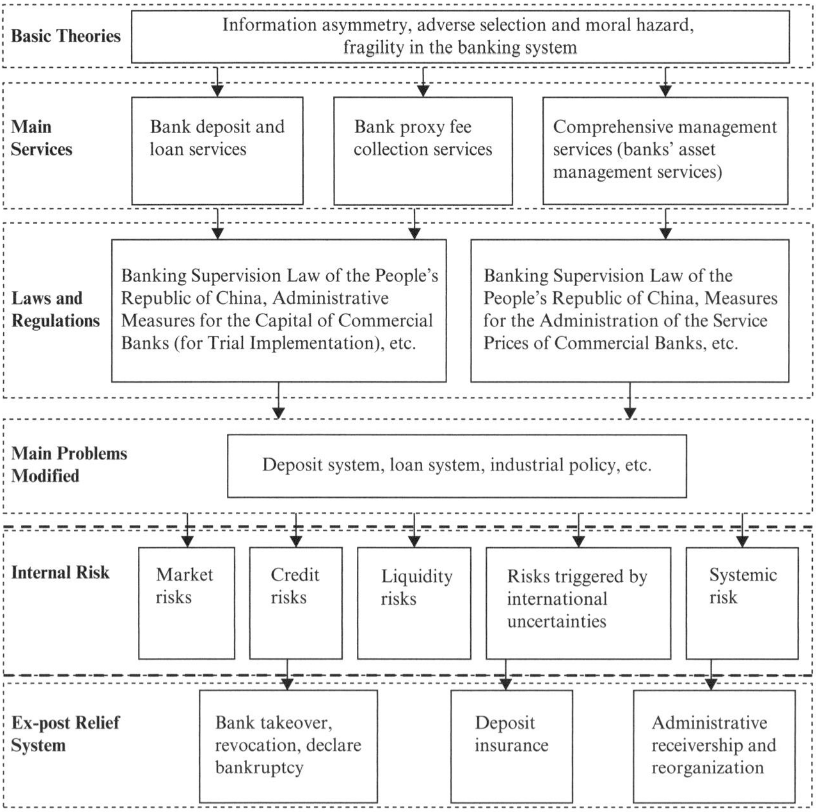

Figure 2.1 Analytical Framework for the Commercial Banking Law

literature on banking risks and practices for coping with financial risks in the United States. Section 3 analyses comprehensive management issues in the Law of Commercial Banks. Section 4 addresses the issues in the commercial banking law that are relevant to banks and their borrowers. Section 5 analyses the deposit insurance system in the commercial banking law. Section 6 concludes.

2. THE RISKS IN THE BANKING SECTOR: A BRIEF REVIEW OF THE LITERATURE

There are three major theories explaining commercial banking risks. The first relates to adverse selection and moral hazard problems in banking.

Joseph E. Stiglitz and Andrew Weiss used an information asymmetry approach to analyse and interpret the risks generated by commercial bank credits.[8] The credit market generates adverse selection problems before corporate borrowing takes place and moral hazard problems after corporate borrowing takes place. Commercial banks cannot obtain private information such as the probability of repayment by financiers and expected returns prior to lending; accordingly, they determine the corporate interest rate based only on the average rate of repayment of all financing firms.[9]

The second theory is a bank-run model. Diamond and Dybvig's classic 1983 paper[10] establishes a formal model that identifies the conditions in which banks operate normally and the conditions in which bank runs occur. Fragility in the banking system is primarily caused by uncertain depositor demand for liquidity and the lack of liquidity in bank assets compared with bank liabilities, which is attributable to information asymmetry among the banks, depositors, and borrowers. Governments have established deposit insurance systems to address the issues of bank runs and banking panics.[11]

The third theory relates to banks' fragility. Minsky adopts an economic cycle perspective to analyse the relationships between commercial banks and different categories of loan firms such as hedge-financed firms and speculation-financed firms. During economic booms, the firms' expected returns increase and borrowing expands. Among borrowers, the proportion of high-risk speculative firms and Ponzi firms quickly increases, but the proportion of hedge-financed firms decreases. When the economy becomes sluggish, the high-risk speculative firms and the Ponzi firms find it difficult to make repayments, which may cause credit default, and banking fragility becomes increasingly serious.[12]

With banking fragility, sudden events – such as bank runs – can lead to a financial crisis. Only the legislative system can guard against such financial risks. The experiences, lessons, and practices of the United States can be used as a reference. In the period 1929–1932 that country's financial crisis also caused an economic crisis. In 1933 the US Congress promulgated the Banking Act of 1933 (commonly referred to as the Glass–Steagall Act). This Act established a financial system in which banking, securities, and insurance services were operated and supervised separately. Over the next

---

8 Stiglitz and Weiss (1981).
9 See Stiglitz and Weiss (1981).
10 See Diamond and Dybvig (1983).
11 See Chang and Ren (2004).
12 See Minsky (1992).

66 years of economic development and financial innovation, the United States gradually expanded financial innovation through ceaseless abolishment, amendment, and passage of laws until the US Congress promulgated the Gramm–Leach–Bliley Act of 1999 (Public Law 106-102).[13] This Act repealed the separate operation system established in the Glass–Steagall Act and established a comprehensive management system for financial holding companies in which a financial holding company can establish banking subsidiaries, securities subsidiaries, and insurance subsidiaries to achieve a model of comprehensive management by the financial holding company and separate operation by the subsidiaries.

In other words, from 1933 to 1999 the United States relied upon separate operation; in 1999, however, after 66 years of legislative tinkering, it legalized comprehensive management.[14] Nevertheless, in 2007, after only seven years of the comprehensive management regime, the United States experienced another financial crisis, which was caused by a subprime crisis. Theorists, practitioners, the federal government, and Congress have repeatedly debated the root causes of this financial crisis, and eventually a societal consensus was achieved that blamed a lack of regulatory supervision of financial derivatives.[15] Subsequently, after endless attempts to pass legislation, the US Congress introduced the Dodd–Frank Wall Street Reform and Consumer Protection Act of 2010, Public Law 111-203, in 2010. This Act included financial derivatives within the scope of supervision. The financial crisis was an issue of both financial innovation and financial supervision. Comprehensive management as such did not cause the financial crisis.[16]

Chinese scholars have learned from the theory of financial fragility. Huang emphasizes that financial risk is different from financial fragility. He believes that financial fragility and financial risk have similar meanings but different points of emphasis. Strictly speaking, financial risk refers to the possibility of a potential loss. Financial fragility includes not only possible losses but also those that have already happened. A narrow sense of financial fragility emphasizes 'immanence' as an inherent characteristic of the financial sector. The fragility of banks is rooted in the temporal

---

13 See Gramm–Leach–Bliley Act of 1999, Public Law 106-102, SEC. 101. Glass–Steagall Act Repeals, (a) Section 20 Repealed.—Section 20 of the Banking Act of 1933 (12 U.S.C. 377) (commonly referred to as the "Glass–Steagall Act") is repealed. (b) Section 32 Repealed.—Section 32 of the Banking Act of 1933 (12 U.S.C. 78) is repealed.

14 See Xi (2005).

15 See Barr (2012).

16 See Coffee (2011).

separation between the use and repayment of credit. However, risk has been used extensively in China, and it is often difficult to clearly distinguish risk from fragility.[17]

Liu has performed an empirical analysis of the fragility of China's banking system and believes that the impact of macroeconomic variables on the banking system's fragility surpasses that of financial and other variables. In China's financial transition process, reform of state-owned commercial banks lags behind; accordingly, they have not yet been transformed to conform to the modern enterprise system. These banks do not have actual corporate property rights and have yet to establish an internal standardized corporate governance structure; therefore, there are hidden institutional factors that can cause fragility in the banking system.[18] Xu and Qian have constructed banking fragility indicators based on relevant data from China for the period 1990–2011, have defined the credit upsurge, and have empirically studied the influence of credit upsurge factors on the fragility of Chinese banks. Their analysis has shown that a credit upsurge alone not only decreases the banking system's robustness but also tends to increase the negative impact of the financial system's structural features on banking fragility.[19] The above theories explore the causes and mechanisms that generate banking risks. Based on these previous studies, the following sections further analyse the three major issues faced by the Law of Commercial Banks.

3. SEPARATE OPERATION AND COMPREHENSIVE MANAGEMENT

3.1 The Costs and Benefits of Comprehensive Management

Commercial banks mainly provide three types of services. The first is bank-operated traditional services, such as absorbing deposits, extending loans, handling settlements, and so on. In traditional banking services, the bank has a debtor–creditor relationship with depositors and borrowers. The second type is the bank's agency services, including proxy fee collection for electricity bills, water bills, telecommunications bills, and so on. Banks also act as agents for insurance and investment funds, which is prone to cause conflicts of interest. According to the relevant

---

17 See Huang (2001b).
18 See Liu (2002).
19 See Xu and Qian (2013).

regulations, a debtor–creditor relationship does not arise out of the collection of service fees charged by the bank. The third type of service is bank-launched comprehensive management services. The bank establishes an investment banking division, securities subsidiary, insurance subsidiary, trust subsidiary, and asset securitization division and launches investment banking services, trust services, and insurance services within a division or a subsidiary of the bank.

In the context of these three types of banking services, if risk is generated by the bank's traditional services and triggers a bank run, in the separate operation mode even a banking panic is limited to the banking industry and to those banks linked by their business with each other. Banking risks do not easily cross over to securities, insurance, and trust businesses. The bank's intermediate proxy services (strictly defined as a fee collection agency service) do not produce debtor–creditor relationships and do not affect the bank's balance sheet; instead, they merely provide the bank with additional revenue.

A bank's comprehensive management services are important. From a micro perspective, a bank realizes its cross-industry management services, expands its business scope, adjusts its sources of funds, and improves its income structure, while increasing various risk-generation mechanisms. From a macro perspective, both the financial system and financial supervision are involved. If comprehensive financial management is implemented, the definition of legal properties and legal relationships in the bank's investment banking services, insurance services, and trust services must be resolved under separate operation and supervision systems; however, investment banking services, insurance services, and trust services must be operated under consolidated and functional supervision. Because each part has different regulations related to the capital adequacy ratio and different risk-generation mechanisms, in theory comprehensive management increases a bank's likelihood of internal risk contagion.

3.2 The Legal Foundation for Adopting Comprehensive Management in China

Since China's reform and opening up in 1978, the banking industry has supported more than thirty years of rapid economic growth, and no financial crisis has occurred. Therefore, China's financial regulation organizations have no experience in responding to a financial crisis. Most Chinese commercial banks conduct separate operation systems under the existing regulations, but several financial conglomerates conducting comprehensive management also exist as a result of statutory exceptions – for example, where the holding companies are financial conglomerates and their subsidiaries (divisions) carry out separate operations. However, the Law of Commercial Banks does not explicitly provide the legal form of financial holding companies; instead, it delegates the authority for this to the State Council. What factors restrict the establishment – whether by law or administrative regulation – of financial holding companies?

Through both regulations and normative documents, the People's Bank of China, the China Banking Regulatory Commission, the China Securities Regulatory Commission, and the China Insurance Regulatory Commission have already designed institutional arrangements for bank-launched comprehensive management services. First, commercial banks can establish fund management companies. In 2005 the first three regulatory agencies jointly issued the Administration of Pilot Projects for the Establishment of Fund Management Companies by Commercial Banks Procedures,[20] which regulated the fund management companies established and funded by commercial banks.

The following provisions were included:

(1) provisions for direct funding by commercial banks as enterprises that are legal persons;
(2) provisions for comprehensive management by banking groups and separate operation by a legal person;
(3) provisions for bank applications to establish fund companies and for audits, approval, and supervision by the China Securities Regulatory Commission; and
(4) provisions related to risk isolation, including personnel isolation, site isolation, service isolation, and financial isolation.

Pursuant to a system of separate operation and supervision, the banks achieved a system of comprehensive management by the group, separate operation by a subsidiary legal person, and functional supervision implemented by supervising institutions.

Second, commercial banks are allowed to provide financial services. In 2005 the China Banking Regulatory Commission issued Temporary Regulations on Administration of Commercial Banks' Personal Financial Service Management. Article 9 clearly defines personal financial services as a banking service that is built upon the foundation of the principal–agent

---

[20] See Measures for the Pilot Management of Establishing Fund Management Companies by Commercial Banks (Shangye Yinhang Sheli Jijin Guanli Gongsi Shidian Guanli Banfa), issued by The People's Bank of China, China Banking Regulatory Commission and China Securities Regulatory Commission, 2005, No. 4 (PRC).

relationship.[21] In 2014 the China Banking Regulatory Commission issued the Notice on Improving the System for Organization and Management of the Wealth Management Business of Banks in 2014,[22] which requires banking and financial institutions to launch multidivisional structural reform for financial services to comply with requirements related to separate accounting, risk isolation, behavioural norms, centralized management by specialized departments, and so on; to establish operating divisions for specialized financial services; and to assume responsibility for focusing on the unified management of the entire bank's financial services. Under a system of separate operation and supervision, the banks achieved a system of comprehensive management by the group and separate operation by business units, accomplished an institutional separation of their different businesses, and built a firewall system to isolate risks occurring in different businesses.

Third, commercial banks can sponsor financial derivative services. A financial derivative is a direct buy–sell transaction contract. Those who are risk-averse directly transfer risks, such as price risk, interest rate risk, exchange rate risk, credit risk, and so on, to risk recipients. In 2004 the China Banking Regulatory Commission issued Interim Measures for the Management of the Dealings of Derivative Products of Financial Institutions (henceforth Interim Measures), which were subsequently revised in 2006 and released in 2007.[23] Article 3 of the Interim Measures relating to the concept of derivatives included the following guidance: 'The term derivative product in these measures is a financial contract whose value depends on one or more basic types of underlying assets or indices. The basic contract categories include forward contracts, futures, swaps

---

21 See Interim Measures for the Administration of Commercial Banks' Personal Financial Management Services (Shangye Yinhang Geren Licai Yewu Guanli Zanxing Banfa), issued by China Banking Regulatory Commission 2005, No. 2 (PRC), and Guidelines for the Risk Management of Personal Financial Management Services Provided by Commercial Banks (Shangye Yinhang Geren Licai Yewu Fengxian Guanli Zhiyin), issued by China Banking Regulatory Commission 2005, No. 63 (PRC).

22 See Notice on Improving the System for Organization and Management of the Wealth Management Business of Banks (Zhongguo Yinjianhui Guanyu Wanshan Yinhang Licai Yewu Zuzhi Guanli Tixi Youguan Shixiang De Tongzhi), issued by China Banking Regulatory Commission 2014, No. 35 (PRC).

23 See Decision of China Banking Regulatory Commission on Amending the Interim Measures for the Business Management of Derivative Product Transactions of Financial Institutions (Zhongguo Yinhangye Jiandu Guanli Weiyuanhui Guanyu Xiugai <Jinrong Jigou Yansheng Chanpin Jiaoyi Yewu Guanli Zanxing Banfa> De Jueding), issued by China Banking Regulatory Commission 2007, No. 10 (PRC).

(exchanges), and options.' Compared with general buy–sell contracts or reciprocity contracts, the biggest difference in derivative contracts is 'current contracting, future performance', which refers exclusively to a temporal separation between contracting and performance. It substantially changes the function of a contract by transfiguring it from a legal instrument aiming to promote trade into a tradable financial product.

Fourth, commercial banks can provide insurance services. China's Banking Regulatory Commission issued a Notice on Further Strengthening the Sales Compliance and Risk Management of the Bancassurance Business of Commercial Banks,[24] which stipulates that when a commercial bank establishes an insurance agency, it should separate the sale of products such as savings deposits, funds, and banking financial management products, and it must explain to customers that the management body for the insurance products is an insurance company that has a principal–agent relationship with the bank.

Fifth, commercial banks can offer asset securitization services. In 2008 the People's Bank of China and the China Banking Regulatory Commission jointly issued Administrative Measures for the Pilot Project on Securitization of Credit Assets,[25] which established a business mode for credit asset securitization sponsored by banks. According to Article 2 of the Pilot Administrative Measures, banking and financial institutions that are part of the originating institution give a credit asset trust to the trustee, and the trustee both issues beneficiary securities to the investment institutions in the form of asset-backed securities and also pays the returns on the asset-backed securities using cash generated by that property. The trust relationship between the originating institution, trustee, and investment institutions is the core of credit asset securitization. The primary legal relationship of asset securitization is in the nature of a trust.

By providing financial, derivative, insurance, and asset securitization services, the bank and the customer may have either a trust relationship or a buy–sell contract relationship. From a legal perspective, a trust relationship exists between all of the parties involved in a commercial bank's

[24] See Notice of China Banking Regulatory Commission on Further Strengthening the Sales Compliance and Risk Management of the Bancassurance Business of Commercial Banks (Zhongguo Yinjianhui Guanyu Jinyibu Jiaqiang Shangye Yinhang Daili Baoxian Yewu Hegui Xiaoshou Yu Fengxian Guanli De Tongzhi), issued by China Banking Regulatory Commission 2010, No. 90 (PRC).

[25] See Administrative Measures for the Pilot Project on Securitization of Credit Assets (Xindai Zichan Zhengquanhua Shidian Guanli Banfa), issued by The People's Bank of China and China Banking Regulatory Commission (2005), No. 7 (PRC).

non-standardized asset products. In essence, non-standardized asset products are used as a channel both to disguise potential indirect financing and to change it into actual direct financing. Generally speaking, a trust relationship is a more mature legal relationship. It is likely that bringing the bank's non-standardized assets into a trust relationship will be the future for asset management.

3.3 Reforming the Business Scope of Commercial Banks

Chinese financial regulators have introduced normative documents related to comprehensive management, have standardized comprehensive management services, have isolated associated risks, and have established a framework for comprehensive management by the banking group and separate operation by subsidiaries (divisions) since 2006. In practice, supervisors have not only accumulated experience in regulating financial conglomerates, but have also improved their supervision capabilities. However, the comprehensive management system primarily consists of normative documents, including notices, guidelines, measures, and suggestions, with low legal and institutional-level fragmentation; these elements do not form a unified framework for a comprehensive management law. Consequently, the time is ripe to modify the provisions of the Law of Commercial Banks related to market access and comprehensive management because it is both necessary and feasible to do so.

Article 3 of the Law of Commercial Banks mainly regulates the business scope of Chinese banks, which could provide 13 different services. Article 43 uses two prohibitive clauses to restrict commercial banks to engaging in traditional banking services, albeit with the provision that the restriction exists 'except as otherwise provided by the State', thus reserving space for commercial banks to develop comprehensive management.[26] We suggest combining and modifying Articles 3 and 43 of the Law of Commercial Banks and defining banking services according to their legal relationships and nature. In bank implementation of comprehensive management, the risk that is borne varies because of differences in the nature of the financial product, differences in the legal relationship between the bank and the customer, and differences in rights and obligations. A bank's credit service involves indirect financing, whereas its asset management service

---

[26] See Article 43 of the Commercial Banking Law: 'Commercial banks are not allowed to make trust investment, trade in shares or make investment in fixed assets of non-self-use or in non-banking institutions and enterprises, unless it is otherwise prescribed by the state.'

involves direct financing. Article 3 could be divided based on the nature of the service.

First, Article 3 addresses bank deposit and loan services, including: (1) absorbing deposits from the public; (2) extending short-, medium-, and long-term loans; (3) conducting domestic and foreign settlements; (4) managing bill acceptance and discounts; (10) providing bank card services; (11) providing letter-of-credit services and guarantees; and (13) providing safety-deposit box services. The legal system for deposit insurance includes a deposit insurance system that partially guarantees bank deposits.

Second, Article 3 further stipulates the proxy fee collection services of banks, which include collecting payments for electricity bills, water bills, natural gas bills, telephone bills, all school fees, and all types of fines. In addition, commercial banks can (6) act as an agent for issuing, cashing, and underwriting government bonds; (7) buy and sell government bonds and financial bonds; (9) buy, sell, and act as an agent for buying and selling foreign currency; and (12) act as an agent for receipts and payments and for insurance services. Based on Article 16 of the Measures for the Administration of the Service Prices of Commercial Banks, banks should not be allowed to collect fees from units or individuals other than the commissioning party.[27] This aspect of banking services is a typical principal–agent arrangement in which there is no debtor–creditor relationship between the bank and the customer.

Third, Article 3 also addresses banks' asset management services. All types of non-standardized credit asset and interbank services, regardless of whether the asset is traded on the interbank market or the securities market, are included within the scope of 'non-standardized credit asset'. Trust products, fund products, securities dealer products, and all equity class products listed in the exchange are included within the scope of non-standardized credit assets.[28]

After the amendment of Article 3, banks will be able to conduct

---

[27] See Measures for the Administration of the Service Prices of Commercial Banks (Shangye Yinhang Fuwu Jiage Guanli Banfa), issued by China Banking Regulatory Commission and National Development and Reform Commission 2014, No. 1 (PRC).

[28] See Article 1 of the Notice of the China Banking Regulatory Commission on Relevant Issues Concerning Regulating the Investment Operation of Wealth Management Business of Commercial Banks (Guanyu Guifan Shangye Yinhang Licai Yewu Touzi Yunzuo Youguan Wenti De Tongzhi), issued by China Banking Regulatory Commission 2013, No. 8 (PRC): 'Non-standardized debt assets' refer to the debt assets that are not traded in the interbank market or the stock exchange market, including, but not limited to: credit assets, trust loans, entrustment credit

comprehensive management. To prevent risk contagion among comprehensive management services, a division of service, product, personnel, and finance should be strictly implemented among different units. A system of comprehensive management by the group and separate operation by a subsidiary legal person (division) is established to effectively prevent risk contagion among the various services. This isolation has the same function as the 'Volcker rule' in the US and the Vickers 'ring-fencing principle' in the UK.[29] In addition, the isolation of different products between asset management services is strictly implemented and function supervision is performed according to the nature of the asset management product.

4. THE RELATIONSHIP BETWEEN COMMERCIAL BANKS AND THEIR BORROWERS

4.1 The Legal Relationship between Commercial Banks and their Borrowers

A loan contract is an agreement in which a bank transfers all of the rights to a certain amount of money to the borrower and the borrower returns the same amount of money plus interest within an agreed period. Civil law on such lending practices determines that a behavioural precondition of such a transaction is the existence of a depositor who has transferred all of the rights to the money that he or she has deposited in the bank; otherwise, the bank either cannot transfer ownership of that money to the borrower or it can only ask the borrower to return the original currency.[30]

A bank loan is classified as a form of indirect finance. Enterprises obtain funding through bank loans. In the bank loan contract, the bank is the creditor and the borrower is the debtor. The object of the loan contract is the loan amount and interest. The content of the loan contract includes both the direction of the loan investment – that is, it will specify where the loan funds will be invested and what will be produced – and repayment dates. Therefore, the borrower's capital investment direction forms the industrial structure, and the value form of the industrial structure constitutes the capital stock.

---

rights, acceptance bills, letters of credit, accounts receivable, various beneficial interests (or rights to income), and equity financing with a buy-back clause.

[29] See Jia and Zhi (2014).

[30] See Cao (2000).

We assume that a bank makes loans based on the principles of market competition, using profit maximization as the operating target. The bank pays deposit reserves to the Central Bank in line with all of the capital adequacy standards stipulated by the China Banking Regulatory Commission. The bank's liabilities are the depositors' savings. The bank's assets are the borrowers' loans. The minimum guarantee of banking operations is the scheduled payment of the depositors' principal and interest. The guarantee condition requires the borrowers to repay the loan principal and interest on time. Loan interest rates are higher than deposit interest rates, and the difference between these is the bank's profit.

Because of information asymmetry, banks and lending companies cannot control the post-loan business activities of enterprises and business risks may occur, including market risks, credit risks, and risks triggered by international economic and social uncertainties. The first is the risk caused by product price fluctuation. Industry restructuring causes a phase-out of the products of a borrowing enterprise. As a result, it is possible that the borrowing enterprise will reduce production and personnel, the bank then stops lending, and the borrowing enterprise's payment is strained. Or the borrowing enterprise's capital chain breaks, the enterprise stops production, and the staff either wait for work or look for work elsewhere. Finally, the borrowing enterprise completely ceases production, there is an overstock of the enterprise's inventory, and the borrowing enterprise cannot repay the loan principal and interest within the life of the loan, generating a bad loan for the bank.

The second is the risk caused by interest rate adjustments. Because of policy controls on real estate, the Central Bank tightens the money supply. Commercial banks reduce real estate business loans, the interest rate adjusts, and real estate development enterprises either find it difficult to make payments on time or cannot both pay their upstream suppliers and also fund the products of their downstream suppliers. Overcapacity has already emerged in industries associated with real estate development, including the cement, steel, glass, and coatings industries; overcapacity has increased following the contraction in real estate development. Next, production reduction, cessation, or transformation emerges in industries related to real estate development; alternatively, bankruptcies and job losses appear. In the four basic types of risks experienced by commercial banks – credit risk, interest rate risk, liquidity risk, and exchange rate risk – the interest rate risk will gradually become the primary risk.[31]

The third is the risk caused by international economic and social

---

[31] See Huang (2001a).

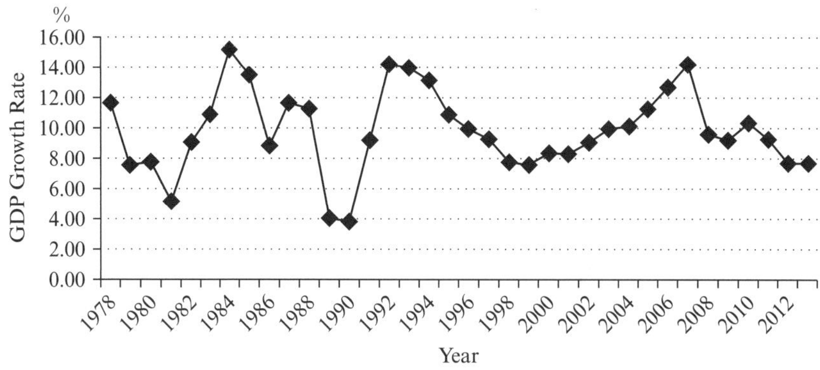

Figure 2.2 *Three major economic fluctuations in China from 1978 to 2013*

uncertainties. If the borrowing enterprise primarily produces or invests in products for the international market, international economic and social uncertainties become the primary risks that affect the borrowing enterprise's operations. These uncertainties include international financial crises; the importing nation's monetary policy, especially exchange rate fluctuations; and political turmoil in the importing nation, especially coups, wars, natural disasters, and so on. If international economic and social uncertainties occur in any of the aforementioned circumstances, they may cause the borrowing enterprise to experience a decline in product exports, reduced orders, production cessation, or even bankruptcy. When domestic enterprises experience reduced exports and orders because of international market changes, economic growth will slow down. For example, the 1997 Southeast Asian financial crisis and the 2007 US subprime mortgage crisis (which evolved into a financial crisis) directly reduced Chinese imports and exports. Declining economic growth in China has caused three major economic fluctuations since China's reform and opening up in 1978 and has formed three economic troughs, which are shown in Figure 2.2.

According to the risk analyses set out above, despite a bank's internal risk-prevention mechanisms, bank loans are based on expectations of future corporate credit and market presence. Future expectations contain uncertainty factors. These uncertainties can be transformed into price risk, interest rate risk, or the risk of an international financial crisis. Who will bear these risks? Commercial banks can only achieve unity in rights and obligations under the constraints of market rules in the main players' behaviour, factor pricing, and decision-making behaviour. Only by weighing the security and risk and the costs and benefits of each transaction can the banks be liable for operating losses or failures. Bank operating losses or even bankruptcies result from the rules of market competition.

That said, the commercial banking law's arrangement in relation to loan systems is inconsistent with the competition principles of a market economy. The law may have limited competition among commercial banks, or it may have imposed policy on commercial banks, either by giving commercial banks the ability to shirk responsibility or by exacerbating moral hazard in commercial banking operations. Accordingly, the economic and social conditions that require amendment to the commercial banking law's loan system already exist.

4.2 The Regulation of the Loan-to-deposit Ratio

The loan-to-deposit ratio refers to the amount of commercial bank deposits available for extending loans. The upper limit stipulated by the loan-to-deposit ratio contains a prerequisite: among the commercial banks' various funding sources, only deposits can be used to extend loans. Even if a commercial bank has other funding sources (for example capital, bonds, or interbank loans), those sources cannot be used to extend loans.

The stipulation relating to the supervision of the upper limit of the loan-to-deposit ratio was established in the period 1993–1995. First, economic growth was rapid, with an inflation rate reaching 24.1 per cent in 1994 and 17.1 per cent in 1995.[32] The central government unleashed a macro-control policy for tightening credit to curb inflation. Second, bank deposits were insufficient. Commercial banks relied on the Central Bank to refinance loans. The loans from the Central Bank to the commercial banks were often two to three times the amount that the commercial banks had deposited with the Central Bank. Third, various specialized banks began to transform themselves into commercial banks.[33] Based on this background, Article 39(b) of the Law of Commercial Banks stipulates that 'the proportion of loan balance and deposit balance shall not exceed 75 per cent'.[34]

---

32 See National Bureau of Statistics (2012) *China Statistical Yearbook 2012*, Beijing: China Statistics Press, p. 315.

33 See Huang (2013).

34 See Article 39 of the Commercial Banking Law: '(1) Capital sufficiency rate must not be less than 8 per cent; (2) The ratio between the balance of loans and the balance of deposits must not exceed 75 per cent; (3) The ratio between the balance of circulating assets and the balance of circulating liabilities must not be lower than 25 per cent; (4) The ratio between the balance of loans of one borrower and the balance of capital of the commercial bank must not exceed 10 per cent; and (5) Other stipulations of the banking regulatory organ of the State Council governing such ratios.'

When the Tenth National People's Congress amended the commercial banking law, Article 39 on commercial bank loan compliance with the provisions for the loan-to-deposit ratio was not modified. At the end of 2013 the commercial bank loan-to-deposit ratio was 74.47 per cent.[35]

There are several issues relating to the loan-to-deposit ratio stipulation that are worthy of discussion. First, banks must have deposit sources before extending loans, and they must comply with the loan-to-deposit ratio stipulation. Accordingly, banks need to attract deposits, even when interest rates are high. For example, commercial banks issued principal-guaranteed financial products (principal-guaranteed financial products are neither deposits, nor are they non-standardized financial management). Second, the loan-to-deposit ratio is an administrative stipulation; accordingly, bank debt management loses autonomy and the ratio is shackled to commercial banking asset liability management. Third, the loan-to-deposit ratio stipulation conflicts with the new Basel Accord. The focus of the new Basel Accord is on the supervision of the capital adequacy ratio and liquidity indices. Supervision of the capital adequacy ratio values the supervision of all banking risks rather than that of the proportional relationship of the loan-to-deposit ratio. Consequently, it is recommended that the Standing Committee of the National People's Congress amend Article 39 of the Law of Commercial Banks based on liquidity supervision indices of commercial banks, set the loan-to-deposit ratio as an elasticity index, and empower the China Banking Regulatory Commission to make adjustments according to the various liquidity risks of commercial banks.

4.3 The Conflicts between Market Incentives and National Industrial Policy

Article 34 of the Law of Commercial Banks stipulates that 'commercial banks launch loan services according to national economic and social development needs under the guidance of national industrial policy'. An analysis of the relationship between law and policy reveals that this provision is inconsistent with the law. To provide market players with stable economic and social expectations, the law provides an arrangement system with normative principles for establishing rules. Policy is formulated according to economic and social development conditions; it is flexible and phased, offers guidance, and can be adjusted by government agencies

[35] See China Banking Regulatory Commission (2014) *Annual Report of China Banking Regulatory Commission 2013*, Beijing: China CITIC Press, p. 7.

if the right opportunity presents itself. If a legal system is stipulated in accordance with the implementation of a national industrial policy, then the relationship between law and policy is reversed.

An analysis of the relationships among the main players in banks and loan firms reveals that they do qualify as contractual relationships between civil agents. The lending contract between a bank and an enterprise is a commercial contractual relationship between parties subject to civil law. All of the contract's clauses, including loan purpose, loan amount, loan interest, loan collateral valuation, loan term, liability for breach of contract, and so on, represent the consensual agreements between the bank and the borrower following a consultation. The contract establishes the debtor–creditor relationship between the bank and the borrower.

Whether the bank loan can recover the principal and interest at maturity depends on future expectations when the loan contract was signed; however, the future has uncertainties. Corporations borrow for the future production of products; alternatively, corporations take medium- to long-term loans for investment in infrastructure. For them, too, the future is uncertain. Therefore, in the face of future uncertainties, banks and enterprises must bear risk. Assuming all other conditions remain unchanged, banks and enterprises choose between the industrial policy and the market. An analysis of the risk/liability relationship between banks, enterprises, the industrial policy, and the market reveals the following predictions, which are shown in Figure 2.3.

Whether the industrial policy is compatible with market supply and demand trends or not	**Execution**	**Non-execution**
Compatible	Prediction 1: The enterprise recovers loan principal and interest normally.	Prediction 3: If the enterprise operation fails, the enterprise bears the risk and liability.
Incompatible	Prediction 2: If the enterprise cannot return the principal and interest, who will bear the liability and risk?	Prediction 4: If the enterprise operation fails, the enterprise bears the risk and liability.

Whether the bank executes industrial policy or not

Figure 2.3 The matrix for the relationship between banks, enterprises and industrial policies

First, if the bank executes the industrial policy and the industrial policy is compatible with market supply and demand trends, an enterprise borrows from the bank and invests in an industry stipulated by the national industrial policy. Under this assumption, the judgements of the bank, industrial policy, and enterprise are consistent. The subsequent problem of not recovering the loan principal and interest does not occur. Second, the bank executes the industrial policy, but the industrial policy is not compatible with market supply and demand trends. An enterprise borrows from the bank and invests in an industry stipulated by the national industrial policy. Under this assumption, the judgements of the bank, industrial policy, and enterprise are inconsistent. If a market problem occurs, the enterprise cannot return the principal and interest to the bank at maturity. Between the bank, industrial regulators, and the enterprises, who will bear the liability and risk for the loan?

Third, the bank does not execute the industrial policy, but the industrial policy is compatible with market supply and demand trends. An enterprise borrows from the bank and invests in industry as agreed between the bank and the enterprise. If the enterprise operation fails, the enterprise bears the risk and liability. Fourth, the bank does not execute the industrial policy and the industrial policy is not compatible with market supply and demand trends. An enterprise borrows from the bank and invests in industry as agreed between the bank and the enterprise. If the enterprise operation fails, the enterprise bears the risk and liability.

In examining the above theoretical predictions, the bank extends loans based on the principles of market competition. If there is a loss, the bank bears the risk and liability. The risks and liabilities are clear. There is no room for shirking responsibility. If the bank extends loans according to the guiding principles of the industrial policy and there is a loss to the bank, the bank can push the responsibility for the loss onto the national industrial policy. By the same token, the enterprise applies for loans based on market supply and demand and market investment expectations. If the enterprise operates at a loss or is bankrupt, there is no room to shirk responsibility. This is a problem of enterprise operation and production. If the enterprise borrows according to national industrial policy principles and suffers a loss or becomes bankrupt, it can shirk its responsibility, as anticipated by the national industrial policy.

Therefore, the commercial banking law is unsuitable for directly stipulating that commercial banks conform to the national industrial policy. State regulation of economic targets should not be achieved by the mandatory requirement that commercial organizations comply with state industrial policy.[36] We recommend the simple deletion of the provisions of Article 34 of the Law of Commercial Banks, which requires that policy-based banking, national debt, and financial allocations should follow the guidance of the national industrial policy. A corresponding liability- and risk-sharing relationship between policy-based banking, national debt, financial allocation, and enterprises should be established.

5. ESTABLISHING THE DEPOSIT INSURANCE SYSTEM

The deposit insurance system is the basic institution for the marketization of banking operations. A State's implicit deposit guarantee can generate a moral hazard problem for depositors and eliminate banks' screening and supervision role. Moral hazard can also be generated for the banks in lending to high-risk investment enterprises, while having the State bear ultimate responsibility for the deposit risk. Three key systems are involved in transforming national credit in banking deposit into bank credit: first, the marketization of bank deposit interest rates; second, banking industry market exit mechanisms; and third, a deposit insurance system.

Viewed from the history of US and EU financial development and the evolution order of financial marketization, interest rate marketization reform and market exit mechanisms for banks can be implemented through a deposit insurance system. This resolves two basic institutional problems in the marketization of banking operations. The first problem involves bank runs or bankruptcy in banking operations caused by interest rate marketization. A deposit insurance system safeguards the depositors' interests. The second problem involves takeover, revocation, and court-declared bankruptcies that occur during the marketization of banking operations. In this situation, a bank's exit from the market is orderly.

5.1 A Framework for Establishing a Deposit Insurance System

On 30 November 2014 the Legal Affairs Office State Council published the 'Deposit Insurance Regulation (Solicit Opinion Draft)' (hereafter the Solicit Opinion Draft), which was drafted by the People's Bank of China. The Solicit Opinion Draft constructed an administrative and regulatory framework for a deposit insurance system and established a basic institution for the marketization of banking operations.

---

[36] See Li (2008).

Article 3 of the Solicit Opinion Draft stipulates the definition of deposit insurance:

> In this regulation, deposit insurance refers to a system in which insured institutions pay premiums to the deposit insurance fund management institution to form a deposit insurance fund, the deposit insurance fund management institution then reimburses the insured deposits to depositors in accordance with the provisions of this regulation and takes necessary measures to safeguard deposits and the security of the deposit insurance fund.

This definition defined the legal relationships in the deposit insurance system and stressed the substance of the deposit insurance system, the key to which is that when a bank fails in its operations, there is guaranteed payment of the depositors' insured deposits.[37]

The legal relationships involved in deposit insurance include the insurer, the insured, and the insurance object. The insurer is the deposit insurance fund management institution. The insured include commercial banks, rural cooperative banks, rural credit cooperatives, and other deposit-absorbing banking and financial institutions stipulated in Article 2 of the Solicit Opinion Draft; these entities are also known as the insured institutions. The deposit insurance stipulated in the Solicit Opinion Draft is a mandatory insurance scheme. Banks that absorb deposits must be insured with deposit insurance. The insurance object is the insured deposit, which includes renminbi (RMB) and foreign currency deposits absorbed by the insured institutions.

Article 5 stipulates the implementation of a deposit insurance payment limit. The maximum reimbursement limit is RMB 500,000. According to estimates based on 2013 deposit conditions, the maximum reimbursement limit of RMB 500,000 can cover the full deposit of 99.63 per cent of depositors. This implies that most depositors' entire deposit can be safeguarded and they will not suffer loss. Of course, the RMB 500,000 maximum reimbursement limit is not fixed and unchanging. Based on factors such as economic development, deposit structure changes, and financial risk status, the People's Bank of China and relevant departments at the State Council can adjust the maximum reimbursement limit.[38]

A deposit insurance system can easily cause moral hazard in banks. As a result of the implementation of deposit insurance, a bank may relax auditing on high-risk loans. Moral hazard can also occur among depositors. Because deposits are insured, depositors lack the incentive to check the

---

[37] See Xie et al. (2001).
[38] See Wu (2010).

credentials of the banks in which they deposit their money. Moral hazard can also occur among borrowers. Subsequent to the implementation of a deposit insurance system, borrowers tend to borrow from high-risk banks. After the bank goes bankrupt, liquidation and repayment can be delayed. Therefore, the key to a deposit insurance system is weighing the two goals of protecting the depositors' interests against preventing banking moral hazards.[39] The deposit insurance system should only cover a proportion of the loss, and the banks, depositors, and borrowers together share the risks of implementation and prevent the generation of moral hazard. In the insurance mechanism, the banks, depositors, and borrowers share the implementation risks and prevent the generation of moral hazard.

5.2 The Effects of Implementation of a Deposit Insurance System

After implementing the deposit insurance system, the depositors will select banks based on the robustness of the bank's operations. Even if the bank fails, the depositor's money can be safeguarded within the scope of the deposit insurance coverage. Because there is a limit to the insurance, any part of the deposit exceeding the deposit insurance limit may not be reimbursed. The insurance mechanism resulting from the deposit insurance limit increases the bank selection mechanism for the depositor in the market.

From a short-term perspective, bank payment of insurance premiums to obtain deposit insurance from the deposit insurance institution increases the bank's operating costs. From a long-term development perspective, this promotes the bank's competition mechanism in relation to the marketization of deposit interest rates because the amount of deposit, the level of interest rates, and the security and convenience of withdrawal determine banking competition. When banks fail, administrative receivership, reorganization, or judicial proceedings are implemented. A direct exit from the market is the real mechanism for implementing 'survival of the fittest' in the banking market. As a result of the implementation of a deposit insurance system, the original national credit is changed to bank credit, ending policy-based bank bankruptcy.[40] National financial policy no longer subsidizes the payment of deposit credits of failed banks, thus rationalizing the relationships between banks, depositors, the market, and the State.

---

[39] See Liu and Li (1999).

[40] The costs of bailing out banks with insufficient liquidity are always high; for example, this cost has reached 30 per cent of GDP in Japan and 27 per cent in Mexico. See Maskin and Xu (2000).

6. CONCLUSION AND RECOMMENDATIONS

China's Law of Commercial Banks was enacted in 1995 and its third amendment was completed in 2015. With the fast economic and social development in China, particularly reform of the banking system and financial deepening, which increase access to financial services, the commercial banking law needs to adapt to the new practices, set aside space for banking reform pilot projects, and reserve space for amending laws through the elastic clause 'except as otherwise provided by the State Council'. Institutional arrangements established by the Law of Commercial Banks, such as bank access, comprehensive management, the bank and depositor relationship, the bank and borrower relationship, the deposit interest rate, industrial policy, deposit insurance, market exit mechanisms for banks, and so on, must comply not only with China's actual financial development, but also with China's financial supervision capacity. In addition, the risks of different products should be isolated, and the various legal relationships generated by different services must be defined. Finally, the commercial banking law is the subject of constant legislative tinkering to address the evolving economic and social problems.

However, the Law of Commercial Banks is only one part of the financial system. For the legal system to operate effectively, other economic and social support systems are absolutely necessary. According to Lu and Yao, '[o]n China's financial development, the reform of the banking system, especially the gains arising from interest rate liberalization, may far exceed the gains from improving the rule of law'.[41] We agree with their view because although money, the market, interest rates, and risk are factors that are endogenous to bank operations, the legal system is composed of institutional rules that regulate the healthy development of endogenous factors. The issue of how to measure the effects of the commercial banking law on banks, individuals, enterprises, and the government, and how to measure the effects of the commercial banking law on bank credit services, bank proxy fee collection services, and bank asset management services, are issues for further discussion.

Finance is the nucleus of any development in a market economy. Banks are the lifeblood of the development of a market economy. Financial products are important elements that determine the balance in supply and demand in the financial market. A financial crisis is like a flood. If it occurs, it will instantly wash away society's accumulated wealth, resulting in unemployment, bankruptcy, and economic depression, and will cause

---

[41] Lu and Yao (2004), p. 55.

social unrest. The commercial banking law is a large institutional dam that prevents a financial crisis being triggered by financial risks.

REFERENCES

Allen, Franklin, Jun Qian, and Meijun Qian (2005), 'Law, Finance, and Economic Growth in China', *Journal of Financial Economics*, 77(1), 57–116.

Allen, Franklin, Chenying Zhang, and Mengxin Zhao (2012), 'China's Financial System: Opportunities and Challenges', in Fan, F. and Morck, R. (eds), *Capitalizing China*, Chicago: University of Chicago Press, 63–143.

Barr, Michael S. (2012), 'The Financial Crisis and the Path of Reform', *Yale Journal on Regulation*, 29, 91–119.

Barth, James, Gerard Caprio, and Ross Levine (2013), 'Bank Regulation and Supervision in 180 Countries from 1999 to 2011', *Journal of Financial Economic Policy*, 5, 111–219.

Cao, Xinyou (2000), 'Lun Cunkuan Suoyouquan De Guishu (About the Ownership of Deposit)', *Xiandai Faxue* (*Modern Law Science*), 22, 63–6.

Chang, Wei and Shaohua Ren (2004), 'Diamond-Dybvig Yinhang Jidui Moxing Shuping (Review of Diamond-Dybvig Model)', *Jingjixue Dongtai* (*Economic Perspectives*), 1, 77–81.

Coffee, John C. (2011), 'Systemic Risk after Dodd-Frank: Contingent Capital and the Need for Regulatory Strategies beyond Oversight', *Columbia Law Review*, 111, 795–847.

Diamond, Douglas W. and Philip H. Dybvig (1983), 'Bank Runs, Deposit Insurance, and Liquidity', *Journal of Political Economy*, 91, 401–19.

Huang, Jinlao (2001a), 'Lilv Shichanghua Yu Shangye Yinhang Fengxian Kongzhi (Market-oriented Interest Rate and Risk Control of Commercial Banks)', *Jingji Yanjiu* (*Economic Research Journal*), 1, 19–28.

Huang, Jinlao (2001b), 'Lun Jinrong Cuiruoxing (Study for Financial Fragility)', *Jinrong Yanjiu* (*Journal of Financial Research*), 3, 41–9.

Huang, Jinlao (2013), 'Gaijin Cundaibi Shangxian Jianguan Zhengce (Improve the Regulatory Policy of the Loan-to-Deposit Ratio's Upper Limit)', *Zhongguo Jinrong* (*China Finance*), 3, 26–8.

Jia, Yingying and Fengyin Zhi (2014), 'Jinrong Jianguan Gaige De Hexin Yaosu (The Core Elements of Financial Regulatory Reform)', *Zhongguo Jinrong* (*China Finance*), 16, 9–11.

La Porta, Rafael, Florencio Lopez-De-Silanes, and Andrei Shleifer (2002), 'Government Ownership of Banks', *Journal of Finance*, 57, 265–301.

Li, Jinze (2008), 'Shangye Yinhang Shouxin De Falv Guizhi Yanjiu (Research for Legal Regulating of the Commercial Bank Credit)', *Fashang Yanjiu* (*Studies in Law and Business*), 2, 106–16.

Liu, Shiyu and Peiyu Li (1999), 'Guanyu Jianli Zhongguo Cunkuan Baoxian Zhidu Ruogan Wenti De Yanjiu (Several Problems with Establishing China's Deposit Insurance System)', *Jinrong Yanjiu* (*Journal of Finance Research*), 11, 61–5.

Liu, Weijiang (2002), 'Zhongguo Yinhang Tixi Cuiruoxing Wenti De Shizheng Yanjiu (A Positive Study of Chinese Bank System Fragility)', *Guanli Shijie* (*Management World*), 7, 3–10.

Lu, Feng and Yang Yao (2004), 'Jinrong Yayi Xia De Fazhi, Jinrong Fazhan He Jingji Zengzhang (Legality, Financial Development and Economic Growth under Financial Repression)', *Zhongguo Shehui Kexue* (*Social Sciences in China*), 1, 42–55.

Maskin, Eric and Chenggang Xu (2000), 'Ruanyusuan Yueshu Lilun: Cong Zhongyang Jihua Dao Shichang (Soft Budget Constraint Theory: From Central Planning to Market)', *Jingji Shehui Tizhi Bijiao* (*Comparative Economic and Social Systems*), 9, 1–27.

Minsky, Hyman P. (1992), 'The Financial Instability Hypothesis', The Jerome Levy Economics Institute Working Paper 74, 1–8.

Prasad, Eswar S. and Raghuram G. Rajan (2006), 'Modernizing China's Growth Paradigm', *American Economic Review*, 96, 331–36.

Stiglitz, Joseph E. and Andrew Weiss (1981), 'Credit Rationing in Markets with Imperfect Information', *The American Economic Review*, 71, 393–410.

Wu, Xiaoling (2010), 'Cong Meiguo Jinrong Jianguan Gaige Kan "Daerbudao" Wenti De Chuzhi (Experience of Solving "Too Big to Fall" from American Financial Regulation)', *Zhongguo Jinrong* (*China Finance*), 16, 8–10.

Xi, Tao (2005), 'Fuza De Shichang, Manchang De Gaige-Meiguo Cong Fenye Jingying Dao Zonghe Jingying De 66 Nian Jingrong Tizhi Yanbian De Qidi' (Complicated Market, Meticulous Amendment and Lengthy Reform: The Enlightenment of the American 66 years' Financial System Evolution from Separate Operation to Comprehensive Management)', *Guoji Jingji Pinglun* (*International Economic Review*), 5, 22–5.

Xie, Ping, Suzhen Wang, and Wei Yan (2001), 'Cunkuan Baoxin De Lilun Yanjiu Yu Guoji Bijiao (Theoretical Study and International Comparison of Deposit Insurance)', *Jinrong Yanjiu* (*Journal of Financial Research*), 5, 1–12.

Xu, Lu and Xuesong Qian (2013), 'Xindai Rechao Dui Yinhang Cuiruoxing De Yingxiang-Jiyu Zhongguo De Lilun Yu Shizheng Yanjiu (The Influence of Credit Booms on Bank Fragility from Chinese Theoretical Models and Empirical Analyses)', *Guoji Jinrong Yanjiu* (*Studies of International Finance*), 11, 84–96.

3. Rethinking China's capital market and financial stability after the global financial crisis: the significance of institutional investors

Jiye Hu and Yang Chen*

1. INTRODUCTION

Institutional investors, mostly mutual funds, insurance corporations and pension funds, are considered to have a positive effect on capital market stability because of their long-term investment strategy and funding. But in China's capital market, institutional investors remain few. The percentage trading value of individual investors declined from 87.4% in 2007 to 85.6% in 2012.[1] The performance of individual investors may intensify the volatility of the capital market in China and they are often described as 'noise traders'.[2]

Many scholars believe that institutional investors contribute to the stability of capital markets. Analysing the internal relationship between institutional investors and capital markets, Shleifer and Vishny concluded that in a corporation with many small shareholders, the owners did not have the motivation to monitor the performance of management. Only large shareholders – to a great extent institutional investors – have the incentive to supervise the company's executives, because such monitoring would be beneficial for their large investments. Institutional investors are

* Hu Jiye appreciates the helpful comments on earlier versions of this chapter from Michael Faure and Niels Philipsen of Maastricht University, Stefan Weishaar of University of Groningen, Laura-Marie Töpfer of Oxford University, Yu-wei Hu of Renmin University, Yang Yansui of Tsinghua University, Xi Tao and Xu Wenming of the China University of Political Science and Law. Zhang Yingnan and Zhang Wenxiu have done excellent assistant work on this chapter. None of the above should be held responsible for any errors or omissions.

1 Shenzhen Stock Exchange (2016).

2 DeLong et al. (1987), Trueman (1988), Paul (1995).

believed to have exclusive access to technology and information capable of indicating valuable improvements to the incumbent's operating strategy. More effective supervision in turn promotes the development of the capital market.[3] Lakonishok, Shleifer and Vishny find that, with the growth of institutional ownership, extra layers of agency problems may explain the differences between mutual funds and pension funds.[4] Walker and Lefort found that pension fund assets can reduce the dividend ratio and increase the ratio of stock price to book value, which in turn results in reducing the cost of capital and promoting the development of the capital market.[5] Meng and Pfau show that the size of pension fund assets has a positive impact on the depth and liquidity of the stock market and on the depth of the bond market.[6] Hu finds that there is a significantly positive correlation between pension fund assets and market capitalization, especially for emerging economies in Asia, where pension fund assets have a positive impact on long-term capital market liquidity.[7] Coffee argues that institutional investors have the ability to hold large equity shares and are locked into the market.[8] Chopra, Lakonishok and Ritter (1992) find that the institutional investment behaviour of institutional investors may counteract irrational trading by individual investors, which helps to maintain price stability.[9] Davis believes that the growth of institutional investors is a key financial innovation, as they tend to enhance the stability of the financial system, even though sporadically they may exacerbate market volatility or liquidity problems.[10] The US subprime crisis and its impact on financial market stability revealed significant systemic risks and interconnections between movements on financial markets and institutional investors' investment behaviour.[11] Callen and Fang present evidence that institutional investor stability is negatively associated with the one-year-ahead stock price crash risk, a result which is shown to be robust in the face of alternative empirical specifications, estimation methods and endogeneity concerns. In addition, they find that institutional ownership by public pension funds is significantly negatively associated with future crash risk, which is consistent with the findings that pension funds more

---

3 Shleifer and Vishny (1986).
4 Lakonishok et al. (1992, 1994).
5 Walker and Lefort (2002).
6 Meng and Pfau (2010).
7 Hu (2012).
8 Coffee (1991).
9 Chopra et al. (1992).
10 Davis (2003).
11 Krišto et al. (2014).

actively monitor management than other types of institutions.[12] The arguments of these scholars focus on the importance of institutional investors for the volatility of capital markets, as well as for financial stability.

In contrast to the above, other scholars believe that an increase in the share of institutional investors will not stabilize the capital market. Friedman believes that increasing institutional ownership has probably increased the market's volatility in the context of occasional large price movements; the increasing prevalence of defined contribution pension plans, especially 401k plans, has resulted in an increased market price of risk.[13] Sias, Starks and Titman argue that the price impact of institutional trading is primarily responsible for the documented positive covariance between quarterly changes in institutional ownership and quarterly returns; this price pressure results from information revealed through institutional trading.[14] All these findings seem to argue that institutional investors impact mature capital markets; but it is not clear that in an emerging market like China, where institutional investors are still underdeveloped, similar effects exist.

In a strong emerging economy, China's stock prices frequently deviate from their fundamental values, resulting in high volatility.[15] Many scholars believe that institutional investors are regarded as having the potential to smooth market volatility and to stabilize capital markets. Analysing the lessons from the US's subprime mortgage crisis, which erupted in 2007, and the European sovereign debt crisis from 2009, Hu and Sun identified special relationships between the debt crisis and pension funds: the private pension systems of the European countries affected by the debt crisis were unable to constitute an independent pillar, their capital markets lacked long-term investors and their fiscal systems were exacerbated by heavy reliance on public pensions.[16] Besides pension funds, this chapter will also focus on the impact of other institutional investors such as mutual funds and insurance companies on China's capital markets, so as to identify the differences between China and other developed countries.

At the annual meeting of finance ministers and central bankers from the 188 member countries of the International Monetary Fund (IMF) held in Peru in October 2015, China's economic situation dominated discussions, with participants asking if 'China's economic downturn [would] trigger a

---

12 Callen and Fang (2013).
13 Friedman (1995).
14 Sias et al. (2001).
15 Poshakwale (2001).
16 Hu and Sun (2016).

new financial crisis'.[17] This concern about another financial crisis stemming from China is not surprising as its economy is slowing down and the exchange rate is depreciating; therefore, financial panic can easily ensue. How such a potential crisis can be prevented is one of the top priorities of China's financial regulatory authorities, scholars and the public at large. Examining the role that institutional investors may play in Chinese capital market development provides important insights into how China can maintain stability in its financial system.

The rest of this chapter is organized as follows. Section 2 provides a basic analytical approach by presenting a panel data analysis of institutional investors and capital markets in OECD member countries from 2001 to 2013. Section 3 compares institutional investors in China and the United States, the two largest economies in the world. Section 4 focuses on the comparison of institutional investors in two groups of OECD countries, that is the Netherlands, Australia, Switzerland and the UK (NASU), and Italy, Greece, Portugal and Spain (IGPS). Section 5 analyses the potential impact of China's newly published normative state documents for the development of institutional investors.

2. AN EMPIRICAL TEST OF THE IMPACT OF INSTITUTIONAL INVESTORS ON THE STABILITY OF THE CAPITAL MARKET IN OECD MEMBERS

According to the OECD classification, institutional investors can be subdivided into three categories: investment funds, insurance corporations and autonomous pension funds (private pensions, hereinafter referred to as pension funds).[18] To verify the effect of institutional investors on the stability of the capital market, we used data from OECD countries for the period 2001 to 2013 to make a panel data regression, to obtain the effect of institutional investors on the stability of the capital market from the empirical analysis. We chose the panel data regression method because cross-section data is not sufficient to obtain a significant regression conclusion. At the same time there are a large number of factors which influence capital market stability; we cannot solve the problem of missing variables using cross-section data regression. However, panel data regression is an effective way of solving this problem, as it can address

---

17 Kaletsky (2016).
18 OECD (2014).

individual factors, which we cannot observe. We used data from 2001 to 2013 because this period reflects a complete economic cycle: the economy grew and the financial market developed better at the beginning of this timeframe, before the global financial crisis broke out in 2007–2008, and the European debt crisis broke out in 2009, following which stability was gradually restored in most countries. So this period is a good representation of an economic cycle.

Regarding the selection of specific indicators, we selected the annual fluctuation rates of each country's stock market composite index volatility (stock price volatility, SPV) as an indicator of capital market stability. The index serves as the explained variable of the model; we selected each country's GDP per capita (lng*dp*) as the control variable, to control time factor impacts on market stability. We used the percentage of investment funds accounted for financial assets (*inv*), the percentage of insurance corporations accounted for financial assets (*ins*) and the percentage of pension funds accounted for financial assets (*pen*) as explanatory indicators of institutional investors.

The regression model is as follows:

$$SPV_{it} = \beta_0 + \beta_1 inv_{it} + \beta_2 ins_{it} + \beta_3 pen_{it} + \beta_4 \text{lng}\, dp_{it} + u_i + e_{it}$$

Here i means the OECD member countries; t is the year – a total of 13 years (2001–2013) were used; u_i is the individual unobserved factor that does not vary with time, e_{it} is the random disturbance term that changes with time and countries.

First, we tested the correlation between each explanatory variable, and the results are as shown in Table 3.1.

As can be seen from Table 3.1, there is little correlation between any two indicators, so the problem of multi collinearity does not arise. From the data we find that investment funds, insurance corporations and pension funds are positively related to the GDP per capita. Yet the correlation coefficient between investment funds and the GDP per capita is very small (only 0.25). We can therefore conclude that there is little correlation between the investment fund scale and the development of the national economy attributable to the different financial structures, or residents' different investment preferences in the various countries. However, the correlation coefficient between insurance corporations and pension funds to GDP per capita is 0.58 and 0.40 respectively. This means that the more developed a country's economy is, the higher the share of insurance corporations and pension funds there are in its capital market.

We used a panel data fixed effect model to build the stepwise regression. The result is shown in Table 3.2.

Table 3.1 Correlation test between GDP per capita, investment funds, insurance corporations and pension funds

	GDP per capita	Investment funds	Insurance corporations	Pension funds
GDP per capita	1.0000			
Investment funds	0.2494	1.0000		
Insurance corporations	0.5891	0.4833	1.0000	
Pension funds	0.4026	0.3236	0.5808	1.000

Source: stock market volatility and GDP per capita data is taken from the World Bank's official website; institutional investor data is taken from the OECD official website; collated by the authors.

Table 3.2 Fixed effect model regression of institutional investors' panel data in OECD member countries

	Explanatory indicator used			
	Investment funds	Insurance corporations	Pension funds	Institutional investors
GDP per capita	2.805951 (0.141)	1.998153 (0.251)	4.378388 (0.092)*	4.425581 (0.019)**
Investment funds	–0.0896977 (0.286)			0.0108774 (0.909)
Insurance corporations		–0.321271 (0.000)***		–0.2548683 (0.018)**
Pension funds			–0.2697357 (0.000)***	–0.1876172 (0.010)***
Observed value	246	304	278	227

Note: To overcome the different variance, we use the logarithmic GDP per capita; P values are given in parenthesis; we use respectively *, * *, * * * as the 10%, 5%, 1% significance level.

Source: stock market volatility and GDP per capita data is taken from the World Bank's official website; institutional investor data is taken from the OECD official website; collated by the authors.

From Table 3.2 we can see that the p-values of investment funds are 0.286 and 0.909. It can be seen that the impact of investment funds on stock price volatility is not significant and cannot pass the t-test. Consequently, we can say that the impact of investment funds on the volatility of stock prices is not verified and we cannot explain the relationship between investment funds and the stability of the capital market through this model. The reason for this may be that most investment funds are open-end funds. Open-end investment funds have particular properties: when the capital market is sluggish or fluctuates greatly, a large number of fund holders will choose to be redeemed. This may interfere with our conclusion concerning the effects of pension funds and insurance corporations on the market. Moreover, the result of the stepwise regression shows that the coefficients of insurance companies and pension funds are approximately –0.32 and –0.27 respectively. So in the statistical sense, we could say that when the percentage of insurance companies accounting for the financial assets increases by 1%, the stock price volatility rate will decrease by 0.32%; when the percentage of pension funds accounting for the financial assets increases by 1%, the stock price volatility rate will decrease by 0.27%.

At the same time, institutional investor trade has a greater impact on stock price because institutional investors have more information and hold more stocks than individual investors. Respective regression results show that the p-values of insurance corporations and pension funds are far below the 1% significance level; so we can conclude that they have a significant impact on price volatility. The coefficients are negative, which means that the higher the percentage of financial assets that insurance corporations and pension funds account for, the smaller the volatility in stock prices. We can find further that insurance corporations and pension funds play an important role in reducing the volatility of stock prices, and thus support the stability of the capital market. Perhaps the reason for this is that insurance corporations and pension funds can take advantage of long-term investment and asset–liability matching, which means their revenue can be predicted and payments can be actuarial; their investment strategies can reflect their long-term strategy, which in turn benefits market stability. These companies will thus not massively overweight or underweight with the volatility of the market. This also verifies the conclusion of Sias, Starks and Titman: there is strong correlation between the quarter changes of institutional investors' ownership and the influence of trading price.[19]

From the above analysis we can conclude that, based on data from OECD member countries, the institutional investors represented by insurance corporations and pension funds can reduce price volatility in the capital market and they play an important role in maintaining the stability and advancing the development of the capital market.

---

[19] Sias et al. (2001).

3. INSTITUTIONAL INVESTORS IN CHINA AND THE UNITED STATES: COMPARISON AND EXPERIENCE

Institutional investors are considered rational and risk neutral,[20] while human beings by contrast are assumed to have bounded rationality. Legal persons or institutional investors control vast sums of money in global capital markets, which affects the stability of the financial system;[21] they can be seen as rational and stable investors. Yet the impact of institutional investors on China's capital market is still unclear.

Given the general lack of institutional investors in China, its stock market performance in mid-2015 to early 2016 experienced a lot of volatility. In June to August 2015, after nearly one year of steady increases, the Shanghai Composite Index (SCI) doubled in mid-June, but began an unexpected decline and lost over 30% in only three weeks. This amounted to a loss of nearly US$4 trillion in market capitalization. By 8–9 July 2015, over 1,400 companies, or more than half of those listed on the Shanghai Exchange, filed for a trading halt in an attempt to prevent further losses.[22] Major aftershocks occurred around the 'Black Mondays' of 27 July and 24 August. The value of Chinese stocks continued to drop, giving rise to the sharpest decline in since 2007, despite all government efforts to stabilize the market.[23]

Financial regulators like the People's Bank of China (the Central Bank), the China Security Regulatory Commission, the China Banking Regulatory Commission, the China Insurance Regulatory Commission and even the Ministry of Public Security, as well as almost all securities institutions, announced that they would buttress the stock market to avert a potential financial crisis. The Chinese government enacted many measures to stem the tide and avoid the crash. Financial regulators limited the ability of investors to sell short under threat of arrest.[24] Large mutual funds and pension funds pledged to buy more stocks. The government stopped initial public offerings, and provided cash to brokers to buy shares, backed by the Central Bank. Despite these efforts, these measures had only limited effect upon the capital markets. In January 2016 China officially introduced the 'circuit-breaker mechanism', which means that during trading, when a specified target price range is attained,

---

20 Hutchinson et al. (2015).
21 Coffee and Black (1994).
22 Duggan (2015).
23 Gough (2015).
24 Colombo (2015).

trading will be suspended. If the 5% threshold is triggered during a late period (from 14:45 to 15:00) or if the 7% threshold is triggered any time during a trading day, trading will be suspended until closing that day. This is similar to the way in which a fuse blows automatically when excess current runs through it, so as to prevent appliance damage. Unfortunately, the circuit-breaker mechanism affects market volatility rather than stability. For instance, in contrast to rising prices, falling share prices more easily lead to collective irrationality. When the market's decline approaches the threshold, investor anxiety that the circuit breaker may take effect may be created, and this panic may result in share dumping. Trading was eventually halted on 4 and 7 January 2016 after the market fell 7%, on the latter date within 30 minutes of opening.[25] Therefore, establishing the threshold requires a delicate balancing of all possible circumstances.

The crashes in the capital market and resulting panic in China that occurred in the course of 2015 to 2016 attracted the attention of the world; and non-energy commodities and metals experienced a broad-based drop in price, resulting in the weakening of manufacturing activity in China, while agriculture prices were also generally down. From many perspectives, China is very much on the brink of a capital market crisis. This view is seconded by Liu Shiyu, the new chairman of the China Securities Regulatory Commission since 2016: 'the stock market crash is like the bursting of a bubble, especially during the process of a downward trend; China's stock market may behave like a runaway truck that rolls downhill, which may crash at any time.'[26] Why was China's financial regulation not able to maintain stable capital markets? Examining the differences in performance of the Chinese and US capital markets and GDP may offer clues.

Figure 3.1 shows a marked downturn in 2008, which is attributable to the subprime mortgage crisis that had a significant international impact. The stock market in both China and the US fell in 2008; seven years later the S&P 500 index recovered and gained a new high. It was about 1.4 times higher in 2015 than it was in 2007. At the same time the SCI was only 61% of what it was in 2007. The GDP growth ratio draws a very different picture. China's GDP average growth rate during this period was 8.8%, or 6.9% higher than that of the US's growth rate. These differences between the world's largest and second-largest economies are startling. The remainder of this chapter examines the respective roles

---

25 Lahart (2016).
26 Bian (2016).

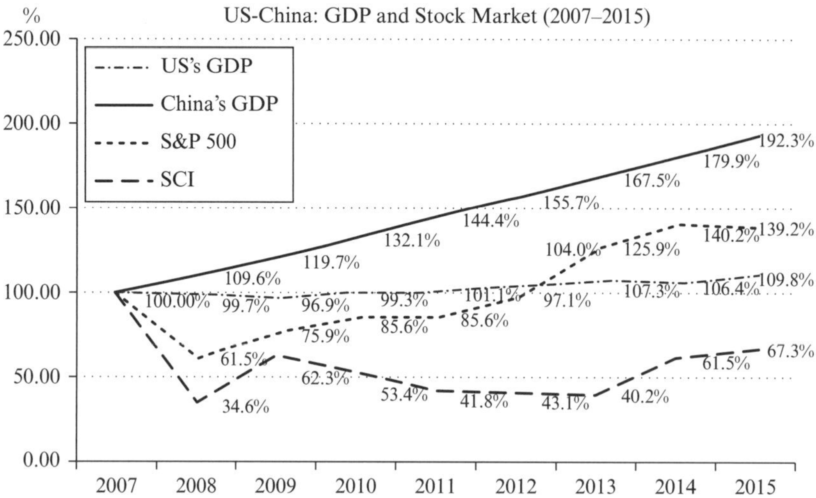

Source: GDP data from http://data.worldbank.org/indicator/CM.MKT.LCAP.CD; SCI from Shanghai Stock Exchange official website: http://english.sse.com.cn/; the US S&P 500 from Yahoo Finance: http://finance.yahoo.com/.

Figure 3.1 Comparison of the Chinese and US Stock Markets and GDP

played by institutional investors in both countries. They are a key reason for explaining the differences in the development of the US and Chinese capital markets.

Compared to China, the United States has a more developed financial regulation system, advanced stock markets and more developed institutional investors. Even after the subprime crisis of 2008, US non-banking financial services and financial markets are still ranked first in the world. Since 2011 the US's main stock market indexes have reached new historic heights.[27] The majority of Chinese investors are retail individuals, who embody the idea of herding behaviour described by Shiller;[28] the deficiency of institutional investors – mutual funds, insurance companies and pension funds – may be one of the principal reasons that explain the difference in performance between the macro economy and capital markets.

A comparison of the Chinese and US economy and capital markets can be made on the basis that there are three types of institutional investor.

---

27 World Economic Forum (2011).

28 Shiller (1995).

Table 3.3 Comparison of institutional investors between China and the US in 2013

Classification		China	USA	USA/China
Unit		RMB billion	US$ billion	
GDP		56,885	16,768	1.8
Mutual funds	Assets	4,221	16,822	24.3
	ARG%	7.2	94.8	
	EIR%	39.3	49.9	
Insurance corporations	Assets	7,687	7,511	5.96
	ARG%	13.1	44.8	
	EIR%	10.2	33.6	
Pension funds	Assets	1,845	16,892	55.8
	ARG%	3.2	100.7	
	EIR%	23.2	50.7	
Total investment by institutional investors		2,871	19,480	41.4
Total market value		23,908	24,035	6.1
Ratio of institutional investors (%)		12.0	81.0	

Key: ARG % = Assets Ratio to GDP %; EIR % = Equity Investing Ratio %.

Source: the total for the American stock market value is derived from the World Federation of Exchanges' annual report: 2013 WFE Market Highlights; the total for the New York Exchange and NASDAQ; institutional investors data is derived from OECD Institutional Investors Statistics 2014,OECD Publishing; China's stock market value is derived from the China Securities Regulatory Commission official website; mutual funds data is from the China Securities Investment Funds Industry Association official website; China's insurance corporations data is from the China Insurance Regulatory Commission official website; China's pension funds data includes the enterprise annuity and the National Social Security Fund (which can be invested in the stock market and the ratio can be weighted), calculated according to the National Social Security Fund Council annual report. The multiple for both countries can be calculated using the exchange rate on 31 December 2013, which was 1:6.0969.

Table 3.3 shows that China's security investment funds are comparable to the mutual funds of the US.

Table 3.3 shows that, as the US has the world's most developed capital market, its assets of mutual funds and pension fund assets are respectively 24.3 and 55.8 times the size of the respective Chinese market. Contrasted to the scale of its economy, this is remarkable: the US's GDP is only 1.8 times that of China. As presented in Table 3.1, the total market value of three types of institutional investors' investment in stocks is close to \$19.48 trillion, accounting for 81% of the total market value of the US, while China's institutional investors' investments only accounted for 12% of the total market value. This shows that the stock market in the US mainly consists of institutional investors, while individual retail investors dominate China's stock market. After the subprime mortgage crisis in 2007–2008, this difference in investment by institutional investors may be one of the most important factors explaining the varying capital market performance between China and the US.

The difference between mutual funds in China and the US is significant. Mutual funds have a history of more than one hundred years in the United States, and include mutual funds, exchange-traded funds (ETFs), closed-end funds and unit investment trusts (UITs) within the United States, and similar funds offered to investors in jurisdictions worldwide. According to the Investment Company Institute's report, there are 801 registered fund companies, whose total holding is US$ 15 trillion, accounting for half of the worldwide mutual funds, while also comprising the main financial investment instruments in the US. More than 22% of American family financial assets were held by mutual funds in 2013, with the average annual investment reaching US$ 368 billion.[29] By contrast, China's mutual funds industry has a history of about only two decades, and by the end of 2013 there were 89 fund management companies. These jointly managed total assets just under RMB 4221 billion, in which the public fund amounted to RMB 3002 billion and private pension assets amounted to RMB 1219 billion.[30]

Table 3.3 shows that the mutual funds assets in the US is US$ 16.82 trillion, which is 24.3 times that of China's, while the stock market capitalization of the US is only 6.1 times that of China's. Mutual funds in both China and the US have invested in capital markets. The huge asset gap may stem from the dominance of individual investors in Chinese stock markets, whose trading behaviour may be characterized as speculative. The stock market depicts strong price fluctuations as individual investors, whose trading behaviour is easily influenced by rumours and lack of rationality, dominate China's stock market. The convergence of their trading behaviour is described by Shiller as 'herding behaviour'.[31] In the US there are mainly institutional investors in the stock market and retail investors account for less than 20% of the market value. Institutional investors are rational and risk neutral, and consequently the US stock

---

[29] Investment Company Institute (2014, 2015).

[30] Data: China Securities Investment Funds Industry Association official website (in Chinese), see: http://www.amac.org.cn/tjsj/xysj/jjgssj/385457.shtml.

[31] Shiller (1995).

market is much more stable than that of China. From the proportion of mutual funds invested in the stock market, it can be seen that about half of mutual funds assets are invested in stocks in the US, while less than 40% of mutual funds assets are invested in stocks in China. There is a long way to go for China's mutual funds industry to catch up with the US because of the huge difference in historical accumulation, the investment ratio and the amount of assets.

As a leading institutional investor, insurance corporations act as long-term investors and invest their assets conservatively and prudently. They thereby provide a stabilizing benefit to society. The total assets of insurance corporations at the global level were estimated at US$ 22.6 trillion in 2009.[32] Life insurance products have a unique nature as they are characterized by long-term investments. Some findings indicate that the stock selection and market timing abilities of life insurance corporations do not differ during bull and bear markets and that they exhibit similar market performance as mutual funds.[33] Insurance depth[34] and insurance density[35] in China are much lower than in the US. The proportion of investment in the stock market is also much lower in China than in the US. Since 2004 China's insurance regulator has gradually increased the proportion an insurance fund is allowed to invest in equity assets from 5% to 30%. As at the end of 2014, insurance corporations invested merely 11.06% in the capital markets.[36] Table 3.3 shows that insurance corporations' assets in the US are nearly six times that of China and around one-third are invested in the capital markets. If China's insurance corporations were to invest in the equity market up to the statutory limit, there would be an additional capital increase in the stock market of RMB 2 trillion. This would make insurance corporations one of the most important institutional investors in China.

Among the three types of major institutional investors, the gap between the Chinese and US pension funds is the largest. The market value of pension fund assets reached a high of US$ 16.89 trillion in 2013. US pension fund assets were 55.8 times larger than those of China and they

---

32 SwissRe (2010).

33 Kleiman and Sahu (1991).

34 Insurance depth means the country's total insurance gross premium to its GDP. It can reflect a country's insurance industry in its importance to the macroeconomy. The index's calculation depends not only on development level of a country's macroeconomy, but also on the development of the insurance industry.

35 Insurance density refers to the insurance expense per capita calculation according to the local population. It reflects the development level of a country's national economy and the insurance industry.

36 China Insurance Regulatory Commission official website: http://circ.gov.cn/web/site0/tab5257/info3948914.htm.

invested 50.7% of their assets in stocks. Because of the maturity of legal protection for investors and capital market regulation, the US's pension fund assets accounted for 57.8% of GDP during the years 1980 to 2008.[37] According to OECD statistics, US pension fund assets reached 100.7% of GDP by the end of 2013, which was more than half of the amount of pension fund assets of all 34 OECD member countries combined.[38] Furthermore, 67% of all US families have individual retirement accounts (IRA) benefiting from preferential taxation schemes. The IRA invested in mutual funds reached US$ 6.5 trillion in 2013.[39] Pension funds therefore have an important stabilizing effect on the US capital market. The capital market is always the most important investment channel for pension funds. Although China's macroeconomic growth rate is much higher than that of the US, its capital market does not perform as well as that of the US. The absence of large-scale private pension fund investment in China may be one of the most important reasons for this. As the largest long-term institutional investors, pension funds account for nearly half of stock marketization and have become the main players in the stock market in order to preserve and increase their value. Financial regulations have helped to protect pensioners and financial consumers effectively and have helped to maintain a competitive, efficient and stable stock market.

From a comparison of mutual funds, insurance corporations and pension funds, it can be seen that in the fields of financial regulations, stock markets and institutional investors, the US is one of the most advanced economies in the world. China can draw valuable lessons for its own capital market development from the US experience.

All of the preceding empirical studies have shown that institutional investors such as pension funds have a huge impact on the capital market. As one of the most marketized sectors in the Chinese economy, the Shanghai and Shenzhen stock markets was established in 1990, China decided to implement a market economy in 1992. Following the decision made by the Third plenary session of the 18th Central Committee of the Communist Party of China in 2013, China adopted institutional changes to allow market forces to play a decisive role in promoting economic growth. Thus the market will play an increasingly important role in the development of the country. In the newly amended draft of the securities law, China seeks to encourage institutional investors to increase their capital allocation in the stock market, while safeguarding investor rights.

---

37 Meng and Pfau (2010).
38 OECD (2014).
39 The Investment Company Institute (2014).

By expanding both the institutional investor base and improving protection for investor rights, this security law amendment contributes to capital market stability.

The above analysis shows that differences in institutional investors can partly explain the varying development of the Chinese and American capital markets. In the US case, key amendments in securities regulations and their respective enforcement also played a decisive role. The US House of Representatives approved the Securities Law (1933) and the Securities and Exchange Act (1934) that involved information disclosure during the process of security issuance, with the aim of protecting outside investors and reducing information asymmetry among small investors and controlling shareholders. The Securities Investor Protection Act (1970) established an insurance scheme (up to US$ 50 million) for investors if they incurred losses on their investments. The Employee Retirement Income Security Act (1974) required firms to comply with minimum standards for pension provisions and imposed additional conditions on the funding of pensions. This Act also set up the Pension Benefit Guarantee Corporation, which guarantees the benefits of funds in default.[40] The tax law amendments of 1978 introduced sections 401(k) and 403(b) to provide tax incentives for employers and employees, encouraging them to invest a portion of salary payments in a pension scheme. This fuelled marked increases in pension assets in the subsequent decades. These assets constituted long-term capital investments that strengthened the US capital markets and Wall Street, a global financial centre. Pension funds became the largest institutional investors and played a significant role in encouraging financial innovation,[41] promoting corporate governance and maintaining capital market stability.

All the relevant laws were not only enacted but also enforced. Coffee (2007) shows that during the years 2003 to 2006 the aggregate financial penalties imposed by the Securities and Exchange Commission (SEC) were 39 times that of UK Financial Services Authority (FSA).[42] Using capital market and related regulations as safeguards, long-term investment of pension funds in the capital market was made possible. This arguably led to a win–win situation for pension funds, which benefitted from higher returns, and for capital markets, which benefitted from more stability. The direct financing of capital markets also allowed for the emergence of a series of technological giants such as Apple, Microsoft and Google, which established and consolidated the US's position as a creative superpower.

---

40 Allen and Gale (2000).

41 Bodie (1990).

42 Coffee (2007).

4. INSTITUTIONAL INVESTORS BEHIND THE EUROPEAN SOVEREIGN DEBT CRISIS

Institutional investors have played a crucial role in the rapid recovery of the capital market following the US subprime crisis. This section examines the role of institutional investors in the context of the European sovereign debt crisis experienced by countries such as Italy, Greece, Portugal and Spain (IGPS) since 2009.

Based on the data from statistical bureaus and the OECD, this section compares and analyses the role of institutional investors in selected OECD countries (the Netherlands, Australia, Switzerland and the United Kingdom – NASU) to that in IGPS.

Table 3.4 shows that institutional investors in IGPS are far behind those in NASU in terms of total capital assets and the percentage share of their capital invested in the capital markets. Furthermore, the three types of institutional investors in IGPS are not strong enough to help the capital markets to resolve the debt crisis.

The number of institutional investors who invested their capital in mutual funds is much larger in NASU than in IGPS. Among all OECD countries, Switzerland has the largest amount of mutual fund assets (86.3% of GDP) and is thus close to the US. The rate for the Netherlands is above 70%, and for the UK and Australia it is 40%. The data clearly show that mutual funds play an important role in NASU capital markets. These capital markets are considered as being among the world's most developed capital markets. In contrast, the asset to GDP ratio of mutual funds in the IGPS economies remains underdeveloped. While Spain had the highest rate (17.8%), Portugal and Italy accounted for only 8.4% and 8.7% respectively. Greece's mutual fund assets accounted for only 2.5% of its GDP.

Mutual funds have invested a large amount of their assets in the stock market: in the case of the Netherlands, Australia and the UK this is more than 50%. In the case of IGPS by contrast, this figure is around 20%–40%. The data show that mutual fund assets differ significantly across NASU and IGPS. This illustrates that the large-scale institutional investors of mutual funds in NASU can influence the capital market through direct investment and help with its stabilization. However, IGPS's relatively weak mutual funds lack this kind of ability. The mutual fund assets to GDP rate in Greece ranked last among the previously mentioned countries, notably because Greece's economy is still struggling to recover from its sovereign debt crisis. As an important index, the mutual funds to GDP ratio between NASU and IGPS shows that the former have a more developed financial level.

Table 3.4 Institutional investors' assets and invested in capital markets ratio in eight OECD countries

Nation		Portugal	Italy	Greece	Spain	Netherlands	Australia	Switzerland	UK
Year		2013	2012	2013	2013	2013	2012	2013	2012
Unit: million		Euro	Euro	Euro	Euro	Euro	AUD	CHF	GBP
GDP		172,345	1,697,437	205,280	1,013,961	643,892	698,405	635,438	1,812,400
Mutual Funds	Assets	14,477	147,677	5,132	180,485	455,876	270,283	548,383	797,456
	ARG%	8.4	8.7	2.5	17.8	70.8	38.7	86.3	44
	EIR%	21.4	29.4	40.9	21.8	57.6	51.6	–	58.3
Insurance Companies	Assets	59,514	548,051	14,921	276,669	425,172	1,644,720	550,463	1,476,748
	ARG%	34.8	33.7	8.2	26.4	66.1	28.2	86.6	89
	EIR%	10.5	25.2	17.6	9.8	31.4	55.8	50.9	23.6
Pension Funds	Assets	14,231	33,828	0	116,361	959,554	1,403,716	655,430	1,572,587
	ARG%	8.3	2.1	0	11.1	149.3	92.3	103.2	95
	EIR%	38.1	53.1	0	20.5	64.2	58.3	68.9	17.6

Key: ARG % = Assets Ratio to GDP %; EIR % = Equity Investment Ratio %.

Note: As with the comparison between the US and China, Table 3.4 shows the relative share of institutional investors in IGPS and NASU. It also shows that they have similar GDPs.

Sources: GDP data from the World Bank's official website; OECD Institutional Investors Statistics (2006–2013), OECD Publishing 2014.

There is also a difference between IGPS and NASU in the area of insurance company assets. Even though insurance markets in all eight OECD countries considered are more developed than that of China, the total insurance corporation assets of IGPS are far less than those of NASU. The insurance corporation assets to GDP ratio in the UK is the highest (89%), followed by Switzerland (86.6%) and the Netherlands (66.1%). The insurance corporations assets to GDP ratio is only 8.2% in Greece, which is the lowest among all the eight countries. At the same time the ratio of insurance corporations assets invested in the stock market is higher in NASU than in IGPS. For instance, Australia's rate is 55.8% and Switzerland's is 50.9%. By contrast, insurance corporations in IGPS only invested approximately 10% to 20% in capital markets. As an important institutional investor, insurance corporations could use their assets in long-term investment to stabilize capital markets. The huge difference in insurance corporation assets between NASU and IGPS could explain the diversity between their respective capital markets and financial systems. Life insurance corporations in particular have asset–liability structures that span decades and should therefore be interested in long-term equity investment instruments, which could benefit the stability of stock markets.

Comparing the pension assets of NASU and IGPS shows significant differences in the ratio to GDP and their investment ratio in the stock market. Regarding pension assets to GDP, the Netherlands ranks number one globally (149.3%), although it suffers from low interest rates and a stock market that did not develop smoothly.[43] The ratio to GDP is also high in Switzerland (103.2%). This is attributable to the Occupational Pension Insurance Act of 1985; Switzerland was the first country in the world to establish a mandatory second pillar in a private pension system.[44] Pension assets have given Switzerland a strong base on which to build one of the world's most developed financial markets. Legislators also reformed the pension system in Australia. In 1992 they introduced the Australian Superannuation System, which constitutes a masterpiece of a compulsory private pension scheme and allows the country to rank first on the global pension sustainability index.[45] This scheme also allowed Australia to catch up with well-developed financial market countries at an astonishing speed. Since October 2012, the UK has transformed its private pension system from voluntary to auto-enrolled, where more than 90% of employees have been auto-enrolled into a workplace pension by their

---

43 OECD (2013).
44 Durand and Gaille (2013).
45 Allianz (2014).

employer. As a consequence, the participation rate has increased from 61% to 83%,[46] allowing the ratio of pension assets to GDP to reach 95%.

The pension system in NASU generally consists of state-level wealth and large-scale private pension assets, which a large proportion of these assets invested inthe capital markets. This has allowed pension funds to grow into the most important institutional investors. In stark contrast to NASU, the pension assets to GDP ratios of IGPS are much lower: Greece has nearly no private pension assets and Italy's pension assets to GDP ratio is a mere 2.1%. Among IGPS, the highest pension asset to GDP ratio is found in Spain (11.1%), but this compares unfavourably with NASU data. The huge gap in pension asset investments in the stock market and the overall differences between pension assets and their ratio to GDP is one of the marked differences between NASU and IGPS.

Table 3.4 shows that institutional investors' influence on the capital market differs significantly between NASU and IGPS, thus between countries that have stable capital markets and those that suffer from a sovereign debt crisis. Institutional investors may therefore be seen as an important explanatory variable for financial stability in the capital market. This relationship is also asserted in the European Capital Requirements Directive that aims at ensuring the stability of the financial system and defines institutional investors as an eligible counterparty or professional client,[47] which is an important element in maintaining financial stability. In order to safeguard financial stability, Directive 2010/76/EU amended existing legislation (Directives 2006/48/EC and 2006/49/EC) in several aspects: (a) it introduced strengthened rules regarding capital requirements for the trading bookend for re-securitizations, and (b) it introduced the supervisory review of remuneration policies, which were areas suffering from a high degree of financial instability.[48] According to Directive 2003/41/EC on the activities and supervision of institutions for occupational retirement provision, these institutions are financial service providers that bear a heavy responsibility for the provision of occupational retirement

---

46 Paterson (2013).

47 Directive 2006/48/EC of the European Parliament and of the Council, Official Journal of the European Union, 14 June 2006, Section 57: 'Supervision of credit institutions on a consolidated basis aims at, in particular, protecting the interests of the depositors of credit institutions and at ensuring the stability of the financial system.'

48 Directive 2010/76/EU of the European Parliament and of the Council of 24 November 2010 amending Directives 2006/48/EC and 2006/49/EC as regards capital requirements for the trading book and for re-securitisations, and the supervisory review of remuneration policies.

benefits and therefore should meet certain minimum prudential standards with respect to their activities and conditions of operation. This kind of requirement for institutional investors to take a prudential attitude will benefit financial stability.[49] All the above directives were meeting the development of the growth of institutional investors in Continental European countries, which tend to focus closely on the long-term sustainability of guarantees being offered on life policies, annuities and pensions. Institutional investors tend to enhance financial system stability, although they may sporadically exacerbate market volatility or liquidity problems.[50]

In the UK it is also the proclaimed objective of the public actors (Financial Services Authority, FSA) to maintain confidence in the financial system.[51] The FSA's successor, the Financial Conduct Authority (FCA) and the Prudential Regulation Authority (Bank of England), are embedding their contribution into financial institutions' assessment of monetary and macro prudential stability.[52] Table 3.4 shows that all types of institutional investors in the UK in 2012 are well developed. Since the 2008 Pension Act came into force in October 2012, all employees have to be automatically enrolled (mandatory in effect) in a qualified pension scheme. As a result the proportion of people with private pension savings could rise from around 40% to around 60% of the working age population, which will increase the proportion of pension fund assets invested in the capital market.[53]

Allen and Gale have argued that differing reactions to the instability associated with financial markets led to two broad types of financial systems – one market based and the other bank based. In the United Kingdom pension funds and insurance corporations are much more important than in the other sample countries.[54] The data presented in this chapter has shown that the financing features of NASU and the US are heavily based on capital markets, while by contrast the banking-dominated system of indirect financing is more widespread in IGPS and in China. Because of the difference in their financial frameworks, NASU and the US

---

[49] Directive 2003/41/EC of the European Parliament and of the Council of 3 June 2003, on the activities and supervision of institutions for occupational retirement provision, L 235/10, Official Journal of the European Union.

[50] Davis (2003).

[51] The UK Financial Services Authority–FSMA 2000 s 3(1): 'The market confidence objective is: maintaining confidence in the financial system.'

[52] Prudential Regulation Authority (2015).

[53] Office for National Statistics, Pension Trends Chapter 6: Private Pensions, 2013 Edition, 16 July 2013.

[54] Allen and Gale (2000).

have better-developed capital markets than IGPS and China. Based on the legal origin hypothesis of La Porta, Lopez-de-Silanes, Shleifer and Vishny, common law countries have better-developed financial markets than civil law countries because they offer better protection to investors and creditors.[55] Australia and the UK are common law countries, but IGPS are all civil law countries. Their underdeveloped capital markets and relatively backward financial development support La Porta, Lopez-de-Silanes, Shleifer and Vishny's legal origins hypothesis. Yet both the Netherlands and Switzerland are top of the league of private pension assets countries, and the performance of their pension policies are proof that even though a country cannot change its legal origin and endowment, it can change pension policies and reform the social security system. Compared to the pay-as-you-go system, a fully funded pension system could promote a country's financial development and economic growth.[56] Table 3.4 shows that all long-term institutional investors, including mutual funds, insurance corporations and pension funds, are better developed in NASU than in IGPS.

To address the problem of ageing populations, the European Parliament and European Council issued a directive on the activities and supervision of institutions for occupational retirement provisions (2003/41/EC), obliging EU member states to adjust their domestic law to the European pension system. In this way the financial market would be promoted and the pension system would become more unified, effective and highly liquid in European countries.[57] Based on this guidance, the European Insurance and Occupational Pension Authority (EIOPA) was aiming to qualify occupational pensions with other traditional financial industries such as banks, securities and insurance. EIOPA's core responsibilities are to support the stability of the financial system and the transparency of markets and financial products, as well as the protection of policyholders, pension scheme members and beneficiaries.[58]

The comparative analysis of the US subprime crisis and the European debt crisis reveals that a key factor behind the sluggish recovery of European debt-ridden economies may be the absence of private pension funds. This is because the rigid public pension payment system served to worsen the impact of the crisis. The situation in Greece is a case in point.

---

[55] La Porta et al. (1998).

[56] Sun and Hu (2014).

[57] Directive 2003/41/EC of the European Parliament and of the Council, on the activities and supervision of institutions for occupational retirement provision, L 235/10, Official Journal of the European Union.

[58] European Insurance and Occupational Pension Authority (2014).

One of the most important requests from the 'Troika' – the European Commission, the International Monetary Fund and the European Central Bank – when granting the Greek bailouts is that Greece must reform its pension system.[59] As a consequence, IGPS have no choice but to seek aid from the Troika, thus creating a spiral of debt entrapment. So it could be seen that pension funds are of vital importance in the financial stability of European countries, while occupational pensions can be compared to traditional financial sectors such as banks, equity and insurance.

5. DEVELOPING INSTITUTIONAL INVESTORS IN CHINA: NORMATIVE DOCUMENTS AS REGULATIONS

From the above, it can be seen that the experiences of developed countries with respect to institutional investors and capital market stability could be a good reference point for China. The US and NASU have more developed institutional investors in their capital markets than IGPS or China, and the former enjoy more stable financial markets; even when both groups suffer similar financial crises, the US and NASU can recover more quickly. In terms of institutional investors, China's securities investment funds, insurance corporations and pension funds all have a relatively young history. Their role in emerging capital markets is thus not on a par with the role such entities play in developed countries.

As legal amendments take a long time, China always relies on governmental normative documents for regulating market participants. According to a modern definition, the notion 'normative document' is generic and may cover various kinds of documents, including those establishing juridical norms and requirements. For example, EU Directives can be adopted in member states as domestic law by means of a variety of legislative procedures depending on their subject matter. China's regulatory instruments in the form of normative documents have been used as a way to modernize Chinese society since the late 1970s.[60] Recognizing the lack of institutional investors, the State Council, China's cabinet, published 'Several opinions on further promoting the healthy development of the capital market (Guo Fa [2014] No. 17[61])', or the 'New Nine Rules' on 8 May 2014. The target of

---

59 International Monetary Fund (2011).

60 Kong (2009).

61 See http://www.csrc.gov.cn/pub/tianjin/tjfzyd/tjjflfg/tjxzfg/201405/t20140513_248868.htm.

these guiding principles is to encourage the national social security fund, pension funds, insurance companies and security investment funds, as well as qualified foreign investment institutions, to invest in the capital markets as long-term investors, which will help to maintain financial stability.[62] So with the current amendment of the security law, the 'New Nine Rules' can guide the development of the Chinese capital market and encourage the growth of institutional investors, which in turn will reduce the volatility of the stock market and help to maintain financial stability.

Among the three types of institutional investors, security investment funds (mutual funds) should be given priority to develop in China, as China has a large proportion of individual investors who exhibit the herding behaviour described by Shiller.[63] Based on the development of public offering of security funds, China will reach a balanced development between exchange trading and OTC trading, public offering and private pension offering, to encourage growth in investment products, including mutual funds, private pension asset management plans, private pension collectives and collective funds trust plans according to the 'New Nine Rules'. Table 3.3 shows that mutual funds in the US are currently 24.3 times the size of those in China, which means that there is still a huge development gap in the Chinese financial market compared to the US financial market. The most important area for improvement remains legal enforcement of investor rights protection to bolster market sentiment sufficiently.

As a key social management tool in advanced economies, insurance remains at the heart of a country's social and economic development. Insurance companies should become a basic tool for managing risk and property for government, companies and the public at large. Accelerating the development of a modern insurance service sector will have great significance for improving and modernizing the financial system, creating employment opportunities, upgrading economic growth, innovating social management, and for safeguarding social stability and security. The State Council published another important normative document titled Opinions of the State Council on Accelerating the Development of the Modern Insurance Industry in August 2014.[64] This document is a useful supplement and amendment of the Insurance Law, under which insurance companies are encouraged to invest (via credit investment plans or equity

---

[62] Xinhua News Agency, 'China issues first capital market guideline'. See: http://news.xinhuanet.com/english/china/2014-05/09/c_126482785.htm.

[63] Shiller (1995).

[64] The State Council (2014).

investment plans) and promote coordinated development in the insurance market, money market and capital market. Insurance companies could fulfil an important support function to the stock market and help it to develop steadily. The new Chinese regulatory framework fosters a deep relationship between insurance companies and the capital market. Insurance companies are therefore likely to become major institutional investors, and will play a much more important role in the corporate annuity, professional annuity and life insurance sectors. As the pioneer of the institutional investors, China's insurance companies assets have increased very quickly since 2004. It took the insurance companies 24 years to accumulate the first RMB 1 trillion in assets; the second trillion took only three years, and the third trillion took less than one year. By the end of 2015 insurance companies assets reached 12.4 trillion; the annual growth rate has been as high as 22% per year since 2006.[65] In the subprime crisis, the US Federal Reserve spent US$ 85 billion to rescue the insurance company AIG after it refused to bailout America's fourth-largest investment bank, Lehman Brothers, in the interest of promoting stability in financial markets and limiting damage to the broader economy.[66] This is an important lesson that China can learn while catching up to developed countries: key firms may need to be bailed out, but not every insurance company. Insurance companies will act as one of the most important institutional investors in the capital market and will foster financial stability.

More significantly, pension funds have huge potential for the development of China's institutional investors. In August 2000 the State Council decided to establish the National Social Security Fund (NSSF) and the National Council for Social Security Fund (SSF) to manage and operate the assets of the NSSF. The NSSF serves as the national social security reserve fund to supplement and adjust social security spending such as social insurance as the population continues to age at an ever-increasing rate. The funding sources of the NSSF include fiscal allocation from central government, the transfer of state-owned capital and fund investment proceeds, and capital raised by other methods approved by the State Council. The total assets of the NSSF reached RMB 1.91 trillion at the end of 2015; the average annual return since 2000 has been as high as 8.82%, and in 2015 reached RMB 790.7 billion investments earning.[67]

---

65 Cao (2016).

66 BBC News, "US government rescues insurer AIG". See: http://news.bbc.co.uk/2/hi/business/7620127.stm.

67 National Council for Social Security Fund (2015).

The State Council promulgated the National Social Security Funds Regulation (The State Council Decree No. 667) in March 2016, so that the NSSF could be entrusted by provincial governments to manage their social insurance funds.

Considering the small number of institutional investors and the small amount of pension assets, the State Council published the Basic Old-Age Insurance Fund Investment Management Approach (Guo Fa [2015] No. 48) in August 2015. This is a regulation to specialize the investment management of the Chinese Social Insurance Law's insurance fund. Under this regulation, a basic pension fund can invest up to 30% of its net assets in the stock market. Additionally, social insurance funds can invest up to 20% of their net assets in the initial public offering of local state-owned enterprises, local industry leaders and provincial finance departments. Fiduciary, custody and investment management agencies must establish a sound internal control system of investment management to safeguard the pension funds.[68]

In addition to the basic pension scheme, a second pillar, a so-called private pension, has also received the attention of the Chinese government. In the Decision of the State Council on the Reform of the Old-Age Insurance System for Government Bodies and Public Institutions (Guo Fa [2015] No. 2), the civil servant and public service unit will set up a compulsory occupational annuity system. The employer will pay 8% of the salary while the individual will need to pay 4% of their income.[69] China currently has 38 million public employees, and the average annual salary is about RMB 15,000, which means that private pension funds will have income from occupational annuities of more than RMB 200 billion per year. China's second pillar pension assets of corporation annuities and occupational annuities will increase in the coming years and will play an increasingly important role in the capital market. For this reason, the development in compulsory enterprise annuity can help firms to build their annuity, and the growth of private pensions in China will herald new opportunities to accelerate the country's capital market development and financial stability. Chinese regulators should follow suit.

In conclusion, it can be seen that in recent years the State Council has published several normative documents to encourage the development of institutional investors in the form of mutual funds, insurance companies and pension funds. From a legal perspective, these normative documents

---

68 Ministry of Human Resources and Social Security, Ministry of Finance (2015).

69 The State Council (2015).

are not only policy papers, but also indications and regulations by which China's institutional investors will enjoy a better policy environment than ever. China's institutional investors are likely to enter a golden era and play an important role in capital market stability. If China's institutional investors become stronger in the near future, perhaps the Chinese capital market will not be so volatile, and the so-called financial crisis will happen (much) later.

REFERENCES

Allen, Franklin and Douglas Gale (2000), *Comparing Financial Systems*, Cambridge, MA: MIT Press.

Allianz (2014), Pension Sustainability Index, Allianz International Pension Papers 1/2014.

BBC News (n.d.), 'US government rescues insurer AIG'. See: http://news.bbc.co.uk/2/hi/business/7620127.stm.

Bian, Yongzu (2016), 'Liu Shiyu answered frankly: Confidence in the steady development of the capital market is firm' (in Chinese), *Sina Finance*, 13 March. See: http://finance.sina.com.cn/stock/t/2016-03-12/doc-ifxqhnev5870910.shtml.

Bodie, Z. (1990), 'Pension funds and financial innovation', *Financial Management*, 19 (3), 11–22.

Callen, Jeffrey L. and Xiaohua Fang (2013), 'Institutional investor stability and crash risk: monitoring versus short-termism?' *Journal of Banking and Finance*, 37 (8), 3047–63.

Cao, Deyun (2016), 'Under the new normal: China insurance asset management's new orientation, new pattern and new development', *China Insurance Assets Management*, No. 1, 2016. (In Chinese), China Insurance Regulatory Commission official website: http://circ.gov.cn/web/site0/tab5257/info3948914.htm.

China Securities Investment Funds Industry Association (n.d.), official website (in Chinese). See: http://www.amac.org.cn/tjsj/xysj/jjgssj/385457.shtml.

Chopra, N., J. Lakonishok and J.R. Ritter (1992), 'Measuring Abnormal Performance', *Journal of Financial Economics*, 31, 235–68.

Coffee, John C. Jr. (1991), 'Liquidity versus control: the institutional investor as corporate monitor', *Columbia Law Review*, 91 (6), 1277–368.

Coffee, John C. Jr. (2007), 'Law and the market: the impact of enforcement', *University of Pennsylvania Law Review*, 156 (2), 229–311.

Coffee, John C. and Bernard S. Black (1994), 'Hail Britannia: institutional investor behavior under limited regulation', *Michigan Law Review*, 92, 1997–2087.

Colombo, Jesse (2015), 'Watch these charts to better understand China's stock market crash', 12 July 2015, Forbes.

Davis, E. Philip (2003), 'Institutional investors, financial market efficiency, and financial stability', European Investment Bank, EIB Papers, Vol. 8, No. 1, pp. 76–107.

DeLong, J.B., A. Shleifer, L.H Summers and R. Waldmann (1987), 'The economic consequences of noise traders', *Social Science Electronic Publishing*, 38 (5), 1–104.

Directive 2003/41/EC of the European Parliament and of the Council of 3 June 2003, on the activities and supervision of institutions for occupational retirement provision, L 235/10, Official Journal of the European Union.

Directive 2006/48/EC of the European Parliament and of the Council, Official Journal of the European Union, 14 June 2006.

Directive 2010/76/EU of the European Parliament and of the Council of 24 November 2010 amending Directives 2006/48/EC and 2006/49/EC as regards capital requirements for the trading book and for re-securitisations, and the supervisory review of remuneration policies.

Duggan, Jennifer (2015), 'Chinese stock markets continue to nosedive as regulator warns of panic', *The Guardian* (Shanghai), 8 July.

Durand, Olivier and Séverine Gaille (2013) 'Switzerland: current retirement system and future prospects', The Geneva Association Life and Pensions, No. 52, March 2013.

European Insurance and Occupational Pension Authority (2014), Board of Supervisors, Annual Report 2014. See: https://eiopa.europa.eu/Publications/Reports/EIOPA_ANNUAL_REPORT_2014.pdf.

Friedman, Benjamin M. (1995), 'Economic implications of changing share ownership', NBER Working Paper No. 5141, June 1995.

Gough, Neil (2015), 'Chinese shares tumble again'. *The New York Times*, 28 July 2015. See: https://www.nytimes.com/2015/07/28/business/international/chinese-stocks-plummet-in-shanghai-and-shenzhen.html?_r=0.

Hu, Jiye and Shouji Sun (2016), 'Lessons from the European sovereign debt crisis for China', in Niels Philipsen et al. (eds), *Market Integration: The EU Experience and Implications for Reform in China*, China–EU Law Series 2, Berlin: Springer Verlag.

Hu, Yuwei (2012), 'Growth of Asian pension assets: implications for financial and capital markets', ADBI Working Paper Series, No. 360, May 2012, Tokyo: Asian Development Bank Institute.

Hutchinson, Marion, Michael Seamer and Larelle (Ellie) Chapple (2015), 'Institutional investors, risk/performance and corporate governance', *The International Journal of Accounting*, 50 (1), 31–52.

International Monetary Fund (2011), 'Greece: third review under the stand-by arrangement', Staff Report, Washington DC.

Investment Company Institute (2014), Investment Company fact book: a review of trends and activities in the US investment company industry (54th edition).

Investment Company Institute (2015), *ICI Research Perspective*, November, 21 (6).

Kaletsky, Anatole (2015), 'China is not collapsing', London: Project Syndicate, 12 October 2015. See: https://www.project-syndicate.org/commentary/why-china-is-not-collapsing-by-anatole-kaletsky-2015-10?barrier=accessreg.

Kleiman, Robert T. and Anandi P. Sahu (1991), 'Life insurance corporations as investment managers: new implications for consumers', *Financial Services Review*, 1 (1), 23–34.

Kong, Qingjiang (2009), 'Conflict of normative documents and its management in China', *Frontiers of Law in China*, 4 (4), 633–46.

Krišto, J., A. Stojanoviić and A. Pavkoviić (2014), 'Impact of institutional investors on financial market stability: lessons from financial crisis', Dubrovnik International Economic Meeting, 2 (1/2), 102–17.

La Porta, R., F. Lopez-de-Silanes, A. Shleifer and R.W. Vishny (1998), 'Law and finance', *Journal of Political Economy*, 106 (6), 1113–55.

Lahart, Justin (2016), 'Why this market meltdown isn't a repeat of 2008: U.S. economy and financial system are in a very different place now', *The Wall Street Journal*, 15 January.
Lakonishok, Josef, Andrei Shleifer and Robert W. Vishny (1992), 'The structure and performance of the money management industry', Brookings Papers on Economic Activity: Microeconomics, pp. 339–91.
Lakonishok, Josef, Andrei Shleifer and Robert W. Vishny (1994), 'Contrarian investment, extrapolation, and risk', *Journal of Finance*, 49 (5), 1541–78.
Meng Channarith and Wade Donald Pfau (2010), 'The role of pension funds in capital market development', National Graduate Institute for Policy Studies Discussion Paper 10-17, Tokyo, Japan.
Ministry of Human Resources and Social Security, Ministry of Finance (2015), "Background of investment management measures of basic old-age insurance fund", 28 August. See: http://www.china.com.cn/zhibo/zhuanti/ch-xinwen/2015-08/28/content_36441785.htm.
National Council for Social Security Fund (2015), The 2015 Annual Report of the National Council for Social Security Fund. See: http://www.ssf.gov.cn/cwsj/ndbg/'01606/t20160602_7079.html.
OECD (2013), Pensions at a glance 2013: Retirement-income systems in OECD and G20 countries, OECD Publishing.
OECD (2014), Institutional Investors Statistics (2006–2013), OECD Publishing, Paris.
Office for National Statistics (2013), Pension Trends, Chapter 6: Private Pensions, 2013 Edition, 16 July.
Paterson, Jennifer (2013), 'Auto-enrolled staff have stayed in pensions', Employee Benefits, 8 August. See: http://www.employeebenefits.co.uk/auto-enrolled-staff-have-stayed-in-pensions/.
Paul, J. (1995), 'Information aggregation without exogenous liquidity trading', Working Paper, University of Michigan, Ann Arbor.
Poshakwale, Sunil S. (2001), 'Foreign investment, market segmentation and volatility in the emerging Chinese stock market', *China Accounting & Finance Review*, 3 (1), 137–66.
Prudential Regulation Authority (2015), Prudential Regulation Authority Annual Report and Accounts for the Year Ended 28 February 2015.
Shenzhen Stock Exchange (2016), 'Investor structure and characteristics of behavioral changes in Shenzhen market: evidence from data of recent years'. See: http://www.szse.cn/main/en/AboutSZSE/SZSENews/SZSENews/39749848.shtml.
Shiller, Robert J. (1995), 'Conversation, information, and herd behavior', *American Economic Review*, 85, 181–5.
Shleifer, Andrei and Robert Vishny (1986), 'Large shareholders and corporate control', *Journal of Political Economy*, 94 (3).
Sias, Richard W., Laura T. Starks and Sheridan Titman (2001), 'The price impact of institutional trading', 25 August. See: http://ssrn.com/abstract=283779.
The State Council (2014), Opinions of the State Council on Accelerating the Development of the Modern Insurance Industry, No. 29. See the official website of the China Insurance Regulatory Commission: http://www.circ.gov.cn/web/site0/tab7561/info3928588.htm.
The State Council (2015), Decision on the Reform of the Old-Age Insurance System for Government Bodies and Public Institutions (Guo Fa [2015] No. 2), 3 January.

Sun, Shouji and Jiye Hu (2014), 'The impact of pension systems on financial development: an empirical study', in Niels Philipsen and Guangdong Xu (eds), *The Role of Law and Regulation in Sustaining Financial Markets*, New York: Routledge.

SwissRe (2010), 'Insurance investment in a challenging global environment', Swiss Reinsurance Company Ltd, Economic Research and Consulting, No. 5.

Trueman, B. (1988), 'A theory of noise trading of security markets', *Journal of Finance*, 43, 83–95.

Walker, Eduardo and Fernando Lefort (2002), 'Pension reform and capital markets: are there any (hard) links?' Social Protection Unit, Human Development Network, The World Bank.

World Economic Forum (2011), 'The Financial Development Report 2011', World Economic Forum USA Inc., Geneva, Switzerland.

Xinhua News Agency (n.d.), 'China issues first capital market guideline'. See: http://news.xinhuanet.com/english/china/2014-05/09/c_126482785.htm.

4. Unpredictable enforcement: a study of the CSRC's approach to insider trading in China

Tianshu Zhou and Wenjing Li*

1. INTRODUCTION

As a result of concentrated ownership structures and weak outside supervision, insider trading has long been a problem in China's capital markets. As Mallin concluded, in Chinese state-owned enterprises (SOEs), even those operating abroad, 'CEOs may be all-powerful and able to take decisions that are not in the best interests of the company and its shareholders and limited disclosure may exacerbate the situation'.[1] Many scholars have expended substantial efforts to explore this topic in the Chinese context, and there are certain subjects upon which agreement has been achieved among these scholars. For example, there is little doubt that, although the insider trading rules of Chinese securities law are (in large part) transplanted from the US, they remain incomplete and inconsistently organized.[2] Furthermore, solid empirical evidence suggests that enforcement of insider trading activities by the China Securities Regulatory Commission (CSRC) remains weak and insufficient.[3]

Beyond these general matters, however, the important issue of tipper liability remains under-researched in China's securities laws. By examining enforcement of tipper liability in China, at least two types of information can be revealed. First, from a purely legal perspective, it remains unclear whether recklessness constitutes sufficient grounds for the CSRC to

* This research is supported by 'Governmental Regulation and Corporate Autonomy: An Empirical Research on China' Securities Markets at China University of Political Science and Law (14ZFQ82004) and by the Program for Young Innovation Research Team at China University of Political Science and Law (16CXTD09).

[1] Mallin (2006), 5.

[2] Howson (2012), 379.

[3] Liebman & Milhaupt (2008), 929.

punish corporate insiders who leak inside information to tippees without an interest-exchange, or whether the CSRC can punish only de facto conspiracies in which the tipper deliberately provides material information to benefit a tippee. It is important that these matters be clarified.

In modern business society, corporate executives rarely engage in insider trading alone. Instead, they tend to employ 'white gloves' to conduct these activities and to thus circumvent legal liability. Furthermore, such executives may use inside information as an important bargaining chip for the exchange of benefits with other parties. Second and more importantly, beyond these sophisticated technical issues, research on the enforcement of tipper liability may also have important implications for China's regulatory and legal institutions. In particular, such research leads naturally to the following broad questions. Is judicial review meant to act as a check on the CSRC's power in a broader balance of powers scheme? Is the regulator equipped with sufficient resources to address the wide range of insider trading activities in China? Finally, is the regulator under the control of powerful insiders or otherwise corrupt?

2. BACKGROUND

Administrative regulation undoubtedly plays the most important role in China's regulatory regime. As one Western scholar has argued, 'rather than existing to provide clear notice to private parties of legal rights and duties, PRC [People's Republic of China] legal enactments exist to facilitate management of a complex society by an administrative state'.[4] Notably, no formal legislation was enacted to govern SOEs in China until 1988. The typical functions of formal corporate legislation – such as protecting creditors and holding managers accountable – were simply performed by state administrative procedures.[5]

This culture of strong administrative regulation has been passed on to the current regulatory regime. The CSRC is the public regulator of China's equity markets. In contrast to some regulators in developed nations, the CSRC is not a quasi-governmental organization. Instead, it is an administrative organization controlled by the central government.[6] In

---

[4] Hutchens (2003), 599 and 625.

[5] Clarke (2003), 496.

[6] The CSRC defines itself as a 'ministerial-level public institution directly under the State Council'; see the CSRC's Introduction on its official website, available at: http://www.csrc.gov.cn/pub/csrc_en/about/intro/200811/t20081130_67718.html.

accordance with China's Securities Law of 2005, the CSRC's powers are divided into three parts: (1) regulation, (2) investigation and supervision, and (3) legal enforcement. Its powers are both proactive and reactive, and it plays an important role in promoting compliance with and enforcing market regulations.[7] First, by enacting quasi-legislation (regulations and guidelines) to implement the principles of the Company Law of 2005 and the Securities Law of 2005, the CSRC contributes considerably to increasing legal certainty regarding corporate governance issues.[8] In general, these regulations and guidelines are legally binding, and all listed companies must comply with them.[9] Second, the CSRC actively exercises supervisory and legal enforcement powers. In terms of proactive enforcement, it is responsible for verifying the Articles of Association of listed companies and ensuring that all the companies in China's securities market meet the required corporate governance standards.

Arguably, the US has developed an intensive regime for regulating insider trading. In the *Texas Gulf Sulphur* case, the US Second Circuit Court of Appeals held that 'all investors trading on impersonal exchanges' should have 'relatively equal access to material information' and 'be subject to identical market risks'.[10] This is the so-called 'equal access of information' doctrine, which was subsequently abolished by later case law. In *Chiarella* v. *United States*,[11] the US Supreme Court rejected the 'equal access policy' in favour of the 'fiduciary duties theory'. Indeed, the Court clearly enunciated that liability could be imposed only if a defendant

---

[7] China first passed a Securities Law in 1998. See Zhonghua Renmin Gongheguo Zhengquanfa [Securities Law of the People's Republic of China], adopted by the Ninth Session of the Standing Committee of the Sixth National People's Congress, 29 December, 1998, effective 1 July 1999. See also Zhonghua Renmin Gongheguo Zhengquanfa 2005 [The Securities Law of the People's Public of China 2005], adopted by the 18th Meeting of the Standing Committee of the Tenth National People's Congress, 27 October 2005, effective 1 January 2006 (hereinafter Securities Law 2005). See Securities Law 2005, chapter 10, articles 179–186.

[8] The Securities Law 2005 does not stipulate that the CSRC has the power to enforce the Company Law 2005. In practice, however, the CSRC enforces some company law doctrines, such as directors' duty of loyalty and directors' duty of diligence. See Xu et al. (2013), 57; Xu (2014), 366–71; and Xu (2016), 23–32.

[9] For regulations that have been issued by the CSRC, see the CSRC's official website, available at: http://www.csrc.gov.cn/pub/newsite/flb/flfg/bmgz/. For a short English summary, see Sekine (2011), 1.

[10] *SEC* v. *Texas Gulf Sulphur Company*, 258 F. Supp. 262 (S.D.N.Y. 1966), affd in part, rev'd in part, 401 F.2d 833 (2d Cir. 1968) (en banc), cert. denied, 394 U.S. 976 (1969).

[11] *Chiarella* v. *United States*, 445 U.S. 222 (1980).

were subject to a duty to disclose prior to trading. Thus, insider trading liability was defined more narrowly. Under the updated doctrine, market analysts are not prohibited from trading equities in accordance with inside information, as they are not subject to a fiduciary relationship with any of the listed companies that they follow. Arguably, the fiduciary relationship doctrine facilitates market analysts' active role in the capital markets. The most recent development in the insider trading doctrine is that inside information is considered an important asset of a company that can be used only in the interests of the company. Under such an understanding, insider trading can be regarded as misappropriation of a company's property. In *U.S.* v. *O'Hagan*, the court confirmed that an insider is prohibited from using 'confidential information for securities trading purposes, in breach of a duty owed to the source of the information', even if the inside trader had no duties to the persons with whom he traded or the issuer of the securities that he traded. This case established the 'misrepresentation theory'.[12]

It seems that Chinese Securities Law has adopted a 'quasi-misrepresentation approach' towards insider trading activities. Article 74 defines a person who is generally considered an 'insider'. According to the law, the following types of persons will be prohibited from trading listed companies' stocks when they have undisclosed material information:

(1) corporate directors, supervisors, other executives, and major shareholders who hold not less than 5 per cent of the shares in a company;
(2) the regulator's staff;
(3) financial intermediary organizations, including staff of such organizations; and
(4) other persons who are specified by the securities regulatory authority under the State Council.

The first tier of 'insiders', who are corporate directors or other executives and majority shareholders, are subject to the 'fiduciary duties theory'. The second and third tiers of insiders generally owe duties to the source of the information; they are subject to the 'misrepresentation theory'. It seems that the last catch-all provision adds some uncertainty to the doctrine. Article 76 further expands the scope of 'insiders' and defines tipper liability. It elaborates on the legal duties of (1) those 'with knowledge of inside information' (the 'insider' is defined by Article 74) and (2) those 'who have misappropriated inside information'; such persons are prohibited

---

[12] *U.S.* v. *O'Hagan*, 21 U.S. 642 (1997).

from (a) purchasing or selling that company's securities, (b) disclosing such information without authority, or (c) suggesting that others should purchase or sell such securities, in each case at any time before such inside information is publicly disclosed.[13] In addition, the Securities Law sets out tipper liability and the corresponding fine in Article 202, which says that if a corporate insider:

> divulges the relevant information or advises any other person to purchase or sell the securities before the information, which may have any substantial impacts on the price of the securities, is publicized, he shall be ordered to dispose of the securities as illegally held thereby according to law. A fine of 1~5 times the illegal gains shall be imposed. Where there are no illegal gains or the illegal gains are less than 30,000 Yuan, a fine of 30,000 Yuan up to 600,000 Yuan shall be imposed.

The current regime seemingly expands the scope of insider trading liability compared with *U.S.* v. *O'Hagan*, which is particularly true of sub-section 2 of Article 76, as it does not require the tipper to have a fiduciary duty to the source of information. Nevertheless, we should note that the US common law regarding insider trading has also developed in recent years. A defendant is not required to have a 'fiduciary duty' to the source of information to be liable if the defendant acquired undisclosed material information using subjective deception. In *SEC* v. *Dorozhko*,[14] the defendant appears to have hacked into a secure server at Thomson Financial, Inc. to gain access to the confidential third quarter earnings of IMS Health, Inc. (which had hired Thomson Financial 'to provide investor relations and web-hosting services'). Learning that the third quarter results were highly unfavourable for IMS, the defendant then purchased short-term put options on IMS, which meant that the options would soon be worthless if IMS's stock price did not fall quickly. On this fact pattern, the defendant had no connection to IMS or to Thomson Financial and clearly owed no fiduciary duty to either. Nonetheless, the Second Circuit panel found that to the extent that the defendant had 'deceptively' gained access to the material, non-public information, he had violated Rule 10b-5.[15]

---

13 Translation by Professor Howson; see Howson (2013), 333.

14 *SEC* v. *Dorozhko*, 574 F. 3d 42 (2d Cir. 2009).

15 Coffee (2013), 281 and 293. According to Rule 10b-5, it shall be unlawful for any person, directly or indirectly, by the use of any means or instrumentality of interstate commerce, or of the mails or of any facility of any national securities exchange, (a) To employ any device, scheme, or artifice to defraud, (b) To make any untrue statement of a material fact or to omit to state a material fact necessary in order to make the statements made, in the light of the circumstances under

A substantial difference between CSRC regulations and the *Dorozhko* case can nonetheless be drawn. As Professor Coffee indicates, *Dorozhko* extends the law of insider trading significantly, but it recognizes that some element of deception must still be present for a defendant to violate Rule 10b-5.[16] However, subsection 2 of Article 76 does not require 'deception', and the CSRC's enforcement also indicates that 'culpable negligence' can constitute grounds for insider trading liability.[17]

To enhance the practicality of the law, the CSRC issued a Guide for the Recognition and Confirmation of Insider Trading Behaviour in the Securities Markets ('Insider Trading Guidance Provisions').[18] Article 6 of the regulation explicitly confirms that 'those who employ illegal methods such as trickery, coaxing, eavesdropping, monitoring, secret trading etc. to gain inside information'[19] should be regarded as 'insiders' and accordingly prevented from engaging in insider trading activities. Furthermore, the CSRC regulation sets forth a broad catch-all provision – 'those who gain inside information through other channels' – as to who should be regarded as 'insiders'. This provision fundamentally enlarges the scope of the CSRC's power with regard to insider trading violations. Subsection 2 of Article 76 uses the term 'misappropriated' (*Feifa Huoqu*), which, if we translate it directly, means 'illegally acquired'. Using this term, the prohibition that is set out by Article 76 does not apply to a person who acquires information without breaking any laws. For example, a taxi driver hears a customer's phone call that mentions the potential takeover of a listed company. Given that he does not know his customer's identity, and he trades the company's stock based on this information, must he bear insider trading liability? In accordance with the securities law, the answer is 'no', as the taxi driver did not breach any laws when he gained this information. The Interpretation of the Criminal Liability of Insider Trading by the Supreme Court sets out a clear standard of tippee liability when they are neither the relatives nor the friends of the tipper. The tippee must know or should know the identity of the tipper and the nature of the

---

which they were made, not misleading, or (c) To engage in any act, practice, or course of business which operates or would operate as a fraud or deceit upon any person, in connection with the purchase or sale of any security.

16 Coffee (2013), 294.

17 See section 3.1 below.

18 Zhengquan shichang neimu jiaoyi xingwei rending zhiyin [Guide for the Recognition and Confirmation of Insider Trading Behaviour] issued by the CSRC in 2007.

19 See note 14.

information.[20] In this hypothetical case, the taxi driver knows none of this information. Accordingly, the person who makes a phone call about the insider information will not be regarded as a tipper. We should also note there is no interest-exchange or any pre-existing economic relationship between the taxi driver and his customer. However, if we apply CSRC regulations to this case, the driver must be held liable. He actually gains 'inside information through other channels' and trades the relevant stocks, although he does not misappropriate the information. As a result, a tipper liability is also imposed on the customer. The CSRC regulations fundamentally alter the quasi-misrepresentation standard that was set out under the Securities Law 2005. Using this catch-all standard, the CSRC adopts an 'equal access information rule'.

Given China's complicated and self-contradictory insider trading law regime, the question of how the CSRC can practically enforce this regime as a coordinated whole has become a fertile topic for research and debate. Using tipper liability as an example, our investigation into Chinese insider trading cases reveals two major findings: first, the standards used by the CSRC to identify insider trading are different from those used in the US, and tipper liability can thus be triggered by 'negligence' in China, while the subjective motivation of tippers can even sometimes be ignored. Second, in some cases the CSRC enforces the law against both the tipper and the tippee, but in other cases with nearly identical facts the CSRC does not hold the tipper liable. In short, it is difficult to summarize a set of stable standards by which the CSRC systematically enforces tipper liability.

3. THE ADMINISTRATIVE ENFORCEMENT OF TIPPER LIABILITY

3.1 The Positive Side: Tipper Liability Enforced by the CSRC

Can either 'negligence' or 'recklessness' be reasonable grounds for the CSRC to hold an insider liable? According to Article 76 of the Securities

---

[20] See Guanyu banli neimujiaoyi xielu neimuxinxi xingshi anjian juti yingyong falv ruogan wenti de jieshi 2012 [Interpretation on Criminal Law of Insider Trading and Divulging Inside Information 2012] issued by the Chinese Supreme Court and Chinese Supreme Procuratorate, Article 2, sub-section 3, which states that the tippee must have the following subjective knowledge: (1) understanding of the nature of the information, namely that the information is inside information, (2) understanding the source of the information, i.e., that the information is divulged by an insider or was obtained by a non-insider illegally.

Law 2005, the insider or the person who has misappropriated insider information is generally prohibited from disclosing the material information or advising other parties to trade based on inside information, and there is no clear requirement for a subjective 'scienter' or 'fault'. The *Kuang Yong* case is representative in that regard.[21] Mr Kuang was an executive of Geli Real Estate (Geli), which proposed that it be listed on the stock market by acquiring a listed company (namely Haixing Technology) and then investing its core holdings in the target company. Following this type of back-door listing, the target company's share price will often increase in the short term. Mr Kuang's wife, Mrs Zhang, made substantial profits by purchasing the target company's shares before this information had been formally disclosed to the general public. In this case, Mr Kuang accepted that although he did not explicitly tell his wife that Geli would take over Haixing Technology's stocks, he had made business calls that contained substantial information about the takeover arrangement between Geli and Haixing Technology at home, and his wife could have obtained this information by overhearing his business calls. Furthermore, she also knew that Mr Kuang frequently made business trips to Xi An City, where Haixing Technology's headquarters were located. In this case, the CSRC held that Mr Kuang, as an executive of Geli Real Estate, was fully involved in the takeover project between Geli and Haixing Technology and therefore comprehensively understood the prospective and potential business consequences of the project. Under such conditions, there is little doubt that Mr Kuang bears a fiduciary duty to the company and should have kept the information confidential. Therefore, when he did not take sufficient steps to protect the confidentiality of the information and leaked the information to his wife, he breached his fiduciary duties, and his conduct should thus be regarded as 'divulging the relevant information', which falls under Article 202 of the Securities Law. In this case, although no solid evidence showed that Mr Kuang deliberately advised his wife to purchase the target company's shares, they had common interests in sharing the insider trading profits, which belong to their marital property. In this sense, Mr Kuang had clear economic motivation to divulge the relevant information to his wife.

In a second case the CSRC further elucidates the standards regarding tipper liability by confirming that the 'culpable negligence' of an insider can be grounds for tipper liability, even if the tipper has no clear economic motivation to advise the tippee to trade particular stocks. Mr Xiao was a director of Shanghai Xinri investment company (Xinri). Ningxia Hengli

---

21 2010 No. 32.

(Hengli) was a listed SOE in Ningxia Province that was undergoing restructuring. Xinri was invited to consult on the restructuring project and to make a substantial investment in the company. Mrs Zhu was Mr Xiao's wife, and she was informed by her husband that Xinri had invested in Hengli to facilitate its restructuring. Nevertheless, it seems that Mr Xiao had no economic motivation to encourage his wife to engage in insider trading activities, since Mr Xiao had previously invested nearly eighty million USD in the listed company through the investment company that he controlled. Illegal insider trading by his family member would impose more potential risk on his investment in this project. When Mr Xiao learned that his wife was engaged in insider trading activities, he asked Mrs Zhu to sell the stocks immediately and returned all the profits to the listed company. In addition, he also resigned from his directorship. Even though Mr Xiao took substantial steps to minimize the negative effects of his wife's illegal activities, the CSRC nonetheless imposed fines on both the tipper and the tippee. First, the CSRC held that although Mrs Zhu was neither a senior executive of the company nor a participant in the restructuring project, she had obtained substantial information through her personal relationship. Under the Securities Law, she had misappropriated inside information. Second, Mr Xiao, who was one of the key participants in the restructuring project, should have borne the responsibility of confidentiality. It was through his 'culpable negligence' (*zhongda guoshi*) that the material information was disclosed to his wife. Therefore, the fine was extended to Mr Xiao and his wife.[22]

Insider information can be divulged not only within marriages but also within friendships. Mr Wu, a manager who worked in an investment institution, called his friend Mr Bao, who worked at Hongda Gufeng, a listed company, to inquire about the future market of precious metals. After finishing their discussion on this topic, Mr Wu asked, 'Should I purchase Hongda Gufeng's stocks?' Mr Bao did not provide a 'yes or no' answer directly; he said only, 'No substantial risk'. At the time, Hongda Gufeng was planning an important takeover action, which had the potential to raise its share price in the near future. Mr Bao, as the chief accountant of the company, was aware of this information. In this case, the CSRC held Mr Bao liable. It said that when Mr Wu inquired about the inside information, Mr Bao did not perform an acceptable level of diligence as a reasonable businessman should, and he divulged the inside information negligently, thereby breaking the law.[23]

---

[22] 2012 No. 22.
[23] 2013 No. 14.

However, the result can be different when the degree of negligence is altered. Huaxing Chuangye (Huaxing) was a listed company that mainly developed computer software. To enlarge the company's business scale, Huaxing was preparing to take over several intelligent technology companies. Mr Cheng, as Huaxing's senior executive, was one of the primary participants in the takeover actions. The CSRC found that Mr Sheng, who was Mr Cheng's colleague, was engaged in insider trading activities. However, Mr Cheng denied that he had shared any inside information with Mr Shen, and said there was no solid evidence to prove that such a communication had occurred. The CSRC found that Mr Shen's workstation was located next to Mr Cheng's office at a distance of less than one metre, which meant that Mr Shen could overhear Mr Cheng's business calls when he discussed the takeover actions with his business partner. Furthermore, Mr Cheng's computer screen was also within Mr Shen's range of vision, which meant that Mr Cheng could obtain confidential information as Mr Shen prepared the takeover documents on his computer. In this case, no fine was imposed on the tipper, and the CSRC punished only the tippee.[24]

The CSRC rarely reveals the reasoning process in its documents regarding administrative punishment on insider trading. Thus, we attempted to draw a logic map tracking the logic of the CSRC's enforcement approach in these four representative cases. It seems that they share one basic similarity, which is that the tippers conveyed sensitive information to the tippee. However, there are also significant differences in the degree of 'negligence' in these cases. In the first case, there is a clear and strong economic motivation for the tipper to disclose the information to the tippee, as their jointly owned family assets would be upgraded by the insider trading activity. This case indicates that economic motivation is an important standard tipper liability under the CSRC's jurisdiction. By contrast, in the other cases there is no clear economic motivation for the tipper. However, as Professor Langevoort has indicated, greed is not the only motivation for insider trading. There are other considerations, such as cultural influences, failure to understand the law and psychological bias.[25] In the second case, it is reasonable to expect that the tipper should foresee the potential risk of his wife's illegal activities when he divulged the information to her. Mr Xiao's disclosure to his wife reasonably gave rise to at least two foreseeable possibilities: she might be motivated by greed to risk insider trading and/or she might gain other benefits by passing such information along to related

---

24 2014 No. 39.

25 Langevoort (2013), 52.

parties. In the third case, although Mr Bao did not explicitly tell his friend that the company was proposing a business activity that might increase the company's share price, he did inform Mr Wu that it was worthwhile to purchase the company's stock at that particular moment, as the profits of the investment overwhelmed the risk based on his insider knowledge. Mr Bao's activity can be regarded as 'investment advice'. Although this advice may be not have been intended to have violated any laws, it is nonetheless prohibited by Article 76 of the Securities Law. In the last case, it seems that Mr Cheng reviewed the business documents and made business calls about the takeover action in his office where it was difficult for him to keep this information confidential, which can be described as non-culpable negligence. In other words, compared with the former two cases, it is far more difficult for Mr Cheng to be aware of or predict that his colleague would misappropriate this information because he worked in his office. Under such conditions, whether 'recklessness' can be viewed as solid grounds for tipper liability remains problematic because there was no 'interest-exchange' between Mr Cheng and Mr Shen.

The standards that applied to the second and third case (and probably also the first) are fundamentally different from US common law, which explicitly requires 'deception and fault' as grounds for tipper liability. For example, in *SEC* v. *Obus*,[26] the Second Circuit summarized the law on tipper liability under Rule 10b-5 as follows:

> a tipper must (1) tip (2) material non-public information (3) in breach of a fiduciary duty of confidentiality owed to shareholders (classical theory) or the source of the information (misappropriation theory) (4) for personal benefit to the tipper.

As we discussed, at least in the case of Mr Xiao and Mr Bao, there was no solid evidence to suggest that the tipper passed the information on to the tippee for personal benefit.[27]

By contrast, a parallel to the Huaxing case can be found in US common law. In *SEC* v. *Yun*[28] a corporate executive and his wife were in the process

---

[26] *SEC* v. *Obus*, 693 F.3d 276 (2d Cir. 2012).

[27] In US common law, the Whitman Court further elaborated the above idea that 'if the only way to know whether the tipper is violating the law is to know whether the tipper is anticipating something in return for the unauthorized disclosure, then the tippee must have knowledge that such self-dealing occurred, for, without such a knowledge requirement, the tippee does not know if there has been an 'improper' disclosure of inside information.' See *United States* v. *Whitman*, No. 12-CR-125, 2012 U.S. Dist. LEXIS 163138 (S.D.N.Y. Nov. 14, 2012).

[28] *SEC* v. *Yun*, 327 F.3d 1263, 1273 (11th Cir. 2003).

of divorcing. The wife called her divorce attorney from her office to tell him that she had just learned from her husband that the stock and options that he owned through his employer were about to decline in value. The purpose of the call was to adjust the valuation of his assets for purposes of the divorce settlement. However, a colleague in the office overheard the negative news and quickly shorted the company's stock, profiting as a result. The SEC sued the executive's wife and her co-worker, probably because it realized that it needed to prove a breach of fiduciary duties by the tipper to hold the tippee liable. Thus, the SEC alleged that the wife had 'recklessly tipped her co-worker'. In all likelihood, the SEC believed that the wife had tipped her colleague knowingly and deliberately as part of a long-standing pattern of their working relationship. However, the Eleventh Circuit dismissed the SEC's claim, and it held that the 'recklessness' charge unfairly prejudiced the defendant and that such conduct by the tipper, when not motivated by any expected benefit from the tippee, was beyond the scope of Rule 10b-5. This case indicates that US insider trading law, §10b and Rule 10b-5 of the Securities Exchange Act require intention, which is a higher standard than negligence.[29] In the Huaxing case, the CSRC may have considered that no liability should attach to Mr Cheng because he simply leaked inside information solely as the result of incidental recklessness with no economic motivation. However, Mr Shen, as Huaxing's employee, did have a fiduciary duty to the company, and he also had clear knowledge of the source of the information. Thus, he is liable when he breached that fiduciary duty by engaging in insider trading.

Unlike US common law on insider trading, which draws a clear line between 'deception' and 'negligence', the CSRC's approach to tipper liability is a more complicated combination of different standards, including the insider's motivation, state of mind and level of negligence. The line between negligence and scienter is blurred by these standards. From the above cases, it seems that beyond the US-style 'scienter requirement', both a 'clear economic motivation' (Mr Kuang and Mrs Zhang) and 'culpable negligence' (Mr Xiao and Mrs Zhu, and Mr Bao and Mr Wu) can be grounds for tipper liability. In other words, only if it can be proved that an insider leaked information with a minimum level of negligence and without clear economic motivation will the CSRC relieve tippers of liability (as in the case of Mr Shen and Mr Cheng). Consistent with the Securities Law 2005 and administrative regulations, the CSRC seems to broadly enforce tipper liability. However, the question remains open as

[29] See note 16.

to whether these standards are applied by the CSRC consistently to all insider trading cases when the CSRC's enforcement of tipper liability is investigated on a macro level.

3.2 The Negative Side: Tipper Liability Ignored by the CSRC

Although the CSRC has made some significant achievements in enforcing tipper liability in insider trading cases, CSRC enforcement continues to exhibit vital weaknesses – it is inconsistent at best. In a 2013 case, Mr Su was a corporate executive of a listed company who learned that a foreign investor would soon make substantial investments in his employer. He disclosed this information to his wife, and his wife profited from trading the company's stock. This case can be compared with Mr Xiao's case, which is discussed above. The key facts of these two cases are similar: a husband tipped off his wife. However, compared with Mr Xiao, it seems that Mr Su's motivation for tipping was stronger, and he did not try to minimize the negative results of the insider trading. Strikingly, the CSRC's judgment in Mr Su's case was different, and it fined only the tippee and not the tipper.[30] This result is hardly fair for other tippers who were fined under similar conditions. Furthermore, the 'negligence standard' that has been set out by the CSRC has been challenged on its face. Mr Zhang was a corporate executive of a listed company. The parent company of a corporate group proposed an investment in some high-quality assets in the listed company. Mr Zhang called a friend and told him this inside information. However, in this case the CSRC relieved the tipper of liability, as the 'leak of information in this case is only a slight negligence'.[31] This decision is difficult to follow, and it is difficult to align it with the case in which the insider made only the merest hint to his friend and was found to be liable.[32]

The problem is even more serious in other cases. Sometimes there is a clear interest exchange relationship between tipper and tippee, and the CSRC does not punish the tipper. Henan Senyuan is a listed company that was obligated to disclose its major profit growth in its quarterly report. Before this information was disclosed to the general public, Mr Chu, who controlled Henan Senyuan, passed this information on to Mr Qi and Mr Zhang. These two persons were business partners of Mr Chu in another business entity. In this case, the CSRC punished only the tippees,

---

30 2013 No. 51.
31 2013 No. 16.
32 Mr Bao and Mr Wu's case, 2013 No. 14.

who made substantial profits. From a subjective perspective, it is not difficult to find the tipper's motivation to convey the information to his business partners, and he deliberately breached his fiduciary duties to his employer.[33] Similar cases are not difficult to find. For example, the CSRC once found that the tipper was the financial consultant of the tippee's company, and the tippee frequently paid service fees to the tipper. Under such an interest-exchange relationship, when the corporate insider tipped his business partner, the CSRC did not fine the tipper.[34] A recent extreme example is the case of Mr Liu, who was an executive of a listed company, who deliberately disclosed important inside information to three of his friends, and the CSRC did not hold him liable.[35] From 2010 to 2014[36] there were 27 cases[37] in which the CSRC punished only the tippees and not the tippers.

As discussed above, US common law requires that the tipper and tippee must be part of a de facto conspiracy in which the tipper breaches his or her fiduciary duty by deliberately communicating the material information to benefit the tippee, either (1) in return for an economic benefit conferred by the tippee on the tipper, or (2) as a gift.[38] Recently, this doctrine was further developed in *SEC* v. *Obus*. The court defined tippee liability as follows:

> Tippee liability requires that (1) the tipper breached a duty by tipping confidential information; (2) the tippee knew or had reason to know that the tipper improperly obtained the information (i.e., that the information was obtained through the tipper's breach); and (3) the tippee, while in knowing possession of the material, nonpublic information, used the information by trading or by tipping for his own benefit.[39]

The above legal standards contain two important pieces of information. First, it seems that even if the tipper does not receive any benefits from the tippee, the tippee would be responsible for breaching insider trading law

---

33 2013 No. 21.

34 2014 No. 36. For a similar case, see 2012 No. 31.

35 See 2013 No. 18, 2013 No. 19, 2013 No. 20, 2013 No. 21.

36 We also investigated all the accessible cases before 2010. However, there was no insider trading case that involved tipper liability.

37 The case numbers are 2011 No. 47, 2011 No. 51, 2012 No. 23, 2012 No. 31, 2012 No. 52, 2013 No. 13, 2013 No. 16, 2013 No. 18, 2013 No. 19, 2013 No. 20, 2013 No. 21, 2013 No. 35, 2013 No. 41, 2013 No. 51, 2013 No. 63, 2013 No. 65, 2013 No. 66, 2013 No. 72, 2014 No. 2, 2014 No. 9, 2014 No. 29, 2014 No. 36, 2014 No. 37, 2014 No. 43, 2014 No. 53, 2014 No. 63, 2014 No. 74.

38 *Dirks* v. *SEC*, 463 U.S. 662 (1983).

39 *SEC* v. *Obus*, 639 F.3d 289.

when solid evidence shows that the tippee knew or had reason to know that the tipper breached his fiduciary duties by disclosing the material information. This approach has been adopted in most of the CSRC's enforcement actions on insider trading. Second and more importantly, a clear connection between tipper liability and tippee liability appears to have been established. One of the pre-conditions of tippee liability is that the tipper breaches his fiduciary duties to his employer when he passes the information to the tippee.

Consequently, the CSRC's enforcement of tipper liability has a major flaw in that it is inconsistent. It uses random legal standards for tipper liability in insider trading cases. This flaw leads to at least two negative results. First, both Article 7 and Article 178 of the Securities Law 2005 require the CSRC to regulate the securities markets in accordance with the laws. Under such conditions, inconsistent enforcement of the law calls into question the CSRC's purported legality as a neutral regulator. The CSRC has been suspected of abusing its administrative power on behalf of various types of market participants. The second negative result is that in a legal technical sense, circumventing tipper liability in insider trading cases triggers a serious logic problem. Tippee liability is triggered by the tipper's breach of fiduciary duties. If the CSRC silently accepts that the tipper is not liable for breaching its fiduciary duties, it means there is no legal basis for the CSRC to hold the tippee liable.

4. THE IMPLICATIONS OF TIPPER LIABILITY IN THE CONTEXT OF CHINA

Although the standards that have been adopted by the CSRC appear to be random, the implications of this phenomenon can be illuminated from different perspectives. There are at least three potential explanations for the random standards of tipper liability: unconstrained administrative power, difficulties in collecting evidence and corruption among senior officials.

4.1 Unconstrained Administrative Power

China's Administrative Litigation Law authorizes the court system to review the CSRC's decisions upon the application of the claimant.[40] This

---

[40] See Zhonghua Renmin Gongheguo Xingzheng Susongfa (enacted on 1 October 1990, amended on 4 November 2014). Article 2 provides that 'a citizen, a legal person, or any other organization which deems that an administrative action

regime does not work well in practice. The Beijing First Intermediate Court and the Beijing High Court are the two courts that have jurisdiction over the CSRC's administrative decisions. From 2008 to 2015 these two courts accepted 39 cases in which the defendant was the CSRC. However, the court held that the CSRC's administrative decision was illegal in only one of those 39 cases.[41] That is to say, private parties enjoyed a 3 per cent winning rate when suing the CSRC. Furthermore, in the one case that was won by a private party, the court set aside the CSRC's decision on procedural grounds, that is the court did not review the CSRC's decision substantively. It has long been argued that in terms of securities law enforcement, the court system in China is a subject of the administrative organ. In accordance with the Supreme Court's Notice,[42] private securities litigation is dependent upon administrative and criminal sanctions. In other words, aggrieved investors can commence civil litigation only against a party who has received an administrative fine from the CSRC or another administrative organ such as the Ministry of Finance on the basis of fraudulent disclosure, or who has been convicted of the crime of misrepresentation by a court. Arguably, these prerequisites reduce the costs of evidence collection for private investors and also keep a check on the floodgates of litigation. Some economic studies have also indicated that the market regulator outperforms courts as a law enforcer when the 'costs of verifying the circumstance of specified cases and interpreting statues are high'.[43] However, the fact that the right of an individual investor to a civil claim is partially controlled by administrative authorities is still problematic from the perspective of procedural fairness. In practice, the ability of a private investor to enforce a claim is tightly restricted by the attitude of the administrative organs towards the fault that is disclosed. It can also be argued that the CSRC – an administrative regulatory body – would adopt different standards to justify whether a disclosure is fraudulent than those tests that are used by a court in hearing a civil litigation. In short, securities

---

taken by an administrative agency or any employee thereof infringes upon the lawful rights and interests of the citizen, legal person, or other organization shall have the right to file a complaint with a people's court in accordance with this Law'.

[41] The only case in which the CSRC was defeated is *Gao Xing Zhong Zi* No. 3699 (2014).

[42] Zuigao renmin fayuan guanyu shouli zhengquan shichang yin sujia chengshu yinfa de minshi qinquan jiufen anjian youguan wenti de tongzhi [The Notice on Relevant Issues Concerning Accepting Civil Tort Dispute Cases Caused by False Statement on Securities and Several Provisions on Hearing Civil Compensation Caused by False Statement on the Securities Market] (hereinafter Notice) issued by China's Supreme Court on 15 January 2002.

[43] Edward et al. (2001), 853.

law enforcement in China is oriented towards the administrative power. For reasons connected with the above phenomena, Professor Clarke has provided an insightful explanation. He argues that:

> The Chinese state prefers direct regulation by government agencies first, and indirect regulation by private litigation in the state's courts next. Regulation by the uncontrolled institutions of the market comes a distant third, and indeed it is hard to find such institutions in China.[44]

To protect publicly listed SOEs, the state endows the CSRC with power that is not subject to outside checks and balances. The court system in general is reluctant to second-guess the CSRC's administrative decisions. Consequently, it is understandable that the CSRC can use random standards regarding tipper liability in accordance with its own preferences.

4.2 Difficulties with Collecting Evidence

Selective enforcement is a more cost-efficient enforcement strategy than complete enforcement for a regulator.[45] The senior officials of the CSRC have admitted that they have considerable difficulty in collecting evidence. A cause–effect relationship between undisclosed information and insider trading behaviour is often difficult to portray. Generally, the CSRC will observe three criteria, namely a 'sensitive period',[46] a 'sensitive identity'[47] and 'sensitive behaviour'. Compared with the first two criteria that have been explicitly elaborated by relevant laws, 'sensitive behaviour' can be divided into two sub-standards: the pre-existing relationship between the trading account and an insider, and deviation from the standard course of dealing. The first standard indicates that the relationship between the securities accounts that are involved in the suspected trading and the insider should be closely related. In many cases, insiders use their relatives' or friends' accounts to engage in insider trading. The second standard indicates that the transaction itself should be sufficiently abnormal, particularly compared with the insider's normal course of transaction activities.

---

44 Clarke (2010), 57.

45 Stigler (1970), 526–36.

46 The sensitive period indicates the period from the time that the inside information is formulated to the time that it is formally disclosed. See Article 5 of Interpretation of Criminal Law of Insider Trading and Divulging Inside Information issued by the China Supreme Court and China Supreme Procuratorate in 2012.

47 See Securities Law 2015, Article 74.

This sub-standard itself consists of two important parts. First, the suspected trading should be considerably different from the normal trading model of the insider. For example, a relative of a director of a listed company director typically trades securities with sufficient caution. From his trading record, the regulator concludes that he is a risk-averse trader. However, in the suspected trading the insider's trading strategy is far more aggressive, for example purchasing a large quantity of stocks over a short period, which indicates a deviation. Second, the fundamentals of the company are also a key test. Given that the public information of a listed company indicates that the company's business and trading activities have not experienced significant improvements and, accordingly, share prices are neither under- nor over-valued, it can be regarded as abnormal when an insider purchases a large quantity of stock at a particular moment. It is assumed that the CSRC may have difficulty collecting evidence of the chain of information between the tipper and the tippee. For example, Mr Ouyang Jiansheng was the vice-director of the CSRC's Inspection Department, which took over responsibility for investigating insider trading violations in 2012. He once told a journalist that inspecting corporate insiders had become increasingly more challenging in recent years, that the chain of insider trading was difficult to determine, and that the most difficult part of an insider trading case was to find where the information came from and how the information was communicated.[48] In this particular area, the only evidence that the CSRC can typically gather is the communication by phone call or physical meetings between tippers and tippees. However, the content of the calls or meetings can be confirmed only by the confession of either the tipper or tippee. A tippee is highly unlikely to confess to his violation, as he will undoubtedly be punished by the CSRC, because the tippee takes active action to engage in insider trading and typically profits from this activity. By contrast, the tipper may be a weak link in this chain, and accordingly has a stronger motivation to confess. In some cases, the tipper only passes the information to another party, but he does not directly trade based on the inside information or exchange interests with the tippees. When the CSRC struggles to gather evidence, it may give preferential treatment to the tipper if they are willing to confess the contents of their communications with the tippee. Therefore, tippers may be relieved from liability in such cases.

Difficulties with collecting evidence are associated with the limited

---

[48] See Neimu jiaoyi chengxian duoyuanhua tezheng [The Diversified Insider Trading, An Interview with Mr Ouyang], available at: http://finance.qq.com/a/20120912/001307.htm.

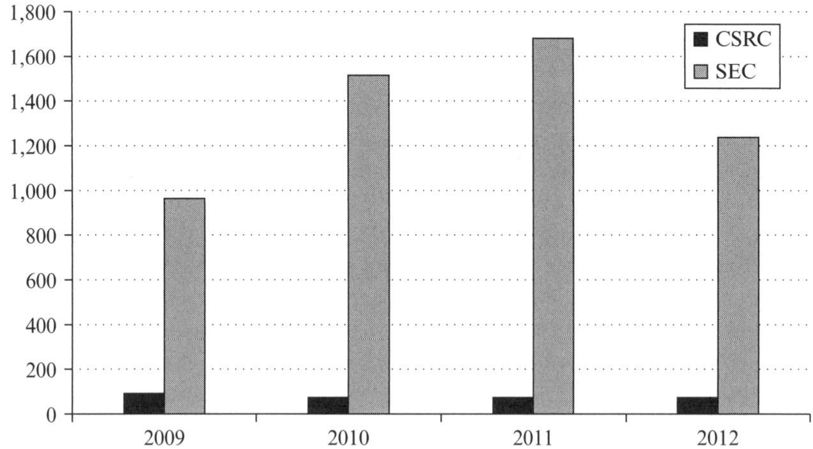

Source: Zhou (2015).[49]

Figure 4.1 Regulatory budgets (inputs) from 2008 to 2012 (million USD), CSRC and SEC

resources allotted to the CSRC. The director of the CSRC, Mr Xiao, claims that the dramatic increase in securities violations, particularly in insider trading cases, has placed substantial pressure on the CSRC. He admitted that there is no effective incentive for officials to enforce the law, and the CSRC's enforcement department has limited resources to fight against the rapidly growing number of securities violations. He further indicated that the CSRC had only approximately 600 law enforcement officers in 2013, compared with the SEC's 1,236 law enforcement officers at the same time.[50] Mr Xiao failed to mention that the CSRC's budget is also far less than that of the SEC, as can be seen in Figure 4.1.

4.3 Corruption among Senior Officials at the CSRC

The random standards associated with tipper liability and unequal treatment may be a by-product of corrupt CSRC officials. Mr Ouyang, who was the vice-director of the CSRC's Inspection Department in 2012, was arrested by the police for assisting in insider trading and the falsification of a public seal in 2015. Mr Ouyang's colleague Mr Liu also made millions

---

[49] For more comprehensive data, see Zhou (2015), 377.
[50] Xiao (2013), 31–3.

of RMB in illegal profits from insider trading and by granting preferential treatment to listed companies. According to media reports, 12 CSRC officials have been arrested on corruption charges from 1994 to 2014.[51] Recently the CSRC vice president Mr Yao Gang and both his assistant Mr Zhang Yujun and former assistant Mr Liu Shufan were arrested in November 2015. Mr Yao was in charge of the initial public offering (IPO) procedure in China's securities markets for nearly 12 years.[52] Although there has been no public announcement of Mr Yao's illegal activities, some reports have indicated that Mr Yao's wife was a successful lawyer and senior partner in one of China's pre-eminent law firms. Not surprisingly, in recent years this law firm has enjoyed a large amount of IPO-related business.[53] Furthermore, Mr Liu Shufan, who was arrested in 2014, engaged in insider trading by approving a public company's proposed private placement of securities and passed this information on to one of his friends, making three million RMB through insider trading. Furthermore, by approving this private placement and maintaining the share price of this public company, Mr Liu received a large amount of bribes (several million RMB) from private parties. Given the above information, it is understandable why CSRC enforcement of insider trading has lacked basic consistency. The officials are corrupt, and they use their power of enforcement for profit. A similar conclusion has been drawn by Liebman and Milhaupt, who argue:

> [T]he CSRC rarely punishes insider trading cases with huge amounts of money, the number of [CSRC] sanctions seem to be rather modest given the ubiquity and severity of the problems with . . . insider trading . . . in China's stock markets. Some evidence found that even the CSRC's officials themselves are engaged in insider trading.[54]

5. CONCLUSION

The above research provides sufficient evidence to illustrate important characteristics of CSRC enforcement of insider trading regulations, which

---

51 Zhengjianhui lizhi guanyuan she neimujiaoyi [The Retired CSRC Officer is Suspected of Insider Trading], available at: http://business.sohu.com/20150826/n419739178.shtml.

52 Yaogang an xin baodao [The Case of Yao Gang], available at: http://mycaijing.com.cn/news/2015/11/16/141013.html.

53 In accordance with Article 11 of the Chinese Securities Law 2015, a pre-IPO company must employ lawyers as sponsors to prepare their legal documents for the IPO.

54 Liebman & Milhaupt (2008), 929.

can be unpacked from a comparative perspective. First, the CSRC's standards for establishing insider trading are broader than those that have been adopted by the US, namely there is no requirement for deception. In other words, insider trading liability can be triggered by negligence. Second, it seems that the CSRC has been endowed with unconstrained power that enables it to enforce tipper liability in insider trading cases using random standards. In short, the CSRC's enforcement of insider trading regulations is not always based solely on the relevant legislation. This research further explores the implications for the way in which CSRC enforces insider trading regulations. Three major constraints may lead to this phenomenon: the absence of judiciary review, difficulty in collecting evidence and corruption of officials. Once again, this research proves the dysfunction of the Chinese regulator in enforcing laws and regulations. Under such conditions, judicial intervention may be expected to play a more important role in enforcing securities law in China.

REFERENCES

Clarke, D. (2003) 'Corporate Governance in China: An Overview', 14 *China Economic Review*.

Clarke, D. (2010) 'Law without Order in Chinese corporate Governance Institutions', 30 *Northwest Journal of International Law & Business*, available at SSRN: http://ssrn.com/abstract=1245803.

Coffee, J. (2013) 'Mapping the Future of Insider Trading Law: of Boundaries, Gaps and Strategies', 2 *Colombia Business Law Review*.

Edward, G., S. Johnson and A. Shleifer (2001) 'Coase v. Coasians', 116 (3) *Quarterly Journal of Economics*.

Howson, N. (2012) 'Enforcement without Foundation? Insider Trading and China's Administrative Law Crisis', 60 *American Journal of Comparative Law*.

Howson, N. (2013) 'Punishing Possession – China's All Embracing Insider Trading Enforcement Regime', in Stephen M. Bainbridge (ed.), *Research Handbook on Insider Trading*, Edward Elgar Publishing Ltd.

Hutchens, W. (2003) 'Private Security Litigation in China: Material Disclosure about China's Legal System', 24 *University of Pennsylvania Journal of International Economic Law*.

Langevoort, D. (2013) 'What Were They Thinking? Insider Trading and the Scienter Requirement', in Stephen M. Bainbridge (ed.), *Research Handbook on Insider Trading*, Edward Elgar Publishing Ltd.

Liebman, B. and C. Milhaupt (2008) 'Reputational Sanction in China's Security Market', 108 *Columbia Law Review*.

Mallin, C. (2006) *Corporate Governance* (2nd edn), Oxford University Press.

Sekine, E. (2011) 'Complete Regulatory Overhaul of China's Capital Market Underway', 2 *Nomura Journal of Capital Markets*.

Stigler, G. (1970) 'The Optimal Enforcement of Law', 78 *Journal of Political Economy*.

Xiao, G. (2013) 'Jianguan Zhifa, Ziben Shichang Jiangkang Fazhan de Jishi', [Enforcement of Regulation: The Cornerstone of Prosperous Stock Markets], 15 *Qiushi [Truth Seeking]*.

Xu, G., T. Zhou, B. Zeng and J. Shi (2013) 'Directors' Duties in China', 14 *European Business Organization Law Review*.

Xu, W. (2014) 'Law Matters? A Bayesian Analysis of the Cross-Country Relationship between Anti-Self-Dealing Rules and Stock Market Outcomes', 21 *Applied Economics Letters*.

Xu, W. (2016) 'Reforming Private Securities Litigation in China: The Stock Market Has Already Cast its Vote', 45 *International Review of Law and Economics*.

Zhou, T. (2015) 'Is the CSRC Protecting a "Level Playing Field" in China's Capital Markets: Public Enforcement, Fragmented Authoritarianism and Corporatism', 15 (2) *Journal of Corporate Law Studies*.

5. Private enforcement of securities law in China: an empirical analysis of the SPC's 2002 Notice on A/B share markets

Jiajia Dai, Shiting Feng and Wenming Xu*

1. INTRODUCTION

The Chinese stock markets are currently under reform and a registration system for the market of initial public offerings (IPOs) will be established.[1] The reform reduces the ex ante efforts of public regulators in screening the quality of listed firms, which functions as an instrument for investor protection.[2] The success of a registration system with lower entry barriers relies heavily on ex post enforcement of the law.[3] With better enforcement,

* We thank Bernard Black, Yun-chien Chang, Jinhua Chen, Xin Dai, Michael Faure, Binwei Gui, Li Guo, Jiye Hu, Hui Huang, Jonathan Klick, Wenjing Li, Kate Litvak, Haitian Lu, Niels Philipsen, Jing-Huey Shao, Yingmao Tang, Lebing Wang, Stefan Weishaar, Chao Xi, Tao Xi, Guangdong Xu, Wei Zhang, Chen Zhao, Tianshu Zhou and seminar participants at the China University of Political Science and Law, the Fuzhou University, the Ocean University of China, the East China University of Political Science and Law, the Hebrew University of Jerusalem and the Peking University for their helpful comments. We also gratefully acknowledge financial support from the Program for Young Innovative Research Team (16CXTD09), Scientific Research Foundation for Young Scholars (1000-10816138) and The Role of Financial Development and Innovation in Facilitating Economic Development of Rural Area (1000-10815013), all of which are granted by China University of Political Science and Law.

1 See Section 3 of the Decision of the Central Committee of the Communist Party of China on Some Major Issues Concerning Comprehensively Deepening the Reform (Zhonggong Zhongyang Guanyu Quanmian Shenhua Gaige Ruogan Zhongda Wenti de Jueding), adopted at the Third Plenary Session of the 18th Central Committee of the Communist Party of China, 12 November 2013) (PRC).

2 Pistor and Xu (2005).

3 Burch (2008).

outside investors are willing to pay more for equity assets, as a result of which more firms are able to finance their investments externally.[4] International best practice has shown that private enforcement through securities class litigation has already become an important external governance mechanism and has helped to regulate corporate officials.[5] Although there is some empirical evidence on private enforcement of securities laws in developed countries,[6] much less is known about reforms conducted in transitional countries.

This chapter addresses this gap in the literature by adopting a "shock-based" event study research design.[7] It investigates the differences in the effects of the Supreme People's Court of the People's Republic of China (SPC)'s 2002 Notice Regarding Accepting Tort Cases Arising from Stock Market False Disclosure (henceforth, the SPC's 2002 Notice),[8] which for the first time explicitly allowed private securities litigations[9] to be accepted on stock price performance in A/B-share markets.[10] Before the SPC's 2002 Notice was enacted, listed companies in China faced no de facto threats

---

4 Cross-country empirical studies have shown that both public and private enforcement of securities laws contribute to stock market development (Jackson and Roe, 2009; La Porta et al., 2006). In addition to enforcement, the "law and finance" scholarship also identifies that the "on the books" investor protection laws facilitate stock market development; see two survey articles, La Porta et al. (2008) and Xu (2011). However, several researchers have commented that the statistical identification is overlooked in this strand of literature (Helland and Klick, 2011; Xu, 2014).

5 Thompson and Sale (2003).

6 For example, there are ample studies on the Private Securities Litigation Reform Act of 1995 in the US. See Choi (2004).

7 A "shock-based" event study can be used to estimate the effects of an exogenous event on the value of listed firms, which event is proxied by the abnormal return of their stocks in the event window. For a thorough discussion on the methodology, see Atanasov and Black (2015).

8 The SPC's 2002 Notice only sets out general features of the private litigation system; a subsequent provision, the 2003 Provisions Concerning the Adjudication of Civil Compensation Securities Cases Based upon Misrepresentation (henceforth, the SPC's 2003 Provisions) was issued to provide detailed guidance to private securities litigation.

9 The private suits governed by the SPC's 2002 Notice include those against misrepresentations in the stock market and exclude those resulting from insider trading and market manipulation.

10 A proportion of listed firms issued both A-shares to raise RMB and B-shares to raise foreign currencies in Chinese stock markets. A/B-shares are ordinary shares with the same voting rights and dividends, but the transactions, dividend payments, trades and quotes of B-shares are conducted in foreign currencies: Shanghai B-shares are denominated in US dollars and Shenzhen B-shares in Hong Kong dollars.

of private litigation, although the "law on the books" generally forbade misrepresentations and provided grounds for civil compensation.[11]

The securities litigation system in China is compensation-oriented and differs significantly from its American counterpart, which combines the functions of both deterrence and compensation.[12] The first difference is that an administrative prerequisite requires that private suits should be based on sanctions of public agencies, mainly the China Securities Regulatory Committee (CSRC), or the criminal judgments of the courts.[13] The enforcement output of the CSRC is limited,[14] which could screen out potential meritorious suits for compensation.[15] In addition, the SPC's 2002 Notice aggravates the collective action problem in shareholder litigations and requires that they should be brought as individual or joint actions, instead of as US-style class actions. Finally, the intermediate-level courts at the place where the defendant firms are located have territorial jurisdiction, which significantly increases plaintiffs' burdens in pursuing such suits.[16]

A unique feature of Chinese stock markets is that a proportion of listed firms issue legally identical "twin A/B-shares", which provides us with an opportunity to examine the market responses to the private enforcement system in different institutional settings. The two types of shares are ordinary shares with the same voting rights and dividends.[17] However, the transactions, dividend payments, trades and quotes of B-shares are conducted in foreign currencies: Shanghai B-shares are traded in US dollars and Shenzhen B-shares are traded in Hong Kong dollars, which leads to different investor structures in these two markets.[18]

The majority of investors in the A-share market are "scattered

---

[11] Hutchens (2003); Liebman and Milhaupt (2008).

[12] Coffee (2006). For a general discussion on functions of tort law, see Philipsen (2007).

[13] Guo and Ong (2009).

[14] The CSRC brought 169 regulatory actions against listed companies in the four years following the introduction of the 1999 Securities Law, that is approximately 42 cases per year; see Chen et al. (2005).

[15] Layton (2008) argues that the administrative prerequisites should bring value to listed firms, considering the capability of the judiciary system and the long history of public-oriented regulation.

[16] Lu (2003).

[17] Chan et al. (2008).

[18] To be specific, we mean investors of tradable shares, which consist of "new shares issued in IPOs and seasoned cash offerings and those derived from tradable shares in rights offerings and stock splits" (Liao et al., 2014: 502). The tradable shares were held mainly by outside investors before the Reform of the Split-Share Structure beginning in 2005. Non-tradable shares were held mainly by the State and legal persons, who are also the controlling shareholders of listed firms.

households", who generally hold trivial interests in listed firms and adopt a speculative strategy.[19] These retail investors suffer from the collective action problem and are "rationally apathetic" to the right to seek compensation.[20] In contrast, investors in B-share markets comprise mainly foreign and domestic institutional shareholders, especially privately managed investment funds raising money from the wealthy in the grey market,[21] who would have enough incentives to overcome collective action problems and file private suits.[22] With litigation rights, institutional shareholders could also employ alternative strategies, such as striking settlement agreements with potential defendant firms, if the costs of going to trial are prohibitive.[23]

We therefore collected a sample of 162 A/B-shares issued by 81 listed firms that undertook their IPOs on the Shanghai Stock Exchange (SHSE) and Shenzhen Stock Exchange (SZSE) before 1 January 2002, and employed regression adjustments, which are shown to significantly reduce potential biases.[24] A significant positive abnormal return for B-shares relative to A-shares is documented, which is approximately 2.08 per cent over the three-day event window after controlling for market liquidity proxy, firm-specific characteristics and industrial dummies. Furthermore, the placebo test presents no significant differences in returns between A-shares issued by our sampled 81 firms and A-shares issued by matched firms issuing only A-shares. We finally find that the magnitude of the abnormal return between B-shares relative to A-shares issued by the same firms is determined by the level of regional judiciary efficiency in the area where listed firms are located.[25]

---

19 Mei et al. (2009).

20 See Black (1990) on shareholder passivity.

21 Bohl et al. (2010).

22 Institutional investors in American markets also leave money on the table, due to the failures in the notification process and monitoring of the custodian to file the claims (Cox and Thomas, 2002, 2005). However, the problem identified may not matter in China, because the information supporting administrative sanctions and criminal judgments is available to the general public. Institutional investors are able to identify those cases satisfying administrative prerequisites.

23 Firth et al. (2011b) survey the lawsuits involving listed firms and report that plaintiff firms suffer from negative abnormal return on the event date, which they ascribe to the daunting litigation costs offsetting the expected return from judgments.

24 Cochran and Rubin (1973); Rubin (1973); Ho et al. (2007).

25 Regional judiciary efficiency is also significant for the expected compensation of settlements because it relates to the comparative bargaining power of the two parties. The minimum benefits of injured investors are the expected compensation of going to trial, which equals the actual loss minus the costs of using the court system. If the regional court system is inefficient, going to trial

Our research is closely related to two recent studies on the private enforcement system of Chinese stock markets. First, Humphery-Jenner conducted an event study on the promulgation of the SPC's 2003 Provisions and argues that given the same regulatory regime, good laws aimed at curbing misrepresentations could cause negative impacts on the information environment of the stock market in China because the negative externality of a new law outweighs its positive externality.[26] Our results provide some counter-evidence that the new private enforcement system at least delivers positive value to investors in the B-share market.

Second, Huang reports that only 25.7 per cent (65/253) of eligible cases, that is those cases with administrative sanctions or criminal judgments against misrepresentation, are brought to court.[27] This ratio is extraordinarily low given that recovery should be straightforward in theory. Liebman and Milhaupt comment that "prospect recovery is simply too small to justify the expense, time and efforts required to bring suit".[28] Aggrieved investors are rationally apathetic to the private litigation rights and "vote with their feet" because collective action problems are severe. Huang argues that the inefficient court system is the major barrier to the effective compensation of aggrieved investors. Our work provides evidence supporting his argument.

The chapter is structured as follows: Section 2 discusses the institutional background to the SPC's 2002 Notice and testable hypotheses, Section 3 presents the data and Section 4 describes the results of our empirical analysis. Section 5 provides some conclusions.

2. INSTITUTIONAL BACKGROUND AND HYPOTHESES

2.1 Institutional Background

Listed firms in China faced few threats of private litigation before the SPC's 2002 Notice was issued, although legal rules "on the books" generally forbade misrepresentations and provided grounds for civil compensation. Compensation for aggrieved investors was overlooked during this time. The SPC even promulgated the Notice Concerning Temporarily

---

could be expected to generate a negative return for investors with small stakes. Anticipating this, rational defendant firms are unlikely to reach an agreement with aggrieved investors.

26 Humphery-Jenner (2013).

27 Huang (2013).

28 Liebman and Milhaupt (2008), 943.

Table 5.1 Staffing and budget levels of the CSRC versus those of the SEC

Year	CSRC				SEC			
	Budget	Budget (std)	Staff	Staff (std)	Budget	Budget (std)	Staff	Staff (std)
2014	155,512.05	14,912.21	3,167	2.32	1,550,513.00	89,012.74	4,150	13.02
2013	156,080.11	16,456.90	3,183	2.34	1,402,477.00	83,639.82	4,023	12.71
2012	134,528.94	15,867.74	2,891	2.14	1,236,057.00	76,473.73	3,785	12.05
2011	118,760.09	15,945.12	2,745	2.04	1,713,531.00	110,422.68	3,844	12.33
2010	112,080.34	18,638.80	2,589	1.94	1,592,638.00	106,428.66	3,748	12.12

Note: The data on annual budget and staffing levels are standardized by annual GDP and population size respectively. The unit for "Budget" is "thousand US dollars", for "Budget (std)" is "per billion US dollars of GDP", for "Staff" is "head count" and for "Staff (std)" is "per million of population".

Source: The data on the CSRC's annual budget is drawn from the website of the State Council of the PRC, available at http://www.gov.cn/; the data on the SEC's annual budget is drawn from the account Total Budgetary Resources in SEC Agency Financial Report Fiscal Year 2011–2014, available at https://www.sec.gov/about/annrep.shtml; the data on the annual exchange rate between RMB and US dollars, GDP and population of both China and the US are drawn from World Development Indicators, available at http://data.worldbank.org/data-catalog/world-development-indicators/.

Not Accepting Civil Compensation Cases Related to Securities (SPC's 2001 Notice) on 21 September 2001, instructing lower courts to refuse acceptance of civil compensation cases related to securities due to legislative and judicial limitations at that time.[29]

It is worth noting that the deterrence function is mainly assumed by the public enforcer of securities laws, the CSRC, which is responsible for investigating potential breaches of securities laws and imposing administrative and criminal liabilities.[30] However, the CSRC appears to be short of disposable resources.[31] In Table 5.1 we report the resources at

[29] The CSRC criticized the SPC's 2001 Notice when it was promulgated; see Pistor and Xu (2005).

[30] The monetary fine imposed by the CSRC is limited. For example, according to Article 177 of the 1998 Securities Law, issuers committing misrepresentation offences face monetary penalties ranging from 300,000 RMB to 600,000 RMB. However, the criminal penalties could be severe. As noted by Chen et al. (2005), those found guilty could be sentenced to death for cooking the books. The CSRC also use the instrument of reviewing applications for public offerings to discipline listed firms (Clarke, 2010).

[31] For more detailed analysis of the public enforcement regime in China, see Xu et al. (2016) and Zhou (2015).

the disposal of the CSRC and US Securities and Exchange Commission (SEC) from 2010 to 2014. The CSRC's budget is only around one tenth of that of the SEC, as is shown in columns 1 and 5. In contrast, the absolute number of CSRC staffing is quite close to that of the SEC, as can be seen in columns 3 and 7. The reason for the coexistence of a small budget and a relatively large staff is probably due to the lower average salary paid to staff members in China than in the US. After adjusting for the annual GDP, the standardized budget of the CSRC is around 20 per cent of that of the SEC, but the staffing level of the CSRC decreases to less than 20 per cent of that of the SEC when the difference in population size of China and the US is taken into consideration.

The staffing and budget levels of the CSRC are also unremarkable when compared with those of public regulators in other countries, as reported by Jackson and Roe.[32] The minimum and median of "Budget per billion US dollars of GDP" reported in their basic sample are 5,576 and 60,675 respectively, and those of "Staff per million of population" are 0.43 and 6.35 respectively. In contrast, the highest standardized annual budget of the CSRC is around 18,638.80 US dollars (2010) and the highest standardized annual staffing number of the CSRC is around 2.34 (2013). It is obvious that the resources at the disposal of the CSRC are considerably limited, and this partially contributes to the smaller regulatory output in China compared to that in the US. The SEC imposed approximately 639 sanctions per year from 2002 to 2004.[33] In contrast, the CSRC performed 169 regulatory enforcement actions against listed companies in the four years following the introduction of the 1999 Securities Law.[34]

The SPC's 2002 Notice was issued about four months after the promulgation of the SPC's 2001 Notice, which completely changed its previous position and allowed private litigations brought on the ground of misrepresentation to be accepted, provided that the CSRC had administratively sanctioned the company. The SPC's 2002 Notice was not expected by the market and was an exogenous event, because public agencies rarely negate their previous decisions within such a short time. In Chinese culture, such inconsistent behavior is considered to be humiliating and detrimental to public authority. Furthermore, the SPC's 2002 Notice was not designed to

---

32 Jackson and Roe (2009).

33 Jackson (2007), 280.

34 Chen et al. (2005); Liebman and Milhaupt (2008). However, this number could underestimate the regulatory output of the CSRC, as two sources of cases are not made public: the CSRC does not disclose cases that do not result in actions and those minor infractions handled by private caution and censure, for example, by issuing "correction orders".

cater to those firms issuing both A-shares and B-shares, because various interested parties, such as law firms, investors and the CSRC, all tried to lobby the SPC to change its decision.

The private securities litigation system has the following features. First, due to the administrative prerequisites for private actions, it is designed to compensate aggrieved investors rather than assume the functions of both deterrence and compensation. Additionally, the SPC's 2002 Notice pays no attention to the collective action problem in shareholder litigation. It instead aggravates that problem and requires that these litigations are brought only as individual actions or joint actions, but not as US-style class actions. At the same time, the intermediate level courts at the place where the defendant firms are located have territorial jurisdiction, which significantly increases the costs of pursuing civil compensation.

Our research relies on the institutional setting where a proportion of listed firms issued legally identical "twin A/B-shares", to which the SPC's 2002 Notice is equally applied. The fact that trading in B shares is conducted in foreign currencies generates an interesting institutional variation that could be employed to test the market evaluations of the private enforcement system.[35] Due to daunting transaction costs, it is highly unlikely that investors could arbitrage between A/B-share markets during the event window. First, there was foreign exchange control in China and buying foreign currencies was regulated at that time. In addition, short-selling is prohibited on both markets. Third, foreign investors were allowed to trade on only the B-share markets. Hence, investors could not short sell A-shares and buy B-shares issued by the same firm and earn the risk-free rate of return.

The majority of investors in the A-share market are "scattered households"[36] with "collective action" problems. These retail investors are "rationally apathetic" to bringing private securities litigations even with administrative sanctions since, given the significant costs of bringing such an action, it would be less cost-effective for them to pursue compensation

---

[35] Before 19 February 2001 the A/B-share markets were completely segmented. Only domestic investors were permitted to trade on the A-share market, whereas foreign investors were permitted to trade on the B-share market. The restrictions were partially lifted thereafter: domestic investors could trade on the B-share market, although foreign investors were still prohibited from trading on the A-share market. A popular strategy for domestic investors is to invest through private managed investment funds, which raise US dollars and Hong Kong dollars from the rich in the grey market.

[36] Hutchens (2003); Mei et al. (2009).

than to sell the stock and "vote with their feet". Hence, the rights to bring private securities litigation are expected to be worthless to the retail investors in the A-share market.

In contrast, both foreign and domestic institutional investors have greater stakes at risk in the B-share market. Bohl et al. have noted that "wealthier Chinese are more likely to have the US dollar accounts necessary to engage in B-share trading", and they usually invest in the B-share market through privately managed investment funds.[37] In their study on investors' trading patterns, Chan et al. confirm that stocks in the B-share market are traded in larger volumes than those in the A-share market, because institutional investors make larger trades in the B-share market.[38]

Those institutional investors consequently have at least two comparative advantages in pursuing civil compensation. First, they hold and trade in larger volume than retail investors in the A-share market do. Given the fixed costs involved in pursuing private securities litigations, their expected returns from these suits are much higher. Second, institutional shareholders usually hold a portfolio of stocks, which results in economies of scale in dealing with private litigations. Moreover, they are likely to handle such suits more frequently and accumulate litigation-specific human resources, which would reduce the average expected costs per action. As a result, investors in the B-share market have higher incentives to overcome the collective action problem, and it is hypothesized that the SPC's 2002 Notice had a disproportional positive impact on the B-share market.

2.2 Hypothesis

As discussed above, we expect the collective action problem to be a major obstacle for retail investors in the A-share market in bringing civil securities cases. However, investors in the B-share market have different payouts, which provide them with incentives to overcome collective action problems. They have higher expected returns from private litigation due to their higher stakes in a given firm, and at the same time, the average expected costs per action are reduced due to economies of scale and accumulated litigation-specific human capital. We, hence, postulate that the

---

[37] Bohl et al. (2010).

[38] Chan et al. (2008). Part of the difference in trading patterns could be ascribed to institutional factors. The minimum trading volume of B-shares is 1,000 shares, approximately ten times greater than that of A-shares on the SHSE. However, the minimum trading volume of B-shares is 100 shares, the same as that of A-shares on the SZSE.

private enforcement system is valued higher in the B-share market than in the A-share market.

- Hypothesis 1 (Collective Action Problem): The portfolio of B-shares gains positive abnormal returns relative to those of A-shares issued by the same firm during the event windows because the collective action problem is better handled in the B-share market.

Because retail investors in the A-share market lack effective instruments to overcome collective action problems, we thus expect that there are no significant differences in cumulative returns between our sampled A-shares and comparable ones selected out of A-shares of listed firms issuing only A-shares during event windows.

- Hypothesis 2 (Collective Action Problem: Placebo Test): The portfolio of A-shares of listed firms issuing both A-shares and B-shares should experience no significant abnormal returns relative to that of matched A-shares issued by listed firms issuing only A-shares during the event windows, because there is a lack of effective instruments to overcome collective action problems in the A-share market and outside investors should be rationally apathetic to the right to seek compensation.

Huang demonstrates that only one-fourth of eligible cases are brought to court and argues that the costs resulting from an inefficient court system outweigh the expected recovery.[39] According to Article 5 of the SPC's 2002 Notice, courts at the place where the defendant firms are located have territorial jurisdiction. Listed firms usually have good relationships with the local government, which controls the court systems. Hence, investors should be willing to pay lower premiums for B-shares of listed firms located in regions with lower court efficiency because they are likely to pay higher costs to obtain civil compensations.

- Hypothesis 3 (Court Efficiency): The magnitude of the abnormal returns of B-shares relative to those of A-shares issued by the same firm is positively correlated with the court efficiency level in the region where listed firms are located.

---

[39] Huang (2013).

3. SAMPLE AND EMPIRICAL STRATEGY

We mainly focused our investigation on a sample of listed firms issuing twin A/B-shares, which are legally identical shares. The following algorithm is adopted to select the sampled shares. First, we collected data for all A/B-shares listed on the SHSE and SZSE, which undertook their IPOs before 31 December 2001, from Wind Information Co., Ltd., one of the major providers of financial data for listed firms in China.[40] Then, we excluded those stocks that suspended trading on 15 January 2002. Finally, those firms issuing only A-shares or B-shares were excluded. As a result, our main data set includes 162 A/B-shares issued by 81 listed firms. Table 5.2 reports the distribution of sampled firms by industry and province. One potential caveat, which could compromise the external validity of our analysis, is that two-thirds of our sampled firms are located in Guangdong Province and the City of Shanghai, where the two exchanges are located.

In our "shock-based" research design, those B-shares expected to be affected significantly by the SPC's 2002 Notice are the treatment group, whereas A-shares are the control group, which also serves as the benchmark when estimating abnormal returns. Hence, a dummy variable TREATMENT was created to indicate whether a given share is a B-share or A-share. If it is a B-share, we set TREATMENT to 1, and 0 otherwise. We utilized two different event windows, 1 day and 3 days [-1, 1], where day 0 is 15 January 2002, to calculate the cumulative return (CR), which was then employed as the dependent variable to test Hypothesis 1 and Hypothesis 2. In addition, to test Hypothesis 3 we utilized the cumulative abnormal return (CAR) as the dependent variable, which is estimated with the controlled share model as follows:

$$\mathrm{CAR_i} = \sum_{T=-\mathrm{t}}^{T=t} \mathrm{CR_{i,1}} - \sum_{T=-\mathrm{t}}^{T=t} \mathrm{CR_{i,0}} \tag{1}$$

where i stands for the ith firm, t equals either 0 or 1, and $\mathrm{CR_{i,1}}$ and $\mathrm{CR_{i,0}}$ represent the raw daily return of the B-share and A-share issued by the ith firm.

To adjust for differences in pre-treatment features, we also controlled for the following set of variables in our multivariate models. First, the A/B-shares issued by the same firm could differ in their liquidity, as a

---

[40] We obtained the data for 1,254 listed A/B-shares, of which 114 are B-shares and 1,140 are A-shares.

Table 5.2 The number of listed firms by industry and province

Industries / Provinces	Materials	Industries	Consumer Discretionary	Consumer Staples	Health Care	Finance	Information Technology	Utilities	Subtotal
Anhui	0	0	2	1	0	0	0	0	3
Beijing	0	0	0	0	0	0	1	0	1
Guangdong	2	5	5	1	1	7	1	1	23
Hainan	0	1	0	0	0	1	0	0	2
Hebei	0	0	0	0	0	0	1	0	1
Heilongjiang	0	0	0	0	0	0	0	1	1
Hubei	2	0	0	0	0	0	0	0	2
Hunan	0	0	1	0	0	0	0	0	1
Jilin	0	0	1	0	0	0	0	0	1
Jiangsu	0	1	2	0	0	0	0	0	3
Liaoning	1	2	0	0	0	0	0	0	3
Neimengru	0	1	0	0	0	0	0	0	1
Shandong	1	0	1	1	0	0	0	0	3
Shanxi	0	0	0	0	0	0	0	1	1
Shanghai	3	11	6	2	2	6	2	0	32
Tianjin	0	1	0	0	0	0	0	0	1
Zhejiang	0	0	0	0	0	0	1	0	1
Chongching	0	0	1	0	0	0	0	0	1
Subtotal	9	22	19	5	3	14	6	3	81

Note: The distribution of 81 sampled firms listed on the SHSE and SZSE are presented by industry and province. The industry classification provided by Wind Information Co., Ltd. has been adopted.

result of which the daily turnover ratio (TURNOVER) averaged over half a year prior to the event date, from 15 July 2001 to 14 January 2002, was included. In addition, given the fixed costs of filing the private litigation, only claims with an expected high value are worth pursuing.[41] Larger firms may also attract more media coverage. Hence, we included the market capitalization (MCAP) of listed firms. Third, those firms reporting higher profits in the previous year are more likely to have enough assets to pay for compensation to aggrieved investors. Consequently, we included the earnings per share (EPS) as reported in the 2001 annual report. Fourth, state-owned enterprises might have a particularly large influence on the local courts, which should increase the expected costs of private litigations and discourage investors from seeking compensation. We therefore included the percentage of shares held by the state in a given firm (STATE).

Fifth, the efficiency of the judiciary system should correlate to the expected costs of bringing private securities litigation.[42] We thus employed the development index of the market intermediaries and legal environment in 2001 as a proxy for the efficiency of local courts (CE2001).[43] Sixth, listed firms having high leverage ratios are found to be more likely to commit financial misrepresentations.[44] Hence, we included the liability to asset ratio (LARATIO) as reported in the half-year report in 2001. Seventh, we also controlled for two financial indicators, the price to book ratio (PB) proxy for growth opportunities and return on equity (ROE), as reported in the 2001 semi-annual financial report. Finally, industrial dummies were included to control for possible industry fixed effects. The descriptive statistics and definitions of these variables are reported in Table 5.3.

4. EMPIRICAL RESULTS

This section presents empirical outputs testing the hypotheses developed in Section 2. Subsection 4.1 and Subsection 4.2 test Hypothesis 1 and Hypothesis 2 on the collective action problem, whereas Subsection 4.3 reports the results testing Hypothesis 3 on the determinants of abnormal returns between A/B-shares issued by the same firm.

---

41 Choi (2007).

42 Huang (2013).

43 Fan and Wang (2003).

44 Firth et al. (2011a).

Table 5.3 Variable definitions and summary statistics

Variable	N	Mean	Std. Dev.	Min.	Max.	Definition
Dependent variables						
$CR_{(0)}$	162	–1.94754	2.307006	–9.9776	1.6227	Raw share price return on the event day.
$CR_{(-1,1)}$	162	–4.19158	4.076124	–27.0434	3.3898	Raw cumulative share price return over the three-day event window.
$CAR_{(0)}$	81	1.2137	2.4496	–3.9880	7.0768	Abnormal return of B-share to A-share issued by the same firm on the event day.
$CAR_{(-1,1)}$	81	2.4204	3.8606	–6.7773	11.3610	Cumulative abnormal return of B-share to A-share issued by the same firm over the 3-day event window.
Independent variables						
TREATMENT	162	0.5000	0.5016	0.0000	1.0000	Dummy variable (=1 for B-share, 0 otherwise).
ABDUMMY	162	0.5000	0.5016	0.0000	1.0000	Dummy variable (=1 for A-share of the firm issuing both A/B-share, 0 for A-share of the firm issuing only A-share).
TURNOVER	162	0.8313	0.4030	0.1186	2.6381	Average daily turnover ratio for a given stock over half a year prior to the event date.
MCAP	162	3.5856	0.2206	3.1765	4.3129	Logarithm of market capitalization in million RMB for a given firm as of 14 January 2002.
EPS	162	0.0999	0.1473	–0.3170	0.9956	Earnings per share as reported in the 2001 semi-annual financial report.
STATE	162	35.6096	21.9391	0.0000	73.5247	The percentage of shares held by the government.
CE2001	162	7.0038	2.4228	2.2900	9.4200	The regional judiciary efficiency level.
LARATIO	162	47.2482	20.2561	8.8966	99.3211	The liability to asset ratio as reported in the 2001 semi-annual financial report.

PB	162	5.001003	7.543794	0.8546	72.5278	The price to book ratio as reported in the 2001 semi-annual financial report.
ROE	162	0.7508	20.9714	–181.3774	15.1682	The return on equity ratio as reported in the 2001 semi-annual financial report.
TURNOVER(B/A)	81	0.1822	0.6093	–2.1592	1.5474	The Napierian Logarithm of the ratio between TURNOVER of a B-share to that of an A-share issued by the same firm.
PB(B/A)	81	–0.5332	0.2132	–1.2285	–0.0209	The Napierian Logarithm of the ratio between PB of a B-share to that of an A-share issued by the same firm.

4.1 Collective Action Problem: Aggregate Treatment Effects

Table 5.4 reports the ordinary least squares (OLS) regression outputs with CRs as dependent variables utilizing our main sample of 162 stocks. Columns 2 and 3 present the basic regressions with 1-day and 3-day CRs against TREATMENT, industrial dummies and a constant term. On the event date, the group of B-shares gains approximately 1.21% more in market value compared to that of A-shares, significant at the 1% level, as shown in the second column. The positive treatment effect for B-shares increases to 2.42% when the event window is set to three days. The outputs of basic regressions are consistent with Hypothesis 1, which states that investors in the B-share market value the right to seek civil compensation higher than those in the A-share market do.

The literature has shown that the potential biases of the estimated treatment effects will be reduced if pre-event features are controlled for. We thus first include the variable TURNOVER proxy for the difference in liquidity between A-shares and B-shares in our model specification. Domestic investors have been allowed to buy and sell B-shares since 19 February 2001, which led to a sharp increase in the trading volume in the B-share market. The average daily turnover ratio for B-shares is 0.87 and that for A-shares is 0.79. Additionally, we include MCAP, EPS, STATE and CE2001 to control for the firm-specific characteristics that could influence the expected costs and benefits of private litigations, the results of which are shown in columns 4 and 5.

The outputs remain similar to those of the basic regressions. In column 4, the treatment effect for the group of B-shares increases to approximately 1.30% on the event date and is highly significant (t-stat=3.82). The variable TURNOVER is shown to have significant negative coefficients, which suggests that more liquid stocks actually gain less on the event date. Furthermore, consistent with the previous findings,[45] larger firms indeed experience higher treatment effects on the event day, as the coefficient of the MCAP is significant and positive. Although slightly insignificant (p-value = 0.138), the variable STATE has a negative coefficient, which is in accordance with the prediction that governmental connections have negative effects on the expected net profits of private litigations. CE2001 is insignificant and indicates that it does not influence the absolute daily returns. In column 5, the coefficient for TREATMENT is increased to 2.45% during the 3-day event window (t-stat=4.07, significant at 1%). The liquidity proxy, TURNOVER, is no longer significant, but the MCAP

45 Choi (2007).

Table 5.4 Regression outputs testing collective action hypothesis

Variable	$CR_{(0)}$	$CR_{(-1,1)}$	$CR_{(0)}$	$CR_{(-1,1)}$	$CR_{(0)}$	$CR_{(-1,1)}$
TREATMENT	1.21373***	2.420431***	1.295873***	2.454306***	1.183505***	2.084638***
	(0.342308)	(0.6094994)	(0.3375841)	(0.6042116)	(0.3537663)	(0.6068643)
TURNOVER			–1.036012*	–0.4272408	–0.9036373	0.2114237
			(0.5672843)	(0.9524042)	(0.6025543)	(0.8940987)
CE2001			0.0130168	0.0722295	0.0145969	0.0886853
			(0.0840954)	(0.1565225)	(0.082744)	(0.152693)
EPS			1.150675	3.902661*	0.5389276	1.702179
			(0.9096238)	(2.258654)	(0.9051433)	(2.216733)
MCAP			1.474869*	3.891488***	1.526744*	3.680032***
			(0.7760931)	(1.237036)	(0.8208349)	(1.302592)
STATE			–0.0118952	–0.0138908	–0.0162278*	–0.0224649
			(0.0079842)	(0.0138408)	(0.0085739)	(0.0142706)
LARATIO					0.0119285	0.0206633
					(0.0105708)	(0.0177688)
PB					–0.03436**	-0.1076038***
					(0.0140337)	(0.0225908)
ROE					0.0147266***	0.0481093***
					(0.0049895)	(0.0088076)
Constant	–1.571865***	–4.322515***	–6.373432**	–18.90978 ***	–6.795192**	–18.57694***
	(0.4178163)	(1.024967)	(2.882236)	(4.722698)	(3.112863)	(5.082238)
Industrial dummies	Included	Included	Included	Included	Included	Included
Observations	162	162	162	162	162	162
R^2	0.1537	0.1397	0.2315	0.2246	0.2528	0.2984

Note:
(a) The model is specified as follows: $CR_{(-t, +t)} = a+b_0*TREATMENT + b_1*X +e$, where "X" represents the vector of controlling variables.
(b) The robust standard error is reported in parentheses.
(c) *, **, *** indicate 10%, 5% and 1% levels of significance, respectively.

proxy for the size of the firm and the EPS proxy for profitability are both significant and positive in magnitude.

Finally, we include controls for additional pre-event financial indicators, LARATIO, PB and ROE, the results of which are reported in columns 6 and 7. Generally speaking, the empirical outputs are consistent with those reported in previous regressions. The coefficients of TREATMENT are positive and significant, but adjusted downwardly. The variable MCAP is significant in both columns, which provides strong evidence for the size effects. The coefficients of STATE are negative. It is significant in column 5, although the reported p-value in column 6 is slightly larger than the 10 per cent significance level (p-value=0.118).

4.2 Collective Action Problem: Placebo Test

In this subsection we test Hypothesis 2 and perform a placebo test comparing the effects of the SPC's 2002 Notice on our sampled A-shares and A-shares of listed firms issuing only A-shares on the SZSE and SHSE. Because retail investors in the A-share market have no incentives to overcome collective action problems, we hypothesize that the CRs of these two groups of shares do not differ significantly. We thus obtain data for 943 A-shares of firms issuing only A-shares and combine them with our 81 sampled A-shares of firms that issue both A/B-shares, forming the full sample of 1,024 shares. A dummy variable ABDUMMY is created to indicate whether the A-share is from a firm issuing A-shares and B-shares. If it is from a firm issuing both types of shares, we set ABDUMMY to 1, otherwise 0.

However, the regression analysis with the full sample runs into the risk that some of the A-shares of firms issuing only A-shares may not be comparable to our 81 sampled A-shares. To reduce the bias brought about by the "extreme counterfactual", a matching algorithm is employed to select those most comparable to our sampled A-shares. We adopt the optimal matching algorithm utilizing propensity scores, which discards 862 unmatched shares.[46] Following Ho et al.,[47] we report the comparison of the mean of each variable for the group of A-shares of firms issuing both A-shares and B-shares with that of A-shares of firms issuing only A-shares before and after optimal matching to check the

---

[46] Rosenbaum (1989). We estimated the propensity score utilizing linear logistic regressions of the dummy ABDUMMY on explanatory variables TURNOVER, CE2001, EPS, MCAP, STATE, LARATIO, PB and ROE.

[47] Ho et al. (2007).

Table 5.5 Remaining covariate imbalances after matching

Variable names	Standardized mean difference for full sample	Standardized mean difference for matched sample	Improvements (percentage)
TURNOVER	0.163	–0.1193	26.8101
CE2001	0.9384	–0.0396	95.7777
EPS	–0.0591	–0.1138	–92.3776
MCAP	0.8521	0.0316	96.2963
STATE	–0.2307	0.1967	14.7692
LARATIO	0.3058	0.0677	77.8586
PB	0.1589	–1.8787	–1,082.3394
ROE	–0.1312	–0.0895	31.7993

Note: The difference in mean is standardized and divided by the standard deviation in the group of A-shares of firms issuing both A-shares and /B-shares.

covariate balance in Table 5.5. This table demonstrates that the optimal matching algorithm significantly improves the covariate balance of our data, except that the imbalance of variables EPS and PB is significantly increased.

Due to the imbalance of some covariates, we apply a regression analysis on the matched sample with multiple controls, instead of relying on only the test of differences in mean CRs. The results are shown in Table 5.6. As a benchmark, we report the outputs of regression analysis with the full sample of 1,024 shares in columns 2 and 3. As shown in column 2, ABDUMMY has a negative coefficient, which is contrary to Hypothesis 2 and suggests that investors of A-shares of firms issuing both types of shares are worse off than those of A-shares of firms issuing only A-shares due to the promulgation of the SPC's 2002 Notice. In columns 4 and 5, we report the regression outputs with the matched sample. In both columns the variable ABDUMMY is not significant, which suggests that there is no significant difference in CRs of A-shares of firms issuing only A-shares and those of firms issuing both A-shares and B-shares. This confirms Hypothesis 2, which states that the collective action problem prevents investors of A-shares from seeking civil compensation, and hence their valuations of the rights to seek compensation have no significant difference.

Table 5.6 Regression outputs of the placebo test

Variable	$CR_{(0)}$	$CR_{(-1,1)}$	$CR_{(0)}$	$CR_{(-1,1)}$
ABDUMMY	–0.50934*	–0.6485316	–0.055624	–0.496487
	(0.3017363)	(0.5187704)	(0.4388186)	(0.6927927)
TURNOVER	0.045315	0.0109858	–0.176226	0.3151355
	(0.0643372)	(0.0959023)	(0.2515735)	(0.4285614)
CE2001	–0.04578	–0.1045726*	–0.562661	–0.281081
	(0.0339729)	(0.0557626)	(0.1118013)	(0.1959544)
EPS	0.55433	2.463096**	1.013084	–0.0162
	(0.6486617)	(1.10426)	(1.417821)	(2.017172)
MCAP	1.075147***	2.134926***	-0.009881*	2.454456**
	(0.2735926)	(0.466066)	(0.6030868)	(1.132379)
STATE	–0.00139	0.0072906	0.0162149	–0.008668
	(0.0031858)	(0.0052275)	(0.0099487)	(0.0141676)
LARATIO	–0.00172	–0.0034167	0.0016035	0.0074591
	(0.0044353)	(0.0069584)	(0.0128024)	(0.020487)
PB	0.00163***	0.0028458*	0.0199834***	0.0054925***
	(0.0001406)	(0.0014804)	(0.0005364)	(0.0008667)
ROE	0.008828	0.0241412	–0.055624***	0.0487941***
	(0.0056867)	(0.0158994)	(0.0064247)	(0.0102974)
Constant	–5.39719***	-11.34248***	–4.622671**	–11.72813***
	(0.9565242)	(1.601486)	(2.183986)	(4.341867)
Industrial dummies	Included	Included	Included	Included
Observations	1,024	1,024	162	162
R^2	0.0407	0.0689	0.1024	0.1024

Note:
(a) The model is specified as follows: $CR_{(-t, +t)} = \alpha + \beta_0{}^* \text{ ABDUMMY} + \beta_1{}^*X + \varepsilon$, where "X" represents the vector of controlling variables.
(b) The robust standard error is reported in parentheses.
(c) *, **, *** indicate 10%, 5% and 1% levels of significance, respectively.

4.3 Court Efficiency Hypothesis

In this subsection we test Hypothesis 3, which supposes that the abnormal returns of B-shares relative to A-shares issued by the same firms are determined by the efficiency of the judiciary of the region where the listed firm is located. The dependent variables are CARs calculated with Equation (1), and thus the sample size is reduced to 81 listed firms. In addition, we calculate the relative turnover ratio and price to book ratio[48]

[48] The difference in price to book ratio between A-shares and B-shares results from the fact that B-shares are traded at a discount relative to A-shares.

between B-shares and A-shares employing the following Equation (2) and Equation (3), respectively:

$$TURNOVER(B/A)_i = LN(TURNOVER_{i,1}/TURNOVER_{i,0}) \quad (2)$$
$$PB(B/A)_i = LN(PB_{i,1}/PB_{i,0}) \quad (3)$$

where $TURNOVER_{i,1}$ is the average daily turnover ratio for the B-shares issued by the ith firm over half a year prior to the event date, $TURNOVER_{i,0}$ is the average daily turnover ratio for the A-shares issued by the ith firm during the same period, $PB_{i,1}$ is the price to book ratio of the B-shares issued by the ith firm, and $PB_{i,0}$ is the price to book ratio of the A-shares issued by the ith firm, both of which are reported in the 2001 semi-annual financial report.

The empirical outputs are shown in Table 5.7. In columns 2 and 3 we present the univariate regressions with 1-day and 3-day CAR against CE2001 and a constant term.[49] The outputs demonstrate that court efficiency is positively correlated with the magnitude of abnormal returns in the event period. CE2001 is significant in both regressions and its coefficients are 0.245 and 0.393 during the 1-day and 3-day event windows, respectively. The results indicate that listed firms located in regions with an efficient judiciary system obtain higher positive abnormal return on the event date, thus providing supporting evidence to Hypothesis 3, which postulates that the efficiency of court systems determines the net expected benefits from civil litigations.

Next we assess whether the results of univariate regressions remain robust with the inclusion of multiple pre-event firm-specific characteristics. First, in columns 4 and 5 we control for the difference in liquidity of "twin shares" and include the variable TURNOVER(B/A). CE2001 still has significant positive coefficients, the magnitudes of which are similar to those reported in columns 2 and 3. However, the coefficients of the variable TURNOVER(B/A) are insignificant in both regressions and present no significant effects on the CARs.

Second, the variables that are proxies for the potential benefits and costs of pursuing the securities litigation are included. Due to significant fixed costs involved in these litigations, only firms above a minimum size will be sued, either frivolously or meritoriously.[50] As a result, we include MCAP to control for such size effects. In addition, those firms suffering

---

[49] All of the industrial dummies are insignificant, and thus we exclude them from our model specification.

[50] Choi (2007).

Table 5.7 Regression outputs testing the court efficiency hypothesis

	$CAR_{(0)}$	$CAR_{(-1,1)}$	$CAR_{(0)}$	$CAR_{(-1,1)}$	$CAR_{(0)}$	$CAR_{(-1,1)}$	$CAR_{(0)}$	$CAR_{(-1,1)}$	$CAR_{(0)}$	$CAR_{(-1,1)}$
CE2001	0.245264**	0.3930957**	0.2307658**	0.3784904**	0.2225717**	0.3422343*	0.2846137***	0.418756**	0.2442264**	0.3328647
	(0.103587)	(0.1791056)	(0.1068921)	(0.1829177)	(0.1078999)	(0.1803831)	(0.1011579)	(0.1964777)	(0.1120288)	(0.2015181)
TURNOVER (B/A)			–0.6154129	–0.6199523					–0.574813	–0.377921
			(0.4678056)	(0.6362394)					(0.5220549)	(0.68628)
MCAP					1.295927	2.921245*			1.038273	3.087565*
					(1.31989)	(1.631505)			(1.338936)	(1.604999)
EPS					2.168463	2.923781			1.595103	3.1702
					(1.468871)	(2.275297)			(1.562925)	(2.567481)
STATE					–0.0046332	–0.0102842			0.0062424	–0.005796
					(0.0133372)	(0.0203214)			(0.0155087)	(0.0239907)
LARATIO							–0.0193386	–0.0110858	–0.018031	0.0015122
							(0.0134453)	(0.021517)	(0.0139167)	(0.0197831)
PB							0.7625371	0.5957403	0.8846481	0.4990285
							(1.309432)	(1.987354)	(1.419989)	(2.23926)
ROE							–0.0019949	–0.0057989	–0.008836	–0.014023
							(0.0066444)	(0.0098428)	(0.006236)	(0.009981)
Constant	–0.5040573	–0.3327432	–0.2904017	–0.1175116	–5.043353	–10.37666	0.5421066	0.3332983	–3.166242	–10.81782*
	(0.7157893)	(1.395711)	(0.747523)	(1.406961)	(4.536107)	(5.962706)	(1.005026)	(1.510122)	(4.833871)	(5.934551)
Industrial dummies	Not included	Not included	Not included	Not included	Not included	Not included	Not included	Not included	Not included	Not included
Observations	81	81	81	81	81	81	81	81	81	81
R^2	0.0592	0.0612	0.0824	0.0707	0.0991	0.1130	0.0869	0.0653	0.1315	0.1219

Note:

(a) The model is specified as follows: $CR_{(-t,+t)} = \alpha + \beta_0 * CE2001 + \beta_1 * X + \varepsilon$, where "X" represents the vector of controlling variables.
(b) The robust t-statistics are reported in parentheses.
(c) *, **, *** indicate 10%, 5% and 1% levels of significance, respectively.

from annual losses may lack the assets to pay civil compensation, as a result of which we include EPS, which is a proxy for the profit level of the listed firms. Finally, it could be extremely costly for aggrieved investors to seek compensation from state-owned enterprises, which usually have good relationships with local governments and, hence, enjoy special advantages in lobbying local courts. Consequently, we include the variable STATE to control for the potential adverse effects from the governmental connection. The results are shown in columns 6 and 7. Again, CE2001 has positive and significant correlations with the CARs. The only variable that has a significant relationship with the dependent variable is MCAP, the coefficient of which is positive in magnitude, as shown in column 7.

Third, we control for the financial indicators of a given firm and include variables LARATIO, PB and ROE, the results of which are reported in columns 8 and 9. The coefficients of CE2001 are consistent with those reported in the previous regressions, and their significance even increases in both regressions. However, none of the financial indicators have a significant relationship with the dependent variables. Finally, we run a "horse race" and include all of these variables in the model specification. The results are presented in columns 10 and 11. In column 10, CE2001 is shown to have a coefficient of 0.244 and is significant at the 5 per cent level. The remaining controlling variables are all insignificant. In addition, the coefficient of CE2001 is approximately 0.333 in column 11, but is slightly insignificant with a p-value of 0.103. Furthermore, MCAP has a significant and positive relationship with the CAR over a 3-day event window.

The empirical outputs reported in Table 5.7 provide supporting evidence to Hypothesis 3 and confirm the positive relationship between the efficiency level of the court and the abnormal return on the event date. The coefficient of CE2001 reported in the last column of Table 5.7 suggests that a one point improvement in the indicator for court efficiency will bring an approximate 0.333 per cent increase in the CAR over a 3-day event window, which means that investors who buy B-shares issued by the firms residing in a region with high court efficiency are willing to pay higher premiums for the right to seek compensation.

5. CONCLUSION

The SPC's 2002 Notice was designed primarily to compensate aggrieved investors suffering from misrepresentations by listed firms. However, this compensatory function has been poorly achieved because of the daunting costs of utilizing the Chinese judiciary system, which are overwhelming compared to the interests held by retail investors. A significant proportion of eligible cases satisfying the administrative prerequisites are not brought to court. Investors intentionally leave money on the table, considering that compensation is expected. In this chapter we have demonstrated that private enforcement rights are more highly valued by investors in the B-share market, where the majority of investors are institutional investors, including foreign institutional investors and privately managed investment funds. Institutional investors hold and trade in large volumes and enjoy economies of scale in handling securities litigation, which partially mitigates the collective action problem. In addition, we have found that regional judiciary efficiency is positively correlated with the magnitude of abnormal returns during the event periods after controlling for various pre-event firm-specific characteristics. Investors of B-shares issued by the firms residing in a region with a more efficient court system are willing to pay higher premiums for the right to seek civil compensation. The empirical outputs anchor the arguments that the inefficiency of the court system imposes significant costs on aggrieved investors seeking civil compensation.

REFERENCES

Atanasov, Vladimir A. and Bernard S. Black (2015), "Shock-Based Causal Inference in Corporate Finance and Accounting Research", *Critical Finance Review*, 5 (2), 207–304.

Black, Bernard S. (1990), "Shareholder Passivity Reexamined", *Michigan Law Review*, 89, 520–608.

Bohl, Martin T., Michael Schuppli and Pierre L. Siklos (2010), "Stock Return Seasonalities and Investor Structure: Evidence from China's B-share Markets", *China Economic Review*, 21, 190–201, doi: http://dx.doi.org/10.1016/j.chieco.2009.12.004.

Burch, Elizabeth C. (2008), "Securities Class Actions as Pragmatic Ex Post Regulation", *Georgia Law Review*, 43, 63–131.

Chan, Kalok, Albert J. Menkveld and Zhishu Yang (2008), "Information Asymmetry and Asset Prices: Evidence from the China Foreign Share Discount", *Journal of Finance*, 63, 159–96, doi: 10.1111/j.1540-6261.2008.01313.x.

Chen, Gongmeng, Michael Firth, Daniel N. Gao and Oliver M. Rui (2005), "Is China's Securities Regulatory Agency a Toothless Tiger? Evidence from Enforcement Actions", *Journal of Accounting and Public Policy*, 24, 451–88, doi: http://dx.doi.org/10.1016/j.jaccpubpol.2005.10.002.

Choi, Stephen J. (2004), "The Evidence on Securities Class Actions", *Vanderbilt Law Review*, 57, 1465–526.

Choi, Stephen J. (2007), "Do the Merits Matter Less after the Private Securities Litigation Reform Act?", *Journal of Law, Economics, and Organization*, 23, 598–626, doi: 10.1093/jleo/ewm014.

Clarke, Donald C. (2010), "Law without Order in Chinese Corporate Governance Institutions", *Northwestern Journal of International Law & Business*, 30, 131–99.

Cochran, William G. and Donald B. Rubin (1973), "Controlling Bias in Observational Studies: A Review", *Sankhyā: The Indian Journal of Statistics, Series A*, 35, 417–46, doi: 10.2307/25049893.

Coffee, John C. Jr. (2006), "Reforming the Securities Class Action: An Essay on Deterrence and its Implementation", *Columbia Law Review*, 106, 1534–86.

Cox, James D. and Randall S. Thomas (2002), "Leaving Money on the Table: Do Institutional Investors Fail to File Claims in Securities Class Actions", *Washington University Law Quarterly*, 80, 855–81.

Cox, James D. and Randall S. Thomas (2005), "Letting Billions Slip through Your Fingers: Empirical Evidence and Legal Implications of the Failure of Financial Institutions to Participate in Securities Class Action Settlements", *Stanford Law Review*, 58, 411–54.

Fan, Gang and Xiaolu Wang (2003), *The Report on the Relative Process of Marketization of Each Region in China*, Beijing: The Economic Science Press.

Firth, Michael, Oliver M. Rui and Wenfeng Wu (2011a), "The Effects of Political Connections and State Ownership on Corporate Litigation in China", *Journal of Law and Economics*, 54, 573–607.

Firth, Michael, Oliver M. Rui and Wenfeng Wu (2011b), "Cooking the Books: Recipes and Costs of Falsified Financial Statements in China", *Journal of Corporate Finance*, 17, 371–90, doi: http://dx.doi.org/10.1016/j.jcorpfin.2010.09.002.

Guo, Li and Allan V.Y. Ong (2009), "The Fledgling Securities Fraud Litigation in China", *Hong Kong Law Journal*, 39, 697–718.

Helland, Eric and Jonathan Klick (2011), "Legal Origins and Empirical Credibility", in: M. Faure and J. Smits (eds), *Does Law Matter? On Law and Economic Growth*, Cambridge–Antwerp–Portland: Intersentia, 99–114.

Ho, Daniel E., Kosuke Imai, Gary King and Elizabeth A. Stuart (2007), "Matching as Nonparametric Preprocessing for Reducing Model Dependence in Parametric Causal Inference", *Political Analysis*, 15, 199–236, doi: 10.1093/pan/mpl013.

Huang, Hui (2013), "Private Enforcement of Securities Law in China: A Ten-Year Retrospective and Empirical Assessment", *American Journal of Comparative Law*, 61,757–98.

Humphery-Jenner, Mark (2013), "Strong Financial Laws without Strong Enforcement: Is Good Law Always Better than No Law?", *Journal of Empirical Legal Studies*, 10, 288–324, doi: 10.1111/jels.12011.

Hutchens, Walter (2003), "Private Securities Litigation in China: Material Disclosure about China's Legal System", *University of Pennsylvania Journal of International Economic Law*, 24, 599–690.

Jackson, Howell E. (2007), "Variation in the Intensity of Financial Regulation: Preliminary Evidence and Potential Implications", *Yale Journal on Regulation*, 24, 253–91.

Jackson, Howell E. and Mark J. Roe (2009), "Public and Private Enforcement of Securities Laws: Resource-Based Evidence", *Journal of Financial Economics*, 93, 207–38, doi: http://dx.doi.org/10.1016/j.jfineco.2008.08.006.

La Porta, Rafael, Florencio Lopez-de-Silanes and Andrei Shleifer (2006), "What Works in Securities Laws?", *Journal of Finance*, 61, 1–32, doi: 10.1111/j.1540-6261.2006.00828.x.

La Porta, Rafael, Florencio Lopez-de-Silanes and Andrei Shleifer (2008), "The

Economic Consequences of Legal Origins", *Journal of Economic Literature*, 46, 285–332, doi: 10.2307/27646991.

Layton, Marlon A. (2008), "Is Private Securities Litigation Essential for the Development of China's Stock Markets", *New York University Law Review*, 83, 1948–78.

Liao, Li, Bibo Liu and Hao Wang (2014), "China's Secondary Privatization: Perspectives from the Split-Share Structure Reform", *Journal of Financial Economics*, 113, 500–18, doi: http://dx.doi.org/10.1016/j.jfineco.2014.05.007.

Liebman, Benjamin L. and Curtis J. Milhaupt (2008), "Reputational Sanctions in China's Securities Market", *Columbia Law Review*, 108, 929–83.

Lu, Guiping (2003), "Private Enforcement of Securities Fraud Law in China: A Critique of the Supreme People's Court 2003 Provisions Concerning Private Securities Litigation", *Pacific Rim Law & Policy Journal*, 12, 781–805.

Mei, Jianping, José A. Scheinkman and Wei Xiong (2009), "Speculative Trading and Stock Prices: Evidence from Chinese AB Share Premia", *Annals of Economics and Finance*, 10, 225–55.

Philipsen, Niels (2007), "Prevention and Compensation of Work Injury in the United States: An Overview of Existing Empirical Evidence", in S. Klosse and T. Hartlief (eds), *Shifts in Compensating Work-Related Injuries and Diseases*, Vienna: Springer Verlag, 197–220.

Pistor, Katharina and Chenggang Xu (2005), "Governing Stock Markets in Transition Economies: Lessons from China", *American Law and Economics Review*, 7, 184–210, doi: 10.1093/aler/ahi008.

Rosenbaum, Paul R. (1989), "Optimal Matching for Observational Studies", *Journal of the American Statistical Association*, 84, 1024–32, doi: 10.1080/01621459.1989.10478868.

Rubin, Donald B. (1973), "The Use of Matched Sampling and Regression Adjustment to Remove Bias in Observational Studies", *Biometrics*, 29, 185–203, doi: 10.2307/2529685.

Thompson, Robert B. and Hillary A. Sale (2003), "Securities Fraud as Corporate Governance: Reflections upon Federalism", *Vanderbilt Law Review*, 56, 859–910.

Xu, Guangdong (2011), "The Role of Law in Economic Growth: A Literature Review", *Journal of Economic Surveys*, 25, 833–71, doi: 10.1111/j.1467-6419.2011.00691.x.

Xu, Wenming (2014), "Law Matters? A Bayesian Analysis of the Cross-Country Relationship between Anti-Self-Dealing Rules and Stock Market Outcomes", *Applied Economics Letters*, 21, 5, 366–71, doi: 10.1080/13504851.2013.861580.

Xu, Wenming, Jianwei Chen and Guangdong Xu (2016), "An Empirical Analysis of the Public Enforcement of Securities Law in China: Finding the Missing Piece to the Puzzle", *European Business Organization Law Review*, 18, forthcoming.

Zhou, Tianshu (2015), "Is the CSRC Protecting a 'Level Playing Field' in China's Capital Markets: Public Enforcement, Fragmented Authoritarianism and Corporatism", *Journal of Corporate Law Studies*, 15, 377–406.

PART II

Social and administrative regulation

6. What can economists learn from contract lawyers?

Qi Zhou

1. INTRODUCTION

A few years ago, I argued in a paper[1] that contract lawyers can learn many valuable insights understanding contract law from economists, even though their main research interests lie in the doctrinal analysis of law. At that time, I was very enthusiastic in applying the economic approach to legal studies. I overlooked many potential contributions which traditional legal scholars can make to law and economics research. Unfortunately, my mistake is shared by many law and economics scholars, in particular young economists. Five years have passed since the publication of that paper. I have not changed my belief that contract lawyers can learn many valuable insights from economists. But I have seen many limitations in the current law and economics literature produced by economists. I strongly believe that economists can also learn many important lessons from lawyers.

I use the term 'contract lawyers' in this chapter to refer to traditional and mainstream legal scholars. Several renowned representatives in the UK are Guenter Treitel, Hugh Beale and Michael Bridge. Contract lawyers take a doctrinal or black-letter law approach. Their research primarily focuses on the interpretation of legal rules, doctrines and principles. The main aims of their research are to understand the law, to clarify ambiguities in the law and to propose solutions to inconsistencies in the law.[2] Their research outputs often take the form of textbooks,[3] monographs,[4] doctrinal analysis in academic legal journals[5] and drafted legislation.[6] The main users of their research are law students, practitioners and judges.

1 Zhou (2011), 157.
2 Smits (2012), 61.
3 Bridge (2014); Peel (2015).
4 Liu (2011); Rowan (2012).
5 Halson (1991), 649; Lord Hoffmann (2010), 47.
6 The Proposal for European Sales Law (CESL).

Many limitations of economic analysis of law can be overcome by the collaboration between economists and lawyers. Economists and lawyers have complementary expertise. Economists are skilled in using advanced analytical tools such as mathematic modelling and statistical analysis. Lawyers have better legal knowledge. They know how the law should be interpreted, applied or used in practice, as well as understanding the problems, ambiguities and inconsistencies in the existing legal system. So, lawyers are in a better position to identify important research questions and to transfer the output of law and economic research into law. The success of law and economics scholarship depends on a mutual respect and close collaboration between economists and lawyers.[7]

The current situation in the law and economics scholarship is less satisfactory.[8] Since the rise of the new law and economics wave beginning in the 1970s,[9] there has been a large body of literature published on almost every legal topic. Special journals on law and economics have flourished. However, publications in these journals are predominantly written by economists, and the mainstream law and economics literature has therefore become highly technical and inaccessible to lawyers. Legal scholars rarely get their works published in law and economics journals unless they use mathematical modelling or statistical analysis in their research. Legal scholarship has been unjustifiably underrated.[10] Many economists do not appreciate the value of legal research, which is unfairly treated as informal and unscientific. At the same time, traditional legal scholars barely read law and economics literature. Even if they are willing to do so, some law and economics literature is beyond their understanding. This is really unfortunate, not only because many valuable insights of law and economics cannot reach their final users – lawyers – but also same flaws persist in the economic analysis of law, which can certainly be remedied by legal scholars. The gap between lawyers and economists in the law and economics scholarship has widened since the 1990s.

In this chapter I argue that lawyers can play a valuable role in the law and economics scholarship as they can correct some persistent flaws in the economic analysis of law. To do so, I will draw a number of examples from the contract law literature. In brief, lawyers can make three valuable contributions. First, lawyers can improve economists' understanding of contracting activities in reality and help them focus on important research

7 Calabresi (2016); Baird (1997), 1129.

8 Posner (2003), 829; Aryes (2003), 881; Craswell (2003), 903.

9 Duxbury (1995), 301.

10 Ogus (2010), 169.

questions. Second, lawyers can correct economists' misunderstanding of the law and improve the quality of their economic arguments. Third, lawyers can evaluate the feasibility and plausibility of legal reforms proposed by economists, and can implement them by designing a suitable legal rule to modify the existing legal system.

The chapter is structured as follows. Section 2 shows legal scholars' contributions to understanding contracting behaviour. Section 3 discusses how legal scholars can improve economists' understanding of legal rules. Section 4 demonstrates the crucial role played by lawyers in implementing economic proposals in legal reform. Finally, Section 5 concludes the discussion by suggesting more collaboration between economists and lawyers on contract law reform in the EU and China.

2. IMPROVING UNDERSTANDING OF CONTRACTING BEHAVIOUR

A proper understanding of contracting behaviour in reality is a prerequisite for any type of economic analysis, in particular for positive economic analysis. Positive economic analysis[11] uses assumptions and economic logics to predict how individuals respond to different legal rules.[12] Take the analysis of efficient breach as an example.

The analyst asks the question how different legal remedies for breach of contract change a party's incentive to commit a breach. To answer this question, the analyst makes a few assumptions: the party by and large acts rationally and has all of the relevant information on which to base his decision. Based on these assumptions, the analyst uses economic logic to predict the party's responses to different legal remedies. A breach of contract may bring a benefit to the promisor, but the remedy for breach of contract also imposes on the promisor a cost. The promisor's decision on whether to breach the contract is based on a cost–benefit analysis. Economic analysis has produced some economic models for predicting incentives to commit a breach.[13] Positive economic analysis has always been criticized for its unrealistic assumptions. Behavioural law and

---

[11] According to Milton Friedman (1953, 4), 'the task of positive economics aims to provide a system of generalisation that can be used to make correct predictions about the consequences of any change in circumstances. Its performance is to be judged by the precision, scope, and conformity with experience of the predictions it yields'.

[12] Ogus (2006), 24; Trebilcock (1999), 12.

[13] Shavell (1980), 446; Birmingham (1970), 273.

economics have convincingly demonstrated the many limitations and flaws of positive economic analysis,[14] and I do not propose to reiterate those criticisms. But it is worth noting the major limitation of positive economic analysis, that is economic models often incorrectly describe contracting behaviour. Positive economic analysis uses economic logics and reasoning to predict contracting behaviour. Economists conducting a positive economic analysis do not always observe actual contracting activities in practice, so their models may incorrectly describe contracting behaviour in reality.

In contrast, lawyers observe contracting behaviour through reading cases and sometimes through their own experience in legal practice. Cases document real legal disputes. The law reports of first instance cases often provide a comprehensive account of the history of the dispute. By reading them, lawyers can better understand how the contract was formed, what went wrong, why there was a dispute and how the parties behaved from the pre-contractual stage until the dispute arose. Often, lawyers themselves are also legal consultants in practice, with direct experience in contracting activities. Lawyers take an empirical approach to studying contracting behaviour.

An incorrect understanding of contracting behaviour may lead economists to overlook some important issues in their analysis and undermines the strength of an economic argument. Let me illustrate this with an example of efficient breach.[15] Economists view a contract as a Pareto-efficient allocation of resources.[16] Both parties to a contract will benefit from the transaction. From an economic perspective, the duty to perform a contract is not absolute. The promisor should breach the contract when the breach is Pareto efficient.[17] This is reminiscent of the famous remark made by renowned American judge Oliver Wendell Holmes:

> the duty to keep a contract at common law means a prediction that you must pay damages if you do not keep it – and nothing else.[18]

A typical example of efficient breach involves three parties. Suppose that a seller sells his car to a buyer for £10,000 and that he can make a profit of £1,000 from the sale. The buyer's subjective value of the car is £11,000. So the buyer can gain a consumer surplus of £1,000. After the conclusion

---

14 Sunstein (2000); Jolls, Sunstein and Thaler (1998), 1471.
15 Zhou (2008), 268.
16 Austen-Baker and Zhou (2015), 104; Coleman (1980), 226.
17 Liao (2015), 45; Birmingham (1970), 273.
18 Holmes (1897), 462.

of the contract, a third party offers £13,000 to purchase the car from the seller. Let us assume that the third party's subjective value of the car is £15,000. If the seller in breach of contract sells the car to the third party and pays the buyer compensation of £1,000, the breach is Pareto efficient, bringing a gain of £2,000 to both the seller and the third party respectively. The buyer, after receiving compensation of £1,000, is put in the position that he would have been in had there been no breach. The breach makes both the seller and the third party better off without making the buyer worse off.

Based on this reasoning, economists have devoted a great deal of effort to the study of different remedies for breach of contract. They seek to answer the question: which legal remedy induces efficient breach?[19] Despite disagreement and controversies, the answer in standard law and economics textbooks is that the remedy of expectation damages is the best remedy for inducing efficient breach. After receiving expectation damages, the promisee would be put in the same position that he would have been in had the contract been performed. At the same time, it gives the promisor an incentive to breach only if he can make a higher benefit from a breach after compensating for loss of the promisee's expectation profit. In contrast, reliance damages may induce too many inefficient breaches[20] and restitutionary damages discourage the promisor from committing efficient breach. Furthermore, the remedy of specific performance may sometimes lead to efficient breach, but it increases transaction costs for the parties.[21]

Based on the above basic propositions, economists have produced some more advanced models. These models incorporate two extra variables in the analysis: the opportunity for renegotiation and transaction costs. But the central question in the economic analysis of efficient breach is the same, that is which legal remedy for breach of contract induces efficient breach and deters inefficient breach.[22]

For a lawyer, the efficient breach theory is incomplete and needs further qualification. Lawyers view legal remedies from their clients' perspectives. When a client comes to a lawyer for legal advice, the first question the lawyer asks is what their client wants to achieve, and then the immediately ensuing question is whether the client's request can be achieved under the current legal system.

---

19 Liao (2015), 89.

20 The remedy of expectation damages may lead to the problem of overreliance by the promisee. See Austen-Baker and Zhou (2015), 128.

21 Austen-Baker and Zhou (2015), 125; Craswell (1988), 628; Ulen (1984), 341.

22 Liao (2015), 79.

A stark difference between analysis by an economist and a lawyer is that the economist focuses on a particular remedy, while the contract lawyer takes a holistic perspective. In other words, the economist asks the question of how the party should respond to a given legal remedy. But the lawyer asks the question: which legal rules can be used to meet my client's need? If contract law is of no help, the lawyer will look into remedies in other branches of law. If we analyse efficient breach from a lawyer's standpoint, efficient breach can rarely happen in practice.

Recall the example discussed above. The seller has sold the car to the buyer. Before delivering the car, the third party offers a higher price to buy the car from the seller. The seller in breach of contract sells the car to the third party. According to the argument of efficient breach, if the seller compensates the first buyer for his expectation losses, the breach is Pareto efficient. However, the lawyer at this moment will pause and ask the question whether his client would be satisfied by receiving only expectation damages from the seller. If his client wanted to claim the profit which the seller makes from the breach, can he find a legal ground on which to do so?[23] The implication of this legal analysis will affect the conclusion of the economic analysis. If remedies in other branches of law allow the buyer to recover the profit which the seller makes from selling the car to the third party, the seller would not have the incentive to breach the contract in the first place. Therefore, even though contract law remedy may induce efficient breach, efficient breach will still not happen in practice.

In English law the buyer may be entitled to claim the seller's profit from the breach. The key legal issue is if the property (in this case the car) has passed from the seller to the buyer. If the property has passed to the buyer, the seller's breach constitutes a conversion in tort law. Instead of suing for breach of contract, the buyer can claim account of the profit which the seller makes from the breach by using the technique of waiver of tort.[24] Section 18(1) of the Sale of Goods Act 1979 provides that where there is an unconditional contract for the sale of specific goods in a deliverable state, the property in the goods passes to the buyer when the contract is made. If the above example is considered under English law, the buyer has become the owner of the car before the seller sells the car to the third party. The seller's breach therefore constitutes a conversion. The lawyer may advise the buyer to claim account of profit instead of damages for breach

---

[23] To my knowledge, this question has not been asked in the law and economics literature except for a paper which I published a few years ago: Zhou (2008), 268.

[24] *Lamine v Orrell (1790) 2 Ld Raym* 1216; 92 ER 303.

of contract. Given this legal claim, the seller would not have an incentive to breach in the first place and efficient breach could not happen.

In addition to suing the seller, the lawyer may advise the buyer to sue the third party. The lawyer may ask his client if he prefers the car to financial compensation. If his client prefers the car to the money, the contract lawyer will investigate whether the third party is a bona fide purchaser. If the third party is not aware of the contract between the seller and the buyer, he may acquire the property in the car through one of the exceptions for *nemo dat quod non habet*.[25] Even in this case, efficient breach may not happen for the reason we just discussed. If the third party is not a bona fide purchaser, he cannot acquire the property in the car. The first buyer as owner of the car can sue the third party to retain the possession of the car in an action of conversion.[26] Given this legal liability, the third party would not have the incentive to make the contract with the seller. Therefore, efficient breach cannot happen.

There is yet another possibility. Even if the buyer intends to claim financial compensation, the contract lawyer may advise the buyer to sue the third party instead of the seller. In practice, the buyer may choose to do this because the seller may become insolvent, or where the third party and the buyer are in the same location, the litigation cost against the third party is lower. The legal question is if this is possible. If the third party is not a bona fide purchaser and intentionally offers the seller a higher price to purchase the car, the third party commits a tortious wrong, that is inducing breach of contract.[27] Tort law provides the legal remedy for the buyer and he can claim damages from the third party. This legal rule also undermines the third party's incentive to purchase the car from the seller. Therefore, efficient breach could not happen.

Economists look at the issue from a different perspective. Some economists aim to examine the impact of a legal rule on people's behaviour. They use models and economic logic to investigate interaction between the law and individuals' incentive to commit a breach. Lawyers, on the other hand, aim to meet their clients' request by the use of legal rules; they

---

[25] Section 24 of the Sale of Goods Act 1979 provides: 'where a person having sold goods continues or is in possession of the goods, or of the documents of title to the goods, the delivery or transfer by that person, or by a mercantile agent acting for him, of the goods or documents of title under any sale, pledge, or other disposition thereof, to any person receiving the same in good faith and without notice of the previous sale, has the same effect as the person making the delivery or transfer were expressly authorised by the owner of the goods to make the same.'

[26] *Jeffries v Great Western Railway Co* (1856) 5 E & B 802.

[27] *Lumley v Gye* [1853] ER 15.

are interested in the question of how a particular legal rule is applied. In practice, it is lawyers rather than economists who advise their clients on negotiation of deals, contract drafting and dispute resolution. Lawyers are the persons who actually engage in a variety of contracting activities and design responses to a 'new' legal rule. When a new legal duty is imposed, lawyers often advise their clients how they can circumvent the law by manipulating the existing legal rules or doctrines. Let me illustrate this with an example of a non-reliance clause.[28]

One of the main legal risks in the pre-contractual negotiation is the legal liability for misrepresentation.[29] In negotiation, many pieces of information are exchanged between the parties. It is impossible for the information provider to check every piece of information, in particular in a long-term negotiation for complicated commercial transactions, such as mergers, takeovers or construction contracts. If one piece of information turns out to be untrue, the party providing the information may face the risk of legal liability for misrepresentation. The other party may rescind the contract[30] and claim damages if the court finds that the misrepresentation was made intentionally or negligently.[31] To establish an action of misrepresentation, the claimant must show that he or she has relied on the misrepresentation.

How do contracting parties respond to the law of misrepresentation? When answering this question, lawyers will consider how the rule can be circumvented by using the existing legal rules. To manage this legal risk in practice, lawyers have created a 'non-reliance clause', which is a clause that usually provides that any party's decision to enter into the contract does not rely on any information provided in the negotiations by the other party. In other words, in agreeing on the non-reliance clause, one party acknowledges that he does not rely on any information provided by the other party. Even if the information turns out to be untrue, the former party is not able to sue the latter party in the action of misrepresentation because the legal requirement of reliance for an actionable misrepresentation cannot be met.

Non-reliance clauses have been widely used in commercial transactions to deal with the legal liability of misrepresentation.[32] To make a non-reliance clause effective, lawyers use the doctrine of estoppel. Where the

---

28 Loi (2015), 346; Braithwaite (2016), 120.

29 Cartwright (2007); Zhou (2009).

30 *Car & Universal Finance Co Ltd v Caldwell* [1965] 1 QB 525.

31 *Doyle v Obly* [1969] 2 QB 158; *Royscott v Rogerson* [1991] 2 QB 297.

32 *Peekay Intermark Ltd v Australia and New Zealand Banking Group Ltd* [2006] EWCA Civ 386; *Springwell Navigation Corp v JP Morgan Chase Bank* [2010] EWCA Civ 1221.

parties have concluded a contract, one party acknowledges that he does not rely on any information provided by the other party. Later, the party making that acknowledgement is estopped from denying the statement made earlier.[33] The use of non-reliance clauses is a legal strategy designed by lawyers to prevent the legal liability for misrepresentation. It is a typical example of lawyers' responses to the law by using other legal rules. In commercial practice, lawyers are the main designer of strategies for responding to new laws.

3. CORRECTING MISUNDERSTANDINGS OF THE LAW

Legal concepts, doctrines and principles are crucial because similar disputes may produce different legal consequences if different legal doctrines are applied. Lawyers spend enormous effort on refining legal concepts. One primary goal of legal research is to clarify the legal rules and to explain how and when a given legal rule should be applied. Where there is an ambiguity in the legal rule or a conflict between two legal rules, it is vital to understand how the rules should be interpreted and which rule should be applied. Lawyers are obsessed with precision of legal concepts. If lawyers do not understand the law correctly and precisely, the law cannot operate smoothly and effectively. Legal uncertainty is a major impediment to economic development[34] and understanding a law correctly is a prerequisite for the economic analysis of law. When studying a particular legal rule, many economists have only a very general level of understanding of law. They often do not give sufficient consideration to legal doctrines and subtleties in a legal rule.

Doctrines are crucial in legal studies. A subtle difference between two legal doctrines may lead to profound implications in practice. A failure to appreciate subtleties in legal doctrines may cause confusion and misunderstanding in communication between economists and lawyers. Let me illustrate it with an example of the penalty clause.

Lawyers have been very enthusiastic in refining the notion of the penalty clause and in differentiating it from another similar legal notion, the liquidated damages clause. Many economists are not interested in such a question. Although they study penalty clauses, their understanding of

---

33 McMeel (2011), 185; Trukhtanov (2009), 648.

34 North (2005), 21.

the law on penalty clauses may be very general. They may not see the vital subtle differences between the two legal concepts.

The issue of penalty clauses is one of the unsettled topics in the economic analysis of contract law.[35] An important economic question is whether it is efficient for the law to permit the use of penalty clauses. Some law and economics scholars argue that the law permitting the use of penalty clauses is efficient.[36] A penalty clause can be used as a signalling strategy to solve the problem of adverse selection. Suppose that there are two types of builder on the market. The reliable builder always finishes the job on time. The less reliable builder may occasionally finish the job late. However, employers cannot distinguish them at the time of contracting; this can only be discerned once the job is done. This is a typical 'market for lemons' problem.[37] If this problem is not solved, the reliable builders will be driven out of the market by price competition. Some law and economics scholars argue that penalty clauses are a solution to this problem.[38] Because the reliable builder always finishes the job on time, he has a strong incentive to distinguish himself from the less-reliable builder. He is willing to agree to a penalty clause that punitive damages are payable on late completion. The reliable builder can use a penalty clause as a signalling strategy to distinguish himself from the less-reliable builder.

Other law and economics scholars disagree.[39] The less-reliable builder may have an incentive to offer the same penalty clause, because he only needs to pay the penalty if he fails to complete the job on time. If this probability is low, the less-reliable builder may gamble on the probability of breach and the credibility of a penalty clause as a signalling strategy will be undermined. In addition, penalty clauses exacerbate the problem of bounded rationality;[40] a contracting party may be irrationally over-confident in the probability of performance and may agree a penalty clause.[41] Furthermore, penalty clauses may impair competition. If a provider of services imposes a penalty on consumers for earlier termination of contracts, this increases the cost of termination for consumers. If another provider offers a better price, and consumers want to switch to the new provider, they have to pay a penalty. Consequently, the penalty

---

35 Walt (2011), 178; Hatzis (2003), 381; Polinsky and Shavell (1998), 869; Cooter (1982), 79; Hylton (1998), 421.

36 Walt (2011), 181; Goetz and Scott (1977), 554.

37 Akerlof (1970), 488.

38 Cooter and Ulen (2014), 314.

39 Aghion and Hermalin (1990), 281; Wagner (2011) 9, 54.

40 Eisenberg (1995), 217; Wagner (2011) 9, 54.

41 Weinstein (1989), 1232.

clause becomes anti-competitive, deterring new firms from entering the market. Accordingly, the law should prohibit the use of penalty clauses. The debate on the topic of penalty clauses still continues. No agreement has yet been reached.

An important issue has been overlooked in this debate. What is the legal definition of a penalty clause? The economist's notion of a penalty clause may be different from the legal definition. Economists often see a penalty clause as a contract term which makes the promisor pays a disproportionate amount of damages to the promisee on breach of the contract: the amount of the penalty significantly exceeds the loss caused by the breach. A penalty does not aim to compensate for loss, but to deter the promisor from breaching the contract. In fact, the distinction between a penalty clause, which is void, and a liquidated damages clause, which is valid, is very subtle.[42] A clause which provides payment of a large financial award is not necessary to make it a penalty. Nor does a clause aim to deter breach of contract. Many agreed damages clauses, which seem to be void penalty clauses, are actually valid in law. Judges are very reluctant to strike down an agreed damages clause, if there is a commercial justification for it. This is illustrated by a recent decision of the UK Supreme Court.

In *Cavendish Square Holding BV v Talal El Makessi* and *Parking Eye Limited v Beavis*[43] the UK Supreme Court consolidated the two appeals and provided a comprehensive legal analysis of a penalty clause. The two appeals are quite different in nature. In *Cavendish*, the dispute arose out of a commercial contract in which the defendant sold a marketing company to the claimant. In the contract there was a clause providing that the defendant should not put himself into a conflicting position. If he did so, he would not be able to claim part of the agreed price. The defendant breached the contract and argued that the clause was a void penalty. The Court gave judgment in favour of the claimant, holding that the clause was not a penalty. When the commercial parties agree on a damages clause without being induced by any unconscionable behaviour, and even if the clause aims to deter breach of contract, the clause is not a void penalty if it is justified for a legitimate commercial interest. In *Cavendish*, the clause aimed to deter the defendant from acting in conflict with the claimant's interests, which were legitimate. Therefore, the clause was not a void penalty.

In *Parking Eye*, the dispute arose from a consumer contract, under which the defendant parked his car in the car park of a shopping mall,

---

[42] *Dunlop Pneumatic Type Co Ltd v New Garage and Motor Co Ltd* [1915] AC 79, 86–7 per Lord Dunedin.

[43] [2015] UKSC 67.

which was managed by the claimant. There was a notice at the entry to the car park stipulating that customers were entitled to two hours of free parking without return within 24 hours. The defendant left his car there more than two hours and the claimant imposed a fine of £80. The defendant argued that this constituted a penalty and should be void. The Court ruled that even though the sum of financial payment was disproportionately high, the term was not a void penalty, because it was used to pursue a legitimate commercial interest, which was defined as the efficient management of the car park.

Both decisions are clearly different from the concept of a penalty clause in the traditional law and economics literature. Rarely do economists consider the doctrine of commercial justification in the economic analysis of penalty rules. However, this doctrine is well known to lawyers. Economists often believe that where an agreed damages clause aims to deter breach by setting the agreed damages disproportionately higher than the reasonable estimation of the actual loss at the time of making the contract, the clause is a penalty. However, lawyers will not reach that conclusion easily due to the doctrine of commercial justification.

Why does the precise understanding of legal rules matter to the economic analysis of contract law? When there is a misunderstanding of a legal doctrine or legal concept, economists cannot effectively communicate with lawyers. Their research subject is unclearly defined. A correct and precise understanding of legal doctrine is vital to prevent confusion in communication and misunderstanding between lawyers and economists.

Furthermore, an incorrect understanding of law may lead the economic analysis to reach a wrong conclusion. Let us look at another example, the doctrine of foreseeability, which is less controversial in the law and economics literature, but has generated great difficulty in legal scholarship. The decision of an old English case, *Hadley v Baxendale*,[44] has always been praised for preventing overreliance and encouraging the sharing of private information by law and economics scholars.[45] In *Hadley*, the plaintiff contracted the defendant to ship a broken shaft of a mill to London for repair. The defendant, in breach of contract, redelivered the shaft late to the plaintiff. As a consequence, the plaintiff's mill could not operate and the plaintiff lost a very profitable contract. The plaintiff sued the defendant to recover damages for loss of the profit from the contract, but the judge ruled that damages for loss of the profit from the contract were irrecoverable. Alderson B held that:

---

44 (1854) 9 Exch. 341.

45 Perloff (1981), 39; Bebchuk and Shavell (1991), 284.

> where two parties have made a contract which one of them has broken, the damages which the other party ought to receive in respect of such breach of contract should be as may fairly and reasonably be considered either arising naturally, that is, according to the usual course of things, from such breach of contract itself, or such as may reasonably be supposed to have been in the contemplation of both parties, at the time they made the contract, as the probable result of the breach of it. [46]

In standard law and economics textbooks, the Hadley Rule has been praised for its efficiency. On the one hand, it prevents the promisee from overreliance because recoverable damages for breach of contract are limited to the foreseeable amount. If the promisee over-relies on the promisor's performance, the losses caused by his overreliance may be irrecoverable because those losses may not be in the contemplation of the promisor at the time of contracting. On the other hand, it encourages the promisee to disclose his private information. In *Hadley*, if the plaintiff had disclosed to the defendant that he had made a profitable contract with another party, the judge would have held that the defendant was liable for the plaintiff's loss of profit. The law limiting recoverable damages to a foreseeable amount therefore creates an incentive for the contracting parties to disclose their private information.[47] The economic argument of the Hadley Rule is based on the understanding that only the amount of loss foreseeable at the time of contracting is recoverable; this is certainly not the correct understanding. There are a number of subtleties in the legal notion of foreseeability, which make it very difficult to apply in practice. As a result, the economic theory of foreseeability has to be qualified.

The economic theory suggests that the promisor is not liable for the promisee's unforeseen loses, unless the promisee discloses to the promisor his private information about his potential losses. This rule would encourage the promisee to share his private information, and then the promisor would be able to manage the risk of breach more effectively and efficiently. However, the validity of this proposition depends on two assumptions. First, the promisee knows the precise actual amount of the loss. Second, if the promisee fails to provide information as to the actual amount of the loss, he is unable to recover it from the promisor. The first assumption has been criticized by some law and economics scholars as unrealistic,[48] which is not our current focus. The question that is considered now is what constitutes a foreseeable loss in contract law.

---

46 *Hadley v Baxendale* (1854) 9 Exch. 341, at 354.
47 Cooter and Ulen (2014), 328.
48 Adler (1999).

Contract law in most common law jurisdictions has never required the parties to foresee the actual amount of loss. It only requires the parties to foresee the type of loss that may occur at the time the contract is concluded. Furthermore, the doctrine of foreseeability does not require that the loss would be a definite result of a breach, but only requires it to be a 'serious probability'.[49] In *Herron II*,[50] the shipowner in breach of contract failed to deliver the goods on time. At the time of contracting, the shipowner did not know that the charterer intended to resell the goods, but the shipowner did know that there was a market for the goods. After the goods were eventually delivered, the market collapsed. The charterer sued the shipowner to claim loss of profit that the charterer would have earned if the goods had been delivered on time. The legal question is whether that loss of profit was foreseeable at the time of contracting. The House of Lords ruled that the charterer was entitled to recover the loss of profit. The loss was foreseeable because the shipowner knew that there was a market for the goods. Therefore, the shipowner knew that there was a 'serious probability' that the charterer intended to resell the goods. The delay in delivery might cause a loss of profit to the charterer.

Does this rule affect the economic theory of foreseeability? The answer is positive. It is reasonable to say that in every commercial contract, both parties should know at the time of contracting that the buyer intends to resell goods – resale would be 'a serious probability'. So, the profit from the resale would be foreseeable at the time of contracting and the intent to resell would be treated as common knowledge between the parties. The buyer would then not have the incentive to disclose information as to the resale.

Both examples of penalty clause and foreseeability show that the validity of economic theories is dependent on a correct and precise understanding of law. Subtleties and details in legal rules may significantly affect the strength of an economic argument. Many law and economic theories in the current literature are by and large based on a general understanding of law. Rarely do economists consider how a small difference in the application of the legal rule affects their economic theories. Lawyers can help economists appreciate vital subtleties in legal rules and enhance the strength of economic theories.

---

49 *Victoria Laundry (Windsor) Ltd v Newman Industries Ltd* [1949] 2 KB 528; *Koufos v C Czarnikow Ltd* (*The Heron II*) [1969] 1 AC 350.

50 [1969] 1 AC 350.

4. EVALUATING PROPOSED LEGAL REFORM

Economists produce not only positive theories to explain legal activities from an economic perspective, but also normative theories that suggest legal reforms. Lawyers' role in normative analysis is irreplaceable. Most of the legal reforms proposed by economists are very general and abstract. To implement these proposals, many important legal issues should be taken into account. There are two vital issues which have been constantly overlooked by many economists.

First, when an economist proposes a legal reform, he often does not give sufficient consideration to the issue of compatibility. In other words, is the proposed legal rule in conflict with the existing legal framework? In any legal system there is a hierarchy of legal rules. A legal rule of a lower order should not contradict a rule of a higher order. For example, if a proposed rule in contract law violates a rule in constitutional law, it should be void. Unfortunately, many economists rarely consider this issue. This problem has been demonstrated beautifully by Professor Anne Van Aaken.[51] Behavioural law and economics has convincingly shown that nudging used as a regulatory means has many advantages over traditional regulatory mechanisms.[52] The term 'nudge' is used to refer to 'a choice architecture' that alters people's behaviour in a predictable way without forbidding any options or significantly changing their economic incentives.[53] Although nudging may be an effective regulatory means, it is not easily adopted into a given legal system. It may be in conflict with constitutional law and the question of legitimacy should be considered. Nudging is often invisible. When nudging is used, people are not aware of their cognitive biases. Nudging actually manipulates people's choice, and this is inconsistent with individual autonomy.[54] Under EU law, nudging may be in conflict with the European Convention of Human Rights (ECHR). Article 8 of the ECHR provides individuals with a right to pursue freely the development and fulfilment of their personality and autonomy. If nudging interferes with decision-making in private matters, it will constitute an infringement of the right to autonomy.[55] Therefore, under the EU law nudging would be illegal if it prohibits personal choices or implicitly restricts personal choices.[56]

---

51 Van Aaken (2015), 83.

52 Thaler and Sunstein (2009); Sunstein and Thaler (2003), 1159; Alemanno and Sibony (2015).

53 Thaler and Sunstein (2009), 6.

54 Van Aaken (2015), 83, 94 and 103.

55 Van Aaken (2015), 105.

56 Van Aaken (2015), 110.

In many cases, a legal reform proposed by economists may be incompatible with the existing legal system. Economists often focus on the efficiency characteristics of law. However, in order to implement a legal reform into an existing legal system, the issue of compatibility must be considered, that is, is a proposed change legitimate so that it can be adopted in the current legal system? Lawyers certainly know the law better. They can help economists to evaluate the legitimacy of a proposal and can advise of potential challenges and resistance to the proposal.

Second, once a legal reform is proposed by economists, it is lawyers who execute it by making proper changes to the existing legal system. Because lawyers understand law better, they are better able to implement the proposed legal reform in the legal system. Often a very straightforward proposal may lead to many significant changes to the existing legal system, a fact that economists often overlook. Take the economic theory of human organ sale as an example. The shortage of human organ supply for transplant has been prevalent in every country. However, the sale of human organs constitutes a criminal offence in most jurisdictions.[57] Many economists suggest legalization of human organ sales.[58] Leaving aside the moral and ethical arguments against human organ sales,[59] there are a number of other challenges. If this proposal were accepted, the current legal system might be inadequate to accommodate such transactions. There would be a number of new legal questions to which the current legal system could not provide answers. Some necessary changes would be necessary. It is not the purpose of this chapter to discuss the technical legal challenges for the legalization of human organ sales, but a few examples in contract law would be adequate to demonstrate the problems.

Let us consider this issue under English law. To allow people to sell their organs, the law should create property rights in human organs. It is most likely that human organs would be treated as goods. Where the parties make a contract for the sale of a human organ, when does the property in the organ pass from the seller to the buyer? The current sales law cannot provide a suitable answer. According to the current law, if it is an unconditional sale and the goods are in a deliverable state, the property in the goods passes from the seller to the buyer when the contract is concluded.[60] This is clearly unsuitable for the sale of a human organ. If this were the rule, it would be possible for the buyer to own the organ while it is still in the seller's body.

---

57 Bilgel (2011), 125 and 182.
58 Becker and Elias (2007), 3; Becker (2003), 897; Spurr (1993), 189.
59 Archard (2002), 87; Sandel (2013).
60 Section 18(1) of the Sale of Goods Act 1979.

Therefore, a special rule on passing property in human organs is needed. Furthermore, if the seller in breach of contract refuses to proceed with the sale, how should damages be calculated? The buyer's losses constitute non-pecuniary losses. The current English law is undeveloped in the quantification of non-pecuniary losses, which often leads to under-compensation. Clearly, this technical question should also be answered before the legalization of human organ sales. Another technical question is related to the validity of the contract. Under the current law, if a party is induced to make a contract by the other party's misrepresentation, the former party may rescind the contract. However, in a contract for the sale of a human organ, this rule needs further consideration. Suppose the seller is induced to sell his kidney to the buyer by the buyer's misrepresentation. When does the seller lose the right to rescission? Can the seller rescind the contract after the transplant? If not, what amount of damages can the seller claim?

In fact, to legalize human organ sales, many technical legal changes to the current legal system need to be considered. However, to my knowledge economists seldom consider these technical legal issues. Without solving these main technical legal issues, the proposed legal reform cannot be adopted. Even if it were adopted, the new legal rule would cause many new problems. Lawyers can certainly play a vital role in this regard. They know the existing legal system better than do economists. They can evaluate a proposal and identify the necessary legal changes for the implementation of the proposal. It is lawyers who draft the law and implement any legal reform. Economists develop theories to understand the law and make proposals for legal reform. Lawyers test to see if the economic theory provides a proper account of legal phenomenon and implement the proposed legal reform by designing proper legal rules.

5. CONCLUSION

The father of modern economics, Adam Smith, started his masterpiece *The Wealth of Nations* by saying:

> The greatest improvement in the productive powers of labour and the greater part of the skill, dexterity and judgement with it is anywhere directed, or applied, seem to have been the effects of the division of labour.[61]

In the law and economics scholarship, lawyers and economists have their own competitive advantages. This has resulted from the division of labour

---

61 Smith (1999), 109.

in the labour market. Lawyers specialize in legal knowledge; economists specialize in economic theories and analytical tools. Lawyers can learn valuable insights from economists. Equally, economists can also learn important legal knowledge from lawyers.

Two projects of contract law reform are in progress in the EU and China, respectively. The collaboration between economists and contract lawyers has therefore become (even) more urgent. In the EU, after the withdrawal of the proposal for a Common European Sales Law (CESL), the reform project has not been abandoned. The drafting of a new version of the CESL is still continuing. It is proposed that the CESL will regulate cross-border sales between traders and consumers.[62] It has been suggested that the modified proposal will give more consideration to legal issues in e-commerce. Law and economics studies have produced many valuable insights into understanding consumer contracts. This is a vital opportunity for lawyers to incorporate law and economics proposals in the CESL. For example, it has been convincingly shown in both theoretical and empirical studies that the mandatory disclosure of information does not necessarily improve consumer protection.[63] This insight challenges the current understanding of consumer protection law, which is by and large based on the rationale of informed decision-making. Certainly, there is an important question to be asked in the making of the European Sales Law: how this finding can be implemented into the legal reform. This is only one of many examples that show how the collaboration between economists and lawyers can improve the quality of the Common European Sales Law.

In China, the drafting of a Civil Law Code has been in progress for many years. Currently, a proposal for the Part on the general principles of Civil Law Code has been discussed with an expectation that it will be formally submitted to the legislature very soon at the time of writing.[64] Unfortunately, few law and economics insights have been incorporated into the current version of the proposal. Clearly, law and economics research can offer many valuable contributions to the drafting of the Chinese Civil Code. For example, there has been a huge amount of law and economics literature on the efficiency of lawmaking,[65] which can certainly improve the efficiency of the drafting of the Chinese Civil Code. In addition, many specific contract law doctrines and rules are under

---

[62] Proposal for a Regulation of the European Parliament and of the Council on a Common European Sales Law, para 1. At http://eur-lex.europa.eu/LexUriServ/LexUriServ.do?uri=COM:2011:0635:FIN:en:PDF.

[63] Ben-Shahar and Schneider (2014); Faure and Luth (2011), 337.

[64] http://www.npc.gov.cn/npc/xinwen/2016-03/05/content_1969089.htm.

[65] Parisi and Fon (2009).

scrutiny, such as the doctrine of change of circumstance, assessment of expectation damages, the doctrine of mistake and rules on swap contracts. Each of these topics has been studied by law and economics scholars. Undoubtedly, many valuable implications for the drafting of a Chinese Civil Code can be drawn from the current law and economics literature.

As this chapter has shown, lawyers can make three contributions to law and economics research. First, lawyers can improve economists' understanding of contracting activities in reality and help them focus on important research questions. Second, lawyers can correct economists' misunderstanding of the law and enhance the quality of economic arguments. Third, lawyers can evaluate the feasibility and plausibility of proposals for legal reform made by economists, and can implement those reforms by designing suitable legal rules. The success of law and economics research is dependent on a mutual respect and close collaboration between lawyers and economists.

REFERENCES

Adler, Barry, E. (1999), 'The Questionable Ascent of Hadley v Baxendale', *Stanford Law Review*, 51, 1547–90.

Aghion, Philippe and Benjamin Hermalin (1990), 'Legal Restrictions on Private Contracts Can Enhance Efficiency', *Journal of Law, Economics, and Organization*, 6(2), 381–409.

Akerlof, George (1970), 'The Market for "Lemons": Quality Uncertainty and the Market Mechanism', *Quarterly Journal of Economics*, 84(3), 488–500.

Alemanno, Alberto and Anne-Lise Sibony (eds), *Nudge and the Law: A European Perspective* (Oxford, UK: Hart Publishing).

Archard, David (2002), 'Selling Yourself: Titmuss's Argument Against a Market in Blood', *Journal of Ethics*, 6, 87–103.

Aryes, Ian (2003), 'Valuing Modern Contract Scholarships', *Yale Law Journal*, 112, 881–901.

Austen-Baker, Richard and Qi Zhou (2015), *Contract in Context* (Abingdon, UK: Routledge).

Baird, Douglas G. (1997), 'The Future of Law and Economics: Looking Forward', *University of Chicago Law Review*, 64, 1129–65.

Bebchuk, Lucian A. and Steven Shavell (1991), 'Information and the Scope of Liability for Breach of Contract: The Rule of Hadley v. Baxendale', *Journal of Law, Economics, and Organization*, 7, 284–312.

Becker, Gary (2003), 'Aspects on the Economics of Organ Transplantation', *Transplantation Proceedings*, 35(2), 897.

Becker, Gary and Julio Elias (2007), 'Introducing Incentives in the Market for Live and Cadaveric Organ Donations', *Journal of Economic Perspectives*, 21(3), 3–24.

Ben-Shahar, Omri and Carl E. Schneider (2014), *More than You Wanted to Know: The Failure of Mandated Disclosure* (Princeton, USA: Princeton University Press).

Bilgel, Firat (2011), The Law and Economics of Organ Procurement (Ph.D. Thesis, Erasmus University of Rotterdam).
Birmingham, Robert (1970), 'Breach of Contract, Damage Measures, and Economic Efficiency', *Rutgers Law Review*, 24, 273–92.
Braithwaite, Jo (2016), 'The Origins and Implications of Contractual Estoppel', *Law Quarterly Review*, 132, 120–47.
Bridge, Michael (ed.) (2014), *Benjamin's Sale of Goods* (9th edn, London, UK: Sweet & Maxwell).
Calabresi, Guido (2016), *The Future of Law and Economics* (1st edn, New Haven, USA: Yale University Press).
Cartwright, John (2007), *Misrepresentation Mistake and Non-Disclosure* (London, UK: Sweet & Maxwell).
Coleman, Julia (1980), 'Efficiency, Exchange, and Auction: Philosophic Aspects of the Economic Approach to Law', *California Law Review*, 68, 221–49.
Cooter, Robert (1982), 'Economic Analysis of Punitive Damages', *Southern California Law Review*, 56, 79–102.
Cooter, Robert and Thomas Ulen (2014), *Law and Economics* (6th edn, Harlow, UK: Pearson).
Craswell, Richard (1988), 'Contract Remedies, Renegotiation, and the Theory of Efficient Breach', *Southern California Law Review*, 61, 629–70.
Craswell, Richard (2003), 'In that Case, What Is the Question? Economics and the Demand of Contract Theory', *Yale Law Journal*, 112, 903–24.
Duxbury, Neil (1995), *Patterns of American Jurisprudence* (1st edn, Oxford, UK: Oxford University Press).
Eisenberg, Melvin A. (1995), 'The Limits of Cognition and the Limits of Contract', *Stanford Law Review*, 47(2), 211–59.
Faure, Michael G. and Hanneke A. Luth (2011), 'Behavioural Economics in Unfair Contract Terms', *Journal of Consumer Policy*, 34(3), 337–58.
Friedman, Milton (1953), 'The Methodology of Positive Economics' in *Essays in Positive Economics* (Chicago, USA: University of Chicago Press).
Goetz, Charles and Robert Scott (1977), 'Liquidated Damages, Penalties and the Just Compensation Principle: Some Notes on an Enforcement Model and a Theory of Efficient Breach', *Columbia Law Review*, 77(4), 554–94.
Halson, Roger (1991), 'Opportunism, Economic Duress and Contractual Modification', *Law Quarterly Review*, 107, 649–78.
Hatzis, Aristides N. (2003), 'Having the Case and Eating It Too: Efficient Penalty Clauses in Common and Civil Contract Law', *International Review of Law and Economics*, 22, 381–406.
Hoffmann, Leonard, Lord (2010), 'The Achilleas: Custom and Practice or Foreseeability?', *Edinburgh Law Review*, 14, 47–61.
Holmes, Oliver W. (1897), 'The Path of the Law', *Harvard Law Review*, 10, 991–1009.
Hylton, Keith (1998), 'Punitive Damages and the Economic Theory of Penalties', *Georgetown Law Journal*, 87, 421–72.
Jolls, Christine, Cass Sunstein, and Richard Thaler (1998), 'A Behavioural Approach to Law and Economics', *Stanford Law Review*, 50, 1471–550.
Liao, Wenqing (2015), *The Application of the Theory of Efficient Breach in Contract Law: A Comparative Law and Economic Perspective* (Antwerp, Belgium: Intersentia).
Liu, Qiao (2011), *Anticipatory Breach* (1st edn, Oxford, UK: Hart Publishing).

Loi, Kelry CF (2015), 'Contractual Estoppel and Non-Reliance Clauses', *Lloyd's Maritime and Commercial Law Quarterly*, 346–67.

McMeel, Gerard (2011), 'Documentary Fundamentalism in the Senior Courts: The Myth of Contractual Estoppel', *Lloyd's Maritime and Commercial Law Quarterly*, 185–207.

North, Douglass (2005), 'Institutions and the Performance of Economics Over Time' in Claude Ménard and Mary Shirley (eds), *Handbook of New Institutional Economics* (Berlin, Germany: Springer), 21–30.

Ogus, Anthony (2006), *Costs and Cautionary Tales: Economic Insights for the Law* (1st edn, Oxford, UK: Hart Publishing).

Ogus, Anthony (2010), 'Law and Economics in the Legal Academy, or What I Should Have Said to Discipulus', *University of Toronto Law Journal*, 60(2), 169–75.

Parisi, Francesco and Vincy Fon (2009), *The Economics of Lawmaking* (Oxford, UK: Oxford University Press).

Peel, Edwin (2015), *Treitel on the Law of Contract* (14th edn, London, UK: Sweet & Maxwell).

Perloff, Jeffrey M. (1981), 'Breach of Contract and the Foreseeability Doctrine of Hadley v Baxendale', *Journal of Legal Studies*, 10, 39–63.

Polinsky, Mitchel and Steven Shavell (1998), 'Punitive Damages: An Economic Analysis', *Harvard Law Review*, 111, 869–962.

Posner, Eric (2003), 'Economic Analysis of Contract Law after Three Decades: Success or Failure', *Yale Law Journal*, 112, 829–80.

Rowan, Solene (2012), *Remedies for Breach of Contract A Comparative Analysis of the Protection of Performance* (1st edn, Oxford, UK: Oxford University Press).

Sandel, Michael (2013), *What Money Can't Buy: The Moral Limits of Markets* (London, UK: Penguin).

Shavell, Steven (1980), 'Damage Measures for Breach of Contract', *Bell Journal of Economics*, 11, 446–90.

Smith, Adam, *The Wealth of Nations*, Books I–III (reprinted edition, London, UK: Penguin 1999).

Smits, Jan M. (2012), *The Mind and Method of the Legal Academic* (1st edn, Cheltenham, UK: Edward Elgar).

Spurr, Stephen (1993), 'The Proposed Market for Human Organs', *Journal of Heath Politics*, 18(1), 189–202.

Sunstein, Cass (ed.) (2000), *Behavioural Law and Economics* (1st edn, Cambridge, UK: Cambridge University Press).

Sunstein, Cass R. and Richard Thaler (2003), 'Libertarian Paternalism Is Not an Oxymoron', *University of Chicago Law Review*, 70(4), 1159–202.

Thaler, Richard and Cass Sunstein (2009), *Nudge: Improving Decisions about Health, Wealth and Happiness* (New York, USA: Penguin Books).

Trebilcock, Michael (1999), 'The Value and Limits of Law and Economics' in Megan Richardson and Gillian Hadfield (eds), *The Second Wave of Law and Economics* (1st edn, New South Wales, Australia: The Federation Press), 12–29.

Trukhtanov, Alexandra (2009), 'Misrepresentation: Acknowledgement of Non-Reliance as a Defence', *Law Quarterly Review*, 125, 648–70.

Ulen, Thomas (1984), 'The Efficiency of Specific Performance: Toward a Unified Theory of Contact Remedies', *Michigan Law Review*, 83, 341–403.

Van Aaken, Anne (2015), 'Judging the Nudge: In Search of the Legal Limits of Paternalistic Nudging in the EU' in Alberto Alemanno and Anne-Lise

Sibony (eds), *Nudge and the Law: A European Perspective* (Oxford, UK: Hart Publishing), 83–112.

Wagner, Gerhard (2011), 'Mandatory Contract Law: Functions and Principles in Light of The Proposal for a Directive on Consumer Rights' in Anthony Ogus and Willem Van Boom (eds), *Juxtaposing Autonomy and Paternalism Law* (Oxford, UK: Hart Publishing), 9–42.

Walt, Steven (2011), 'Penalty Clauses and Liquidated Damages' in Gerrit De Geest (ed.), *Contract Law and Economics: Encyclopaedia of Law and Economics* (vol. 6, 2nd edn, Cheltenham, UK: Edward Elgar), 178–206.

Weinstein, Neil (1989), 'Optimistic Biases about Personal Risks', *Science*, 246, 1232–33.

Zhou, Qi (2008), 'Is a Seller's Efficient Breach of Contract Possible in English Law?', *Journal of Contract Law*, 24, 268–83.

Zhou, Qi (2009), *Economic Analysis of Misrepresentation in English Contract Law* (Saarbrücken, Germany: VDM Publishing).

Zhou, Qi (2011), 'What Can Contract Lawyers Learn From Law and Economics?' *University of Tasmania Law Review*, 30(1), 157–73.

7. Evolving goals of EU State aid policy and possible lessons for China: a law and economics approach

Niels Philipsen

1. INTRODUCTION

This chapter deals with the concept of State aid, a uniquely European concept that is not known in China or any other jurisdiction or trade area. Even in a federation like the United States, there are no provisions at federal level that limit the possibilities of individual States to compete with each other by subsidizing industry. The EU State aid regime does share some characteristics with the World Trade Organization (WTO) provisions on subsidies, although the latter are more limited in scope and lack the strong enforcement regime that the EU has.[1] Moreover, compared to the WTO provisions, the EU concept of 'State aid' has been defined very broadly, and not only includes subsidies but also, for example, tax advantages, capital injections and debt waivers provided by public bodies on a selective basis. All these forms of aid are held to be incompatible with the EU internal market, unless they are exempted or if the aid is of limited scope.[2]

In this chapter I will critically discuss the evolving goals underlying EU State policy, ranging from market integration and other 'objectives of common interest' to efficiency and fiscal discipline. More specifically, I will address the question whether the recent focus on fiscal discipline (sometimes called budgetary discipline)[3] can be supported by economic

[1] Bacon (2013), p. 4. See also more generally Dewatripont and Seabright (2006).

[2] The legal basis is Article 107 Treaty on the Functioning of the European Union (TFEU). For a more elaborate description of the relevant legal provisions and EU State aid policy, see section 3.

[3] See further section 4.2 below.

theory: is avoiding wasteful government spending at the national level a task for the European Commission, even in cases where there is no clear effect on trade in the EU internal market? It should be pointed out at the outset that the approach taken in this chapter follows from economic theory; although references to the relevant legal provisions will of course be made, the methodological framework applied here consists of the economics of regulation (market failure theory and public choice) and the economics of federalism (bottom-up approach to harmonization).

Before the issue of 'evolving policy goals' can be addressed, it is necessary first to discuss, from an economic perspective, the arguments for State aid control. Therefore, section 2 will start by answering two basic questions: (1) why do governments grant aid; and (2) why do we need supranational control on such aid? Subsequently, section 3 provides some basic information on the legal framework concerning EU State aid policy, including a brief discussion of the recent 'more economic approach'. Building on this theoretical and legal framework, section 4 will examine the (changing) goals of EU State aid policy. Possible implications for China and some concluding remarks will be presented in the final section of this chapter.

2. ECONOMICS OF STATE AID

In this section I will first discuss why governments grant aid to private undertakings, focusing both on public interest reasons (efficiency, equity) and public choice explanations (section 2.1). After that, I will discuss the reasons for introducing a supranational control on such aid (section 2.2).

2.1 Why Governments Grant Aid

From a public interest perspective, governments provide subsidies to private undertakings either in an attempt to cure a market failure (*efficiency*), or in order to attain certain social or environmental objectives (*equity*). From a public choice perspective, the role of private interest groups is stressed, including not only lobbying groups representing industry, but also other lobbying groups and the EU bureaucracy itself.

2.1.1 Efficiency

Market failure theory has been extensively discussed in the economic literature, more particularly in the context of the economics of regulation. Market failures like externalities, information asymmetry, market power and public goods may all provide justifications for government

Table 7.1 Market failures and State aid

Market failure	Examples
externalities	R&D&I aid, environmental aid
asymmetric information	risk capital to SMEs
coordination failures	different producers + complementary goods
market power	general aid to SMEs (not recognized)

intervention in the form of regulation, but in some cases these failures can be better corrected by subsidies and other types of State aid.[4] Table 7.1 provides an overview of the market failures that can, in certain conditions,[5] be solved by State aid.

Externalities refer to side effects from production or consumption that are not (or cannot be) taken into account by the party causing these effects. In case of *positive externalities*, the level of production or consumption is too low from a social perspective, as a result of the free-rider problem.[6] Subsidies and other types of aid may solve this problem, making 'internalization' of the positive externality possible. Various authors have mentioned R&D&I (research and development and innovation) aid (subsidies as a means to solving the problem of knowledge spillovers) and environmental aid as examples of categories of aid that can solve market failure in the form of externalities.[7] These categories of aid have also been recognized by the European Commission, as can be seen, for example, from the block exemptions and Guidelines that apply (see further section 3 below).

A second type of market failure that may potentially justify the granting of aid is *information asymmetry* between two parties, for example a bank

---

[4] It should be noted here that other solutions to market failures may include market-based instruments like taxation, or changes in liability rules. For a more detailed discussion of market failure theory, including references to the literature, see Philipsen (2003), pp. 9–45 and Philipsen (2012), pp. 716–19.

[5] Related inter alia to the size and duration of the aid, non-availability of other measures, distortions created in other markets, and so on. See more particularly the discussion of the 'balancing test' in section 3.

[6] The concept of positive externalities is related to another economic concept, 'public goods', which is not discussed separately here. The discussion of Article 106 TFEU, including the concept of 'services of general economic interest', is outside the scope of this chapter. Interested readers are referred to Devroe and Gabathuler (2014).

[7] Nicolaides (2008), pp. 106–27; Quigley (2015), pp. 360 and 378, and many others.

and its customer. Banks are generally not willing to provide loans to low-risk customers if they lack information on the actual risk of that customer. That may occur in particular when the customer is a small or medium-sized company (SME). This will result in the under-provision of certain goods and services, preventing an efficient market outcome from occurring.[8]

The third type of market failure mentioned in Table 7.1, *coordination failure*, refers to the situation when there are two or more undertakings producing goods that are valuable to consumers when used together, but without coordination between the undertakings concerned they would not be produced. Such coordination failure may prevent certain goods or services for which a potential demand exists from reaching the market altogether.[9] This type of market failure is related to information problems (discussed in the previous paragraph).

The fourth type of market failure, *market power*, although mentioned in Table 7.1, is not one that is generally accepted (and certainly not by the European Commission) as a justification for granting subsidies to undertakings. It refers to the fact that, in order to introduce competition into markets where competition is currently lacking, smaller firms could be incentivized to compete with dominant undertakings by means of subsidies.[10] Of course, such artificially created competition goes against the idea of an 'invisible hand', and may also raise serious fairness concerns. Nevertheless, hypothetically this could be an efficiency argument for allowing State aid.

2.1.2 Equity

Governments may also provide advantages to private undertakings in order to obtain certain policy goals, for example in the field of employment, regional cohesion or environmental protection. Economists often use the heading *equity* when referring to State intervention for purposes other than efficiency.[11] Generally, such intervention occurs when market outcomes, even if they are efficient, are not considered socially acceptable, because they lead to regional or social inequalities. Some 'equity' considerations may be shared by the EU as a whole (on that see sections 3.2 and 4.1 below); others follow only from policy at the Member State level, leading to potential conflicts of interest between the European Commission and public bodies at the national level, especially when government intervention at the Member State level leads to negative externalities across the border.

---

8 Bacon (2013), p. 8.
9 Bacon (2013), p. 8.
10 See also Bacon (2013), p. 10.
11 Friederiszick et al. (2008), p. 632.

When discussing equity, it is important to keep in mind that economic theory does not provide an 'optimal' redistribution of wealth and resources across society, as this depends on the preferences of citizens (which, taking a bottom-up approach to lawmaking into account,[12] are best served at the local or national level).[13] Economists agree, at least to some extent, only about the *means* to achieve redistribution; they do not agree about redistributive *ends*.[14]

2.1.3 Public choice arguments

So far we have assumed that governments grant aid in order to serve the public interest. In reality, however, many subsidies, tax advantages and other forms of State aid may also result from *private interest* considerations, ranging from lobbying by private interest groups (such as industry, but also consumer groups or NGOs) to corruption of public officials. As indicated in the public choice literature,[15] government officials may tend to choose those forms of market intervention that ensure them being re-elected, leading to political favours being granted to particular lobbying groups.[16] While some authors such as Becker have indicated that competition between lobbying groups may eventually lead to efficient results,[17] there are many situations where such competition – even though it can be considered democratic – does not lead to improvements in social welfare.

2.2 Why Supranational Control?

Having discussed the reasons why governments grant aid, the question can now be addressed whether (from an economic perspective) a supranational

---

12 See the references quoted in section 4.2 below.

13 Friederiszick et al. (2008), p. 634.

14 Cooter and Ulen (2012), p. 7. For example, progressive taxation and social welfare programmes are likely to target equity goals defined by Member States more efficiently than would reshuffling private legal rights, as they do not rely on crude averages, their effects are more predictable, transaction costs are lower and there are generally fewer distortions. For a more detailed explanation of these points, see Cooter and Ulen (2012), p. 8.

15 For summaries of that literature, see e.g. Philipsen (2003), pp. 23–7, and Boehm (2007).

16 Especially those lobbying groups with low transaction costs, i.e. those which are relatively small (though not too small to prevent successful lobbying) and well organized, and with homogeneous preferences among their members. See Olson (1965).

17 Becker (1983).

Table 7.2 Arguments for and against State aid control

arguments supporting State aid control	counter-arguments
prevention of subsidy wars	not all subsidy races are harmful
avoiding distortions in other markets (static efficiency effects)	static effects are often small
avoiding distortions in other markets (dynamic efficiency effects, including moral hazard)	none, provided that there is a genuine effect on trade and competition in the EU market
transboundary externalities	depends on definition of efficiency (Pareto, Kaldor-Hicks)
EU can better resist lobbying groups	depends on political arena
high costs of State aid	high costs of State aid control
policy transparency and predictability	questionable due to complex rules
avoiding wasteful government spending (budgetary discipline)	not a task for the EU, more particularly when equity and efficiency goals conflict

control on State aid should be introduced. The arguments are summarized in Table 7.2.

Preventing a subsidy war is perhaps the most advanced argument for controlling State aid.[18] This argument is directly related to the prisoner's dilemma in game theory, in which all players (here: Member States) end up being worse off by choosing a strategy (here: providing subsidies) that leads to a net welfare loss. In the context of State aid, the argument holds that States subsidizing an industry with the aim of benefiting their own industry at the expense of that in other countries, or in retaliation to such subsidies provided by other countries, will result in a waste of social resources, while making no-one better off. This is particularly so if industries are subsidized in countries that do not have a real comparative advantage. The solution to such a game would be to introduce the possibility for players to cooperate, or if that is not possible, to involve an external party to solve the conflict. The latter would imply the introduction of transnational rules on subsidies in the form of EU State aid control.[19] Although this argument is well supported in the literature, according to Bacon,

[18] Dewatripont and Seabright (2006), p. 513, pointing also to the WTO rules on subsidies.

[19] Nicolaides (2008), p. 94, also discusses this argument under the heading tit-for-tat strategies. The argument also fits into the economic theory of federalism, where one of the arguments for moving legislation to a higher (transnational) level

'recent economic thinking is less critical towards subsidy races', because (1) not all State aid results in subsidy races, as there is not always an effect on trade, for example when markets are purely national, and (2) sometimes a subsidy race can be considered as 'a market-oriented mechanism to determine the most efficient location of a production facility', implying that it is not a waste of resources.[20]

Saving inefficient firms or subsidizing industries where a country does not have a real comparative advantage may lead to distortions in other markets.[21] This is inefficient from a *static efficiency* perspective. However, recent economic literature has argued that unless State aid is granted to large undertakings enjoying dominant market positions, the static efficiency effects of such aid are often small, and may moreover be offset by positive effects on competition.[22] The latter effects would occur if, because of the aid provided to an existing (small) undertaking or a new entrant, competition in a relatively concentrated market is kept alive or restored.[23]

Distortions of competition are likely to be more serious when *dynamic efficiency effects* are taken into account. For starters, State aid may lead to a crowding-out effect, driving private investors from the market. It may also reduce the incentives for undertakings to compete. Moreover, it may lead to certain expectations by market participants: a 'too big to fail' attitude may arise, leading to excessive risk-taking by undertakings, in the expectation that the government will step in to save them anyway if a risk materializes. This 'moral hazard' effect of State aid has been said to apply, for example, in the banking sector.[24]

Negative spillover effects of State aid that cross country borders have been mentioned as a separate (potential) justification for supranational control on subsidies.[25] Examples of such *transboundary externalities* include negative effects on employment, transboundary pollution and losses of tax income, which occur in countries other than the country that provides the aid. It follows from the economic theory of federalism that, as a starting

---

would be prevention of a 'race to the bottom'. See Cauffman and Philipsen (2015), pp. 258–60.

[20] Bacon (2013), p. 9.

[21] Nicolaides (2008), p. 102 in this respect states that subsidies are raised through taxation, which in itself is a distortion.

[22] Bacon (2013), p. 10; Nicolaides (2008), p. 102.

[23] Note that this relates to the discussion of the 'market power' market failure in the previous section.

[24] Zimmer and Blaschczok (2011). See also Bacon (2013), p. 10.

[25] Nicolaides (2008), p. 94. See also Dewatripont and Seabright (2006), pp. 2–4. It is clear that this argument is related to those discussed above, especially the one on preventing subsidy wars.

point, the presence of transboundary externalities can be one of the reasons to move regulation from a decentralized level to a central level.[26] This argument has been applied in particular in the field of environmental law. However, to the extent that transboundary externalities are created or increased by States subsidizing private industry, this could also be a separate argument for State aid control at the EU level. It should be clear that this argument is linked to those we discussed above in relation to market distortions. Moreover, one could add that it depends on the notion of efficiency that is applied, whether or not certain transboundary externalities caused by State aid have to be 'prohibited'. If there is only a small effect on other countries, while the aid leads to a substantial increase in social welfare (e.g. GDP) of the home country, Kaldor-Hicks efficiency would consider State aid to be efficient if the social welfare of the EU as a whole is considered.[27]

The next argument that has been advanced in the literature follows from public choice theory. The starting point is that the decision-making discretion of governments at the national level makes them vulnerable to lobbying by special interest groups, especially those representing certain sectors of industry. If policy-makers at the national level can shift the blame for certain unpopular or difficult policy decisions, for example not to provide certain tax advantages or other types of support to particular sectors, to a higher level of policy-making (the EU), this will make it easier for them to *resist lobbying efforts*. Under the condition that lobbying would be aimed at increasing private interests ('rent-seeking behaviour') rather than the public interest, introducing supranational control on State aid would indeed be an improvement for social welfare. [28] One could advance the counter-argument that Brussels has become the capital of lobbying, making the European Commission itself extremely vulnerable to lobbying. To some extent this is certainly true. However, here we need to recall that the Commission has adopted many detailed guidelines, providing exactly how a particular horizontal or sectoral aid measure needs to be designed before it can be approved; this not only provides guidance to public policy makers at the national or local level (see the argument on transparency, discussed below), but also makes it easier for the Commission to resist political pressure from lobbying.

---

[26] For details and references to literature, see Van den Bergh (1996), Wagner (2012) and Cauffman and Philipsen (2015).

[27] If the stricter criterion of Pareto efficiency is applied, any State aid causing negative spillover effects abroad would need to be prohibited. For notions of efficiency, see e.g. Cooter and Ulen (2012), pp. 12–14 and 42–3.

[28] See e.g. Nicolaides (2008), pp. 94–5, Friederiszick et al. (2008), p. 652, and Dewatripont and Seabright (2006), pp. 514–15.

Nicolaides mentions yet another argument in defence of the EU State aid policy, namely that supranational rules may serve the purpose of 'introducing *greater transparency and predictability* in the partner countries' policy processes'.[29] From a theoretical perspective, indeed, the legal certainty that results from such policy transparency and predictability will make it easier for business to plan its investments, and for Member States' governments to formulate and implement their policies.[30] Looking at the complexity of the State aid rules (see section 3 below), it is questionable whether this goal is reached.[31]

There is also a *cost argument* that can be invoked to rationalize a supranational control on State aid, which is that the administrative costs of granting subsidies are huge. According to Nicolaides, they have been estimated (by the UK National Audit Office) to account for about 10 per cent of the subsidies granted.[32] Half of these costs (5 per cent) are carried by granting authorities, which need to have the proper administrative infrastructure to process applications and to monitor compliance. The other 5 per cent relates to the costs of the firms that obtain the subsidies, which need to file applications and satisfy reporting requirements. If the number of subsidies granted is reduced as a result of EU State aid policy, that would save many of these administrative costs. While this is undoubtedly true, it is also undoubtedly true that there are huge costs involved in the whole system of State aid control, ranging from the costs of the EU bureaucracy, courts, lawyers, as well as again compliance and application costs for businesses and public authorities in all of the EU Member States.

More recently another argument for supranational control on government spending has appeared, more particularly from EU practice and European Commission documents:[33] *budgetary discipline*.[34] Avoiding wasteful government spending at Member State level seems to have become one of the more important objectives of the EU State aid policy. While this may be in line with the idea of economic efficiency,[35] it also seems to run counter to the economic theory of federalism and the legal principle of subsidiarity,

---

[29] Nicolaides (2008), pp. 94–5.

[30] Nicolaides (2008), pp. 94–5.

[31] This problem of complexity seems to be even more prevalent in relation to tax schemes that fall under State aid scrutiny; see Luja (2014).

[32] Nicolaides (2008), p. 102.

[33] See especially the State Aid Modernization Communication, paras 5, 12 and 14.

[34] Dewatripont and Seabright (2006), pp. 514 and 519–21; Bacon (2013), pp. 10–11.

[35] Especially when taking into account that it is generally difficult to determine what the effects will be of subsidizing a particular sector (i.e. whether industrial economic policies lead to the desired results), and that where there is doubt, it is therefore better not to intervene in a market.

both of which take as a starting point that a bottom-up approach to harmonization should be taken. The economic theory of federalism, built on the classic work of Charles Tiebout,[36] points out that political decisions should be taken as much as possible at a lower level, closest to voters' preferences, unless there are clear reasons for going to a higher level.[37] Moreover, it may lead to conflicts between the different goals of EU State aid policy (other than efficiency), notably internal market concerns and equity. Bacon ventilates this point nicely, by stating that 'the Commission's role in the implementation of State aid control is no longer a form of "internal WTO", but has become, in large part, that of a financial controller with special responsibility for subsidies.'[38] This will be discussed in more detail in section 4.

3. EU LEGAL FRAMEWORK

3.1 Main Provisions on State Aid

Article 107 of the Treaty on the Functioning of the European Union (TFEU) provides the substantive rules on State aid. The first paragraph of that Article holds that:

> [s]ave as otherwise provided in the Treaties,[39] any aid granted by a Member State or through State resources in any form whatsoever which distorts or threatens to distort competition by favouring certain undertakings or the production of certain goods shall, in so far as it affects trade between Member States, be incompatible with the internal market.

Four criteria can be distilled from this provision, which all need to be fulfilled before a measure can be qualified as aid (and hence be held incompatible with the common market):[40]

---

36 Tiebout (1956).

37 These reasons could be transboundary externalities (already discussed above), destructive regulatory competition caused by a race to the bottom (related to the argument on subsidy wars, also discussed above), transaction costs, economies of scale, or non-economic arguments. See Cauffman and Philipsen (2015).

38 Bacon (2013), p. 11.

39 This refers, notably, to Article 106(2) TFEU on Services of General Economic Interest, the procedural provisions in Article 107(2) and (3) TFEU and exceptions provided by Article 346 TFEU, in relation to national security.

40 For a detailed examination and relevant case law on the notion of aid, see e.g. Craig and de Búrca (2015), pp. 1133–9 and (for the most recent and elaborated analysis) Quigley (2015), pp. 3–91.

- the aid confers an economic advantage on the recipient; from case law it follows that this advantage also needs to be selective (meaning that it is provided only to certain undertakings or to the production of certain goods);
- the aid is granted by Member States or through State resources to undertakings (not to individuals or households);
- the aid affects trade between Member States;
- the aid distorts competition in the internal market.

However, the last two conditions, both of which are very important from an economic perspective (as shown in section 2.2 above), are usually dealt with rather quickly and without in-depth analysis. In the words of Kelyn Bacon, 'the Court's case law establishes a very low threshold for [these conditions]. There is no requirement to show that State aid will lead to consumer harm . . . and there is not even, in practice, any need for extensive analysis showing a material distortion to the level playing field.'[41] This is backed by Friederiszick, Röller and Verouden, then chief economists at the European Commission, who wrote that '[d]espite the increased fine tuning of soft law provisions, EU state aid rules remain rather form-based, leaving little room for assessing the impact of the measure on competition and trade'.[42] Instead, as regards the effect on inter-state trade, it is already sufficient that trade *might* be affected.[43]

All measures that constitute State aid need to be notified in advance to the European Commission, pursuant to Article 108(3) TFEU.[44] However, in line with the economic theory discussed in section 2.1, not all aid measures falling under the definition of Article 107(1) are prohibited. The (many) exemptions to the general rule of incompatibility are included in paragraphs 2 and 3 of Article 107. In addition, a *de minimis* Regulation applies, exempting aid that is small in amount from notification to the Commission, for the reason that these small amounts are not considered to fall within the scope of Article 107(1).[45]

Article 107(2) lists a small number of 'automatic exemptions' from incompatibility, the most important being (a) aid to individuals of a social

---

41 Bacon (2013), pp. 12–13.
42 Friederiszick et al. (2008), p. 631.
43 For references to case law, see Craig and de Búrca (2015), pp. 1138–9.
44 Article 108 TFEU is discussed in more detail below.
45 Regulation 1407/2013 of 18 December 2013. This regulation exempts aid amounts of up to €200,000 per undertaking over a period of three years. The exempted amounts are higher in relation to e.g. road transport, while there are also different calculations applying to agriculture and fisheries.

character; and (b) aid to make good the damage caused by natural disasters and exceptional occurrences (flooding, earthquakes, marine pollution, war, etc.).[46]

Article 107(3) provides 'discretionary exemptions'. It concerns types of aid that may be considered (by the Commission) as compatible with the internal market:

(a) aid to promote the economic development of areas where the standard of living is abnormally low or where there is serious underemployment;
(b) aid to promote the execution of an important project of common European interest or to remedy a serious disturbance in the economy of a Member State;
(c) aid to facilitate the development of certain economic activities or of certain economic areas, where such aid does not adversely affect trading conditions to an extent contrary to the common interest;
(d) aid to promote culture and heritage conservation where such aid does not affect trading conditions and competition in the Union to an extent that is contrary to the common interest;
(e) such other categories of aid as may be specified by decision of the Council on a proposal from the Commission.

It goes far beyond the scope of this chapter to discuss the extensive Commission decision-making practice and case law of the Court of Justice of the European Union (CJEU)[47] regarding these discretionary exemptions. Instead, readers are referred to the General Block Exemption Regulation[48] and the many guidelines and frameworks[49] published by the Commission that provide criteria on, for example, the eligible

---

[46] There is case law and soft law on the conditions under which this provision applies. For a discussion, see Quigley (2015), pp. 196–202.

[47] Judicial review in the context of Article 107(2) and (3) is relatively limited. More specifically: such review according to Craig and de Búrca (2015), p. 1130 is limited to verifying whether the Commission complied with procedural rules, whether the facts on which the decision was based were accurately stated, and whether there was a manifest error of assessment or misuse of powers.

[48] Commission Regulation 651/2014 of 17 June 2014 declaring certain categories of aid compatible with the internal market in application of Articles 107 and 108 of the Treaty.

[49] Examples include guidelines on regional aid, energy and environmental protection, risk finance and the Framework on R&D&I. There are many more examples. See the DG COMP website at http://ec.europa.eu/competition/state_aid/legislation/legislation.html.

beneficiaries, maximum aid intensities (the maximum proportion of the costs of a project that can benefit from state aid) and eligible expenses for many different types of horizontal and vertical aid. With these regulations and guidelines, the Commission can declare specific categories of State aid compatible with the Treaty, exempting them from the requirement of prior notification and Commission approval.[50]

The requirement of prior notification is contained in Article 108(3) TFEU, on the basis of which a Member State needs to inform the Commission of all new aid,[51] with the exception of *de minimis* aid, as explained above. Unless the notified aid is (block) exempted, Member States are not permitted to put their proposed measures into effect until the so-called 'preliminary review of new aid' by the Commission (which can take up to two months) has resulted in a decision approving the aid measure. If it is difficult for the Commission to decide whether a particular aid measure is compatible with the internal market, a detailed examination on the basis of Article 108(2) will follow. If such examination leads to the decision that the proposed aid is incompatible with the internal market, the Member State concerned needs to abolish or alter the aid. There are no fines that can be imposed on Member States (let alone on aid recipients), but all unlawfully granted aid needs to be recovered.[52] This can, of course, have huge consequences for the aid recipients involved.

3.2 The 'More Economic Approach' and the Balancing Test

The 'more economic approach' to EU competition law adopted since the early 2000s has resulted in the publication of several new or adapted regulations and guidelines concerning, for example, vertical restraints, behaviour by dominant market undertakings and merger control.[53] Characteristic of this approach is its emphasis on the (efficiency) effects of

---

[50] Council Regulation No. 994/98, amended by Council Regulation No. 733/2013, enables the Commission to adopt so-called Block Exemption Regulations for State aid. The General Block Exemption Regulation of 2014, which replaced and extended an earlier version from 2008, is the most important regulation in this respect. See http://ec.europa.eu/competition/state_aid/legislation/block.html.

[51] There is also a continuous review of 'existing aid', according to Article 108(1) TFEU.

[52] Recovery takes place in accordance with national law. There is very limited scope for defence against recovery. More information on State aid procedures and relevant case law can be found in Craig and de Búrca (2015), pp. 1145–53, and in huge detail in Quigley (2015), pp. 493–657.

[53] See, for example, the communications relating to abuse of dominance (2009/C 45/02) and the application of Article 101(3) TFEU (2004/C 101/08), as

certain business practices rather than considering only market structures or particular types of behaviour. This has led to (somewhat) less reliance by the Commission[54] on 'prohibitions by object', and a more extensive analysis of the actual welfare effects of business practices.[55]

In the field of State aid, the more economic approach (although the term as such was not used) became part of the so-called State Aid Action Plan 2005–2009 (hereafter: SAAP). Following the accession of ten new EU Member States in 2004, the SAAP advocated a fundamental reform of procedures and substantive law, in the form of (1) less and better-targeted aid, (2) a refined economic approach and (3) more effective procedures. This resulted inter alia in a new *de minimis* regulation in 2006 and a General Block Exemption Regulation in 2008 (both were revised in 2014 as a result of the more recent State Aid Modernization – see below), the introduction of a simplified procedure for the approval of certain types of aid, a Notice on the enforcement of State aid law by national courts (2009), and many revised or new Guidelines and Communications.[56] In the meantime, due to the financial crisis, and despite some successes achieved by the SAAP, the percentage of crisis-related aid to GDP had (far) surpassed the percentage of non-crisis aid in the late 2000s.[57]

The SAAP was followed in 2012 by another reform programme, called State Aid Modernisation (hereafter: SAM). SAM again had three closely linked objectives, being (1) to foster growth in a strengthened, dynamic and competitive internal market, (2) to focus enforcement on cases having the biggest impact on the internal market, and (3) to facilitate streamlined

---

well as the guidelines on horizontal and vertical mergers (2004/C 31/03 and 2008/C 265/07).

[54] Many commentators – such as Bishop and Walker (2010) and Craig and de Búrca (2015) – have argued that the CJEU had often been more 'economic' in its analysis than the Commission, at least in previous decades. In this author's view, the more economic approach is therefore likely to lead first and foremost to changes in Commission practice, hopefully also followed/backed by the courts. With regard to the more recently published documents, only time can tell what the effects in practice will be.

[55] See, generally, Bishop and Walker (2010) and Basedow and Wurmnest (2011).

[56] Information compiled from http://ec.europa.eu/competition/state_aid/reform/archive.html and various textbooks. See also Hildebrand (2014), pp. 2–3.

[57] In 2011 EU Member States granted €784 billion of State aid, of which €64 billion consisted of non-crisis aid (aid to industry and services, agriculture, fisheries, transport and rail), €715 billion of crisis state aid, and €5 billion of temporary aid. See the State Aid Scoreboard, available online at http://ec.europa.eu/competition/state_aid/scoreboard/index_en.html and Hildebrand (2014), pp. 4–5.

rules and faster decisions.[58] SAM resulted in, inter alia, a revision of the General Block Exemption Regulation, Procedural Regulation and *de minimis* Regulation, creating a new Enabling Regulation, and a revision and streamlining of the existing guidelines on different types of State aid.[59]

Underlying the SAAP and SAM reforms is the so-called balancing test, so named because its aim is to weigh the positive effects of aid measures against their negative effects. It is on this basis that the Commission has been trying to fill in some of the gaps left by Article 107(3), that is, in deciding which aid measures can be exempted and hence be held compatible with the EU internal market. The balancing test comprises three steps.[60] First, any aid measure needs to be aimed at a well-defined market failure or a well-defined objective of common interest (e.g. growth, employment, cohesion or environment). The fact that both the economic goal of curing market failure and equity goals are mentioned here is particularly interesting in the context of this chapter, and will be taken up again in section 4. As a second step of the balancing test, aid should be well designed, which means that it needs to:

- be *appropriate*, in the sense that no other, better, policy instruments are available to deal with the particular market failure or to achieve the objective of common interest;
- induce a change in behaviour of the aid recipient, that would not have taken place without the aid (i.e. the aid needs to have an *incentive effect*);
- be *proportional*, meaning that aid must be limited to the minimum necessary.

The third step in the balancing test consists of balancing the positive effects of the aid with the negative effects. This in practice means that the distortions of competition and effect on trade need to be limited. The Commission has been trying to integrate the elements of this balancing test in the General Block Exemption Regulation, guidelines and frameworks regarding the different types of aid, and to apply them in deciding

---

58 Communication on State aid modernisation (COM/2012/0209 final), published on 8 May 2012.

59 For a full list of changes, see http://ec.europa.eu/competition/state_aid/modernisation/index_en.html. Hildebrand (2014), pp. 3–8 provides a more elaborate summary of SAM.

60 Nicolaides (2008), pp. 106–9; Hildebrand (2014), pp. 11–12. The balancing test is also described in various Commission documents, most prominently in Commission Staff Working Document (2009).

individual cases of (non-block-exempted) aid.[61] It is not the aim of this chapter to analyse whether it has succeeded in doing so.[62] Rather, the next section will consider the potential conflicts between this shift in focus on efficiency and the other goals of EU State aid policy.

4. EVOLVING GOALS OF STATE AID POLICY IN THE EU

Different goals that have been associated with EU State aid policy include market integration, efficiency and equity, and more recently fiscal discipline. Looking at the recent developments described in section 3.2, the emphasis of State aid control seems to have shifted at least to some extent from internal market concerns to goals of efficiency, while equity ('objectives of common interest' such as cohesion and environmental protection) has always been a separate goal of all EU policy. Efficient government intervention in markets appears to become an ever more important policy concern, justifying whether or not State aid can be held compatible with the internal market. The question whether that recent focus on fiscal discipline is a good development will be assessed from the perspective of the 'economics of federalism' theory in section 4.2. First, however, section 4.1 will elaborate on the different goals mentioned above and potential conflicts that arise.

4.1 Potentially Conflicting Goals

The rules on State aid control were introduced in 1957 as part of the Treaty of Rome. According to Bacon, the main objective was related to *market integration* concerns and was to avoid subsidy races[63] between Member States, more specifically the risk of political damage to economic integration created by subsidy races.[64] Nevertheless, the fact that from the outset DG Competition has been the main actor in the enforcement of State aid provisions indicates that the objective of *avoiding distortions of competition* (which can also be found in the original Treaty) was considered important as well. The sometimes conflicting goals of competition law and internal market policy have been recognized by many authors, who have argued

---

61 See also Hildebrand (2014), pp. 8–12.

62 Interested readers are referred to Friederiszick et al. (2008), Kaupa (2009), Basedow and Wurmnest (2011), and more recently Quigley (2015).

63 See also section 2.1 above.

64 Bacon (2013), p. 4.

that these goals at times have also led to a policy in the field of State aid that is complex and not always coherent.[65]

As stated repeatedly above, *equity* is an important rationale of EU policy. The concept 'equity' is referred to explicitly in the balancing test,[66] and has since found its way into the various Regulations and guidelines in which the balancing test has been incorporated, more particularly via the (pre-existing) notion of 'objectives of common interest'. Some objectives of common interest[67] aim (also) at correcting market failures and thus target efficiency; examples include aid in relation to R&D&I, training, risk capital to SMEs or environmental externalities. In some other cases, however, aid may be provided solely for the sake of equity, thereby ignoring or overriding efficiency concerns. Examples of aid targeted exclusively at objectives of common interest, and which can be – in certain conditions and within certain limits – (block) exempted by the Commission, include:[68]

- furthering economic cohesion by helping to reduce the gap between the development levels of the various regions of the EU;
- safeguarding the provision of services of general economic interest;[69]
- helping disadvantaged/disabled workers to enter or stay in the labour market;
- rescuing and restructuring firms in financial difficulties with the aim of avoiding loss of employment (only under very strict conditions);
- preserving cultural diversity (again under very strict conditions).

The Commission in its assessments requires that equity justifications are demonstrated by statistical indicators that make explicit the social or regional disparities. Such indicators include GDP per capita, unemployment levels, poverty indicators, and so on.

I have already presented the Commission's more economic approach and its stronger focus on *efficiency* in section 3.2. It is clear that efficiency may conflict with equity.[70] Saving jobs, protecting the environment or

---

65 Bacon (2013), p. 5. See also e.g. Bishop and Walker (2010), pp. 7–8, and Ma (2016), pp. 32–4, and references quoted therein.

66 See section 3.2 of Commission Staff Working Document (2009).

67 Where it should be pointed out that the word 'common' also suggests a European element, stretching beyond purely national interests.

68 See Commission Staff Working Document (2009), p. 10.

69 For a detailed discussion, see Devroe and Gabathuler (2014).

70 The former is sometimes referred to as 'the size of the cake', while the latter is referred to as 'the distribution of the cake'. Friederiszick et al. (2008),

promoting the number of female directors in companies, just to mention some random examples of equity goals that can be associated with State aid, can be social objectives determined by policy makers at the national or EU level, even if they are not necessarily efficient in terms of social costs and benefits. In such situations, reaching equity goals, sometimes at large costs, may be at the expense of efficiency, namely when saving jobs means keeping inefficient firms alive, when investments in environmentally friendly technology do not pay off in the long term or are not cost-efficient, or when job positions are no longer filled on the basis of the qualities of job applicants. Of course, one can also think of situations where equity goals are in line with (Kaldor-Hicks) efficiency, for example when income redistribution in order to reduce socio-economic inequality leads to an overall improvement in social welfare, or when large and risky investments in R&D&I in the present lead to an increase in social welfare in the future. However, it is important to keep in mind that preferences about, for example, optimal income (re)distribution or industrial policy are likely to differ between Member States. Ideally, this should have implications also for EU State aid policy. I will come back to this point in section 4.2.

Several authors have argued that the shifts in policy goals (different equity goals, but especially the stronger focus on efficiency and budget discipline) make it particularly difficult to maintain consistency with past decisions in the field of State aid. What this means for the coherence of Commission practice and legal certainty is yet another interesting question.[71]

4.2 Fiscal Discipline by National Governments: A Task for the EU?

As explained above,[72] the SAAP included the aim of having 'less and better targeted aid', often rephrased in the literature as 'curbing wasteful spending', 'budgetary discipline', 'fiscal discipline', and so on.[73] From an economic perspective, it is hard to see why EU intervention should be justified, if it is only to prevent wasteful aid from occurring at the national level, especially when there is a conflict between goals of efficiency and other goals defined by policy makers at the national level. Such EU

---

pp. 634–6 discuss some examples of potential trade-offs between equity and efficiency.

[71] Bacon (2013), p. 5.

[72] Section 3.2.

[73] See Dewatripont and Seabright (2006), Kaupa (2009), Bacon (2013), and references quoted therein.

intervention would go against both the legal principle of subsidiarity and the economic theory of federalism. The latter theory, inspired by the work of Charles Tiebout[74] and applied to EU lawmaking by many law and economics scholars, takes a bottom-up approach to harmonization.[75] A decentralized (national or local) approach is preferred to EU intervention, because people's preferences are best represented at local or national level. Moreover, regulation at the national level avoids creating a monopoly in lawmaking at EU level and leaves room for regulatory competition and mutual learning. [76] People then still have the option to vote or exit to influence decision-making.[77] According to the economic theory of federalism, from an efficiency perspective, moving decision-making to the EU level is recommended only if there are significant transboundary externalities, high transaction costs or when there is a 'race to the bottom'.[78] Applying these criteria to State aid, we recognize some of the arguments presented in Table 7.2 above. The need for 'fiscal discipline' (also when this is in contrast with equity goals defined at the national level) is not recognized as a separate reason for centralized decision-making in the economic theory of federalism.[79]

State aid control has a strong political dimension, as (unlike control of abusive practices and mergers) it is aimed directly at governments of Member States and not at undertakings. This political dimension has undoubtedly influenced the prioritization of the different goals over the years. For example, in recent years it has led to the support at EU level of objectives such as the green economy, the digital agenda and R&D&I. According to Kaupa, focusing on efficiency in the form of fiscal discipline does not make much sense for aid measures that are aimed at

---

[74] Tiebout (1956).

[75] Philipsen and Zhou (2016).

[76] On this point see also Hayek (1968).

[77] See generally Van den Bergh (2000), Faure (2003) and Frey (2009).

[78] Another potential argument for moving to the EU level concerns a 'levelling of the playing field', but it is debated whether this is really an economic argument. Furthermore, the economic theory of federalism also recognizes the non-economic arguments, i.e. those related to equity. For a longer discussion of the criteria for harmonization in the context of competition law, see Cauffman and Philipsen (2015) and Van den Bergh (1996). See also Wagner (2012) for an application of these arguments in the light of the financial crisis.

[79] Although various economists have written about 'fiscal federalism', fiscal centralization does not seem realistic for the EU, especially when taking into account the 2016 'Brexit' vote in the UK and the growing Eurosceptisicm among parts of the population. On fiscal federalism, see e.g. Oates (1999) and – in an interesting application of the optimum currency areas theory to the Euro – Krugman (2013).

non-economic goals. He argues that making the efficiency criterion the primary criterion 'bears a considerable risk that Member States will be limited in their ability to pursue non-economic goals'.[80] More specifically, the trade-offs that have to be made between equity and efficiency objectives at EU level will 'ultimately limit the ability to justify aid measures with arguments of fair distribution'.[81]

Dewatripont and Seabright have provided some supporting theory for the goal of fiscal discipline as part of EU State aid policy, which somewhat resembles the 'public choice' argument for supranational control presented in Table 7.2. Their paper begins by posing the question whether a 'waste of fiscal resources involved [is not] simply a matter of domestic political failure to be resolved by strengthening the mechanisms of domestic political accountability.'[82] After providing an overview of existing evidence of States wasting money by subsidizing industry, they conclude, on the basis of an economic model, that wasteful spending is a by-product of accountability rather than a symptom of its absence. The explanation can be found in public choice theory: politicians tend to fund inefficient projects (i.e. projects that generate real benefits to their host economies but at a disproportionate investment cost) in order to show their diligence, and are rewarded for that with votes. Strengthening only the mechanisms of domestic political accountability will not work under these circumstances; an independent, possibly supranational, control may be called for.[83] However, the question whether the European Commission (and more particularly DG Competition) is best able to provide such independent monitoring is not addressed by the authors.

5. CONCLUDING REMARKS AND POSSIBLE LESSONS FOR CHINA

What can we conclude from this discussion of economic theory and the practice of State aid policy? It follows from section 7.2 that there are certainly good reasons to introduce a supranational control on government spending, including economic (efficiency) reasons. The strongest arguments are those related to preventing a race to the bottom (subsidy war) and dynamic distortions. Other 'efficiency' arguments, as presented in

[80] Kaupa (2009), p. 316.
[81] Kaupa (2009), p. 317.
[82] Dewatripont and Seabright (2006), p. 514.
[83] Dewatripont and Seabright (2006), p. 521.

Table 7.2 above, may hold too, but are (sometimes much) more debated. However, it also follows from the discussion above that the argument of fiscal discipline, that is 'curbing government spending', does not seem very strong in cases where there is a conflict with equity goals defined at the national level (income redistribution, social policy, etc.) and where there is no genuine effect on EU trade. The explanation for this result can be found both in economic theory, in the form of the 'bottom-up approach to federalism' theory, and in the legal principle of subsidiarity.

It is therefore important that one of the crucial steps of Article 107(1) TFEU and the balancing test based on Article 107(3) TFEU, being the effect on trade and competition, are taken very seriously in practice. The most recent developments resulting from the State Aid Modernization– increasing the scope and size of the exemptions and the explicit mentioning of the 'balancing' of pros and cons of aid measures – seem to suggest that the Commission is realizing this, but (as always) we will have to wait and see what the future brings.

Another conclusion of this chapter can be drawn from the discussion on public choice theory: namely, that it remains important to (try to) control the influence of lobbying groups asking for subsidies that do not serve the public interest. The question is whether such control should take place at local, national or EU level. It is too easy to assume that shifting decision-making to a higher level will solve problems of lobbying and regulatory capture. On the contrary, these problems may then merely take a different form.[84] However, addressing these public choice concerns goes beyond the 'mere' question of dealing with conflicting goals of policy and is not the main topic of this chapter.

In China, subsidies provided at the provincial or local level may also distort the competition between undertakings located in different areas, or indeed lead to any of the other problems referred to in Table 7.2 above. Such subsidies exist in the form of tax reductions, political favours (for example, when granting licences) and other advantages, just as in other jurisdictions. Provincial officials may be inclined to provide advantages to local companies in order to create or maintain jobs or GDP, especially if this helps their political career.[85] Even firms listed on the stock exchange may be dependent on government subsidies for their survival.

---

[84] Vaubel (1994), pp. 153–8, shows that certain actors may have an interest in centralization, including EU politicians and bureaucrats, judges of the CJEU, particular pressure groups, and even some politicians and bureaucrats of the lower-level governments.

[85] On tax competition, licensing barriers and the behaviour of local politicians in China, see e.g. Shen and Philipsen (2016) and Shen (2016).

Nevertheless, a system similar to EU State aid control is not available in China in its administrative law, and the possibilities to effectively address distortions of competition created by administrative monopolies (an indirect method of controlling local government spending) in the Anti-Monopoly Law (AML) are also fairly limited.[86] The EU experience in State aid control may therefore provide some valuable food for thought for the Chinese legislator and the enforcement agencies of the AML.

REFERENCES

Bacon, Kelyn (2013), *European Union Law of State Aid*, second edition, Oxford: Oxford University Press.

Basedow, Jürgen and Wolfgang Wurmnest (eds) (2011), *Structure and Effects in EU Competition Law*, Alphen aan den Rijn: Kluwer Law International.

Becker, Gary S. (1983), 'A Theory of Competition among Pressure Groups for Political Influence', *Quarterly Journal of Economics*, 98 (3), 371–400.

Bishop, Simon and Mike Walker (2010), *The Economics of EC Competition Law: Concepts, Application and Measurement*, third edition, London: Sweet & Maxwell.

Boehm, Frédéric (2007), 'Regulatory Capture Revisited – Lessons from Economics of Corruption'. Available at: http://www.icgg.org/downloads/Boehm%20-%20 Regulatory%20Capture%20Revisited.pdf. Accessed 2 February 2016.

Cauffman, Caroline and Niels Philipsen (2015), 'Who Does What in Competition Law?: Harmonizing the Rules on Damages for Infringements of the EU Competition Rules', in Bram Akkermans, Jaap Hage, Nicole Kornet and Jan Smits (eds), *Who Does What? On the Allocation of Competences in European Private Law*, Antwerp–Cambridge–Portland: Intersentia, 245–87.

Chan, Gordon Y.M. (2009), 'Administrative Monopoly and the Anti-Monopoly Law: An Examination of the Debate in China', *Journal of Contemporary China*, 18, 263–83.

Commission Staff Working Document (2009), 'Common Principles for an Economic Assessment of the Compatibility of State Aid under Article 87.3', Brussels: European Commission. Available at: http://ec.europa.eu/competition/state_aid/reform/economic_assessment_en.pdf.

Cooter, Robert and Thomas Ulen (2012), *Law & Economics*, sixth edition, Boston, MA: Pearson Education International.

Craig, Paul and Gráinne de Búrca (2015), *EU Law: Text, Cases and Materials*, sixth edition, Oxford, UK: Oxford University Press.

Devroe, Wouter and David Gabathuler (2014), 'The Evolving Treatment of Services of General Economic Interest under EU Law', in S. Schoenmaekers,

[86] Both Chan (2009) and Weishaar (2011), referring to various other authors, note this problem, and highlight that in this respect the enforcement structure of the AML also makes it difficult to control administrative monopolies.

W. Devroe and N. Philipsen (eds), *State Aid and Public Procurement in the European Union*, Cambridge–Antwerp–Portland: Intersentia, 47–66.

Dewatripont, Mathias and Paul Seabright (2006), 'Wasteful Public Spending and State Aid Control', *Journal of the European Economic Association*, 4, 513–22.

Faure, Michael (2003), 'How Law and Economics May Contribute to the Harmonisation of Tort Law in Europe', in Reinhard Zimmerman (ed.), *Grundstrukturen des Europäischen Deliktsrechts*, Baden-Baden, Germany: Nomos, 31–82.

Frey, Bruno S. (2009), 'A New Concept of European Federalism', LSE 'Europe in Question' Discussion Paper Series, LEQS Paper No. 03/2009, London, UK: London School of Economics and Political Science.

Friederiszick, Hans W., Lars-Hendrik Röller and Vincent Verouden (2008), 'European State Aid Control: An Economic Framework', in Paolo Buccirossi (ed.), *Handbook of Antitrust Economics*, Cambridge, MA and London: MIT Press, 625–69.

Hayek, Friedrich A. (1968), *Der Wettbewerb als Entdeckungsverfahren*, Kiel: Institut für Weltwirtschaft.

Hildebrand, Doris (2014), 'Modernisation of State Aid Rules in the European Union Application of Economic Concepts and Principals', in S. Schoenmaekers, W. Devroe and N. Philipsen (eds), *State Aid and Public Procurement in the European Union*, Cambridge–Antwerp–Portland: Intersentia, 1–18.

Kaupa, Clemens (2009), 'The More Economic Approach – A Reform Based on Ideology?', *European State Aid Law Quarterly*, 3, 311–22.

Krugman, Paul (2013), 'Revenge of the Optimum Currency Area', in Daron Acemoglu, Jonathan Parker and Michael Woodford (eds), *NBER Macroeconomics Annual 2012*, Volume 27, University of Chicago Press, 439–48.

Luja, Raymond H.C. (2014), 'Defining the Scope of State Aid', in Sarah Schoenmaekers, Wouter Devroe and Niels Philipsen (eds), *State Aid and Public Procurement in the European Union*, Cambridge–Antwerp–Portland: Intersentia, 19–32.

Ma, Jingyuan (2016), 'Market Integration as the Goal of Competition Law: The EU Experience and its Implications for China', in Niels Philipsen, Stefan E. Weishaar and Guangdong Xu (eds), *Market Integration: The EU Experience and Implications for Regulatory Reform in China*, Berlin: Springer Verlag, 15–39.

Nicolaides, Phedon (2008), *Essays on Law and Economics of State Aid*, 2008, PhD dissertation, Maastricht: Maastricht University, available at http://arno.unimaas.nl/show.cgi?fid=13483.

Oates, Wallace E. (1999), 'An Essay on Fiscal Federalism', *Journal of Economic Literature*, 37 (3), 1120–49.

Olson, Mancur (1965), *The Logic of Collective Action: Public Goods and the Theory of Groups*, Cambridge, MA: Harvard University Press.

Philipsen, N.J. (2003), *Regulation of and by Pharmacists in the Netherlands and Belgium: An Economic Approach*, Antwerp/Groningen: Intersentia.

Philipsen, Niels J. (2012) 'Regulation of Accountants', in Roger J. Van den Bergh and Alessio M. Pacces (eds), *Encyclopedia of Law and Economics: Regulation and Economics*, Cheltenham: Edward Elgar, 715–42.

Philipsen, Niels J. and Qi Zhou (2016), 'Business Restrictions in the Legal Professions: Do We Need More Market Integration?', in Niels Philipsen, Stefan E. Weishaar and Guangdong Xu (eds), *Market Integration: The EU Experience and Implications for Regulatory Reform in China*, Berlin: Springer Verlag, 211–38.

Quigley, Conor (2015), *European State Aid Law and Policy*, third edition, Oxford and Portland, OR: Hart Publishing.

Shen, Guang (2016), *Regulation of Cross-border Establishment in China and the EU*, Antwerp–Cambridge–Portland: Intersentia.

Shen, Guang and Niels J. Philipsen (2016), 'Regulation of the Inter-Provincial Establishment of Companies: Applying the Private Interest Approach to China', in Niels Philipsen, Stefan E. Weishaar and Guangdong Xu (eds), *Market Integration: The EU Experience and Implications for Regulatory Reform in China*, Berlin: Springer Verlag, 183–210.

Tiebout, Charles (1956), 'A Pure Theory of Local Expenditures', *Journal of Political Economy*, 64, 416–24.

Van den Bergh, Roger (1996), 'Economic Criteria for Applying the Subsidiarity Principle in the European Community: The Case of Competition Policy', *International Review of Law and Economics*, 16, 363–83.

Van den Bergh, Roger (2000), 'Towards an Institutional Legal Framework for Regulatory Competition in Europe', *Kyklos*, 53, 435–66.

Vaubel, Roland (1994), 'The Political Economy of Centralization and the European Community', *Public Choice*, 81 (1/2), 151–90.

Wagner, Helmut (2012), 'Is Harmonization of Legal Rules an Appropriate Target? Lessons from the Global Financial Crisis', *European Journal of Law and Economics*, 33, 541–64.

Weishaar, Stefan (2011), 'Administrative Monopolies, State Aid, Barriers to Entry and Market Integration: Challenges for the Chinese Anti-Monopoly Law', in Michael Faure and Xinzhu Zhang, *Competition Policy and Regulation: Recent Developments in China, the US and Europe*, Cheltenham: Edward Elgar, 98–129.

Zimmer, Daniel and Martin Blaschczok (2011), 'The Role of Competition in European State Aid Control During the Financial Markets Crisis', *European Competition Law Review*, 32 (1), 9–16.

PART III

Environmental regulation

8. Development of a regulatory framework for CDM-enabled offshore carbon capture and storage (OCCS) in China

Roy A. Partain and Michael G. Faure

1. FRAMING REGULATORY DEVELOPMENT AS A RESEARCH PROBLEM

China faces an obstacle course of energy challenges; it needs to identify an efficient pathway to quickly evolve a regulatory framework that meets multiple agendas whilst remaining compatible with Chinese governance institutions. The scholastic literature of law and economics provides insights into that policy problem and suggests potential solutions.

1.1 China's Emerging Need for a CCS Regulatory Framework

China needs more energy, but that will likely involve fossil fuels and greenhouse gas (GHG) emissions. It has been forecasted that even under the most favorable of outcomes from investments into renewable energy sources and gains in energy efficiency, China is still likely to produce over 50 per cent of its electrical power from coal in the year 2030;[1] thus China needs a means to reduce emissions in the face of foreseeable future coal consumption. As is, China is said to have "1,620 large stationary CO_2 point sources that each emits at least 100,000 metric tons of CO_2" each year;[2] those combined emissions exceed 3,890 million tons ($MtCO_2$) a year.[3] And most of those emissions are located within either the North China plain or on industrialized coastal areas.[4]

1 Liu & Gallagher (2009), 3878.
2 Li, X.C. et al. (2009), 2794.
3 Li, X.C. et al. (2009), 2795.
4 Li, X.C. et al. (2009), 2795.

For the foreseeable future China will continue to have greenhouse gas emissions, but China is committed to reducing its overall greenhouse gas emissions. China could use carbon capture and storage (CCS) technologies to reduce emissions,[5] but that would likely precipitate a need for a national regulatory framework to address CCS's unique legal issues.[6] Additionally, many of China's carbon emission points are located in the southeast of China,[7] where few geological structures are optimal for onshore CCS.[8]

However, off the coast of China, from the north in Shandong down to the south off of Guangxi, there are massive offshore deep saline formations suitable for offshore CCS (OCCS) activities.[9] The Bohai Basin off the coast of Shandong has been found to be one of the "best opportunities for CCS development" in China.[10] Similarly, the Pearl River Mouth Basin has been identified as a potential OCCS site; it has been estimated that the Basin could store the CO_2 volumes from two centuries of emissions from major sources in Guangdong.[11] Thus,

---

[5] Liu & Gallagher (2009), 3878–9. See also Huang et al. (2014), 2: "[m]oreover many Chinese scholars consider CCS to be a key bridging technology which reduces the growing CO2 emission [*sic*] . . . in the country.". CCS is known by several monikers: carbon capture and sequestration (CCS), carbon capture and storage (CCS), and as carbon capture, utilization, and storage (CCUS). For the large part, these references are identical. For the purposes of this chapter, CCS will denote onshore, terrestrial, subterranean storage of carbon dioxide within deep earth structures, whereas offshore CCS (OCCS) will be used to denote a similar idea performed offshore but with the carbon stored within deep earth structures akin to the onshore models of CCS. OCCS will not include reference to ocean fertilization or deep sea pooling of carbon dioxide for the purposes of this chapter.

[6] Huang et al. (2014), 2.

[7] Li, X.C. et al. (2009), 2795, Figure 1. See also Dahowski et al. (2009), 2851, Figure 1. See also Huang et al. (2014), 5, wherein they document that Guangdong has led China in energy efficiency gains and renewable investments, but that those efforts will remain insufficient to match the pre-existing demand for fossil fuels.

[8] See Dahowski et al. (2009), 2854: "Indeed, many of these sources are unable to access any suitable CO_2 storage capacity with the 150-mile (241-km) search radius. Storage options do appear to be present in the nearby offshore basin, which would likely offer great benefits to these regions." See also Dahowski et al. (2009), 2853, Figure 2. Even where onshore sites might be found, they would face stiff challenges from land availability and resistance from agricultural and environmental fronts. See Huang et al. (2014), 7.

[9] Li, X.C. et al. (2009), 2796, Figure 2. See also Dahowski et al. (2009), Figure 2.

[10] Li, X.C. et al. (2009), 2800.

[11] Zhou et al. (2011), 316. See also Huang et al. (2014), 6, wherein they report the Pearl River Mouth Basin could store 308 gigatons of CO_2 ($GtCO_2$) and they

China will want to consider offshore CCS activities for much of its CCS needs.

China has many competitive calls on its domestic capital resources, and it could benefit from the financial tools afforded under the Kyoto Protocol's Clean Development Mechanism (CDM) to finance CCS projects.[12] But using those financial tools would obligate China to develop certain forms of regulatory oversight for CCS activities.

Finally, the suggested framework should be able to coordinate with the existing institutions of governance within China to ensure the optimal efficiency of those regulations.

All of those challenges need to be met urgently. How might China meet those challenges, to rapidly provide a full regulatory framework that both coordinates with existing Chinese governing policies and Kyoto Protocol requirements? This chapter, with the application of law and economics to the circumstances of offshore CCS, will endeavor to answer that question of regulatory design.

1.2 Research Methodology

This chapter explores the policy question of how to efficiently, in terms of both time and financial resources, develop regulations that can satisfy the multiple challenges facing OCCS in China. Primarily, legal methodology drawn from the law and economics literature will be utilized to evaluate a variety of regulatory options in consideration of the facts and circumstances of Chinese OCCS options.

First, a general introduction to the need and potential for Chinese OCCS options is provided (section 2). The circumstances of OCCS are reviewed and prepared for later analysis.

Second, the theoretical literature on optimal regulatory planning is surveyed and reviewed (section 3). Theoretical perspectives on both public regulations and private regulations are compared and contrasted. Key findings from the literature are provided. A theoretical model of optimal regulatory governance is provided in light of the circumstances of both China's legal institutions and its offshore CCS opportunities.

Third, an evaluation is made to determine if there are any public and private models of CCS regulatory frameworks to draw upon in

---

state that is equivalent to 150 years of injection volumes at current levels of coastal emissions.

[12] Huang et al. (2014), 13. See also the discussions below in section 2.2 on financial tools in the context of the Clean Development Mechanism.

formulating a regulatory framework for China (section 4). A variety of existing public offshore CCS frameworks are identified and discussed. Similarly, a collection of private or NGO-led efforts to provide private guidance on CCS regulation is provided (section 5).

Finally, it will be concluded that China has ample materials to drawn on to efficiently draft its own regulatory frameworks (section 6). China could build both public and private regulatory systems to benefit from both, and to buttress the efficacy of both.

2. OFFSHORE CCS: AN OPTION FOR CHINA?

2.1 Benefits of Offshore CCS for China

Onshore CCS has been explored for a number of decades and has met certain technological challenges;[13] yet it remains broadly unimplemented. In China, there are only a few experimental onshore CCS sites. Lui et al. report that major onshore CCS projects in China, such as the ShenHua Ordos CCS Project in Inner Mongolia, suffer from low porosity and low permeability.[14] Because of such tight reservoirs, onshore CCS projects might need to utilize fracturing techniques,[15] which could potentially result in fractures that enable CO_2 migration and leakage. Additionally, China's better CCS reservoir areas are close to hydrocarbon and coal projects that remain in operation or development;[16] conversion of those fields into CCS storage sites might place economic volumes of hydrocarbons at risk. Thus, even when onshore storage sites are available, they may lack optimal conditions, further reinforcing the need for non-local sources of carbon emissions to seek storage alternatives.

Offshore CCS (OCCS) provides an alternative for China. OCCS enables a safer geological setting due to several geochemical and geophysical differences in the pore space and pore fluids engaged in the storage systems. For certain regions of China, particularly those close to the industrial areas from Shanghai down towards Hong Kong, offshore CCS sites might be the best option for feasible CCS.

Offshore CCS, under certain conditions, can display very different risk characteristics from onshore CCS. Unlike onshore CCS, OCCS provides

---

13 Li et al. (2011), 6031.

14 Lui et al. (2014), 6907; see also Li et al. (2011), 6034–5.

15 Lui et al. (2014), 6907.

16 Lui et al. (2014), 6908.

several characteristics that could enhance the overall likelihood of secure containment. First, OCCS can benefit from negative buoyancy: the CO_2 does not seek to escape its confinement vertically, unlike the CO_2 volumes stored in terrestrial CCS.[17] Second, OCCS can benefit from the formation of CO_2 hydrates, which transform the injected volumes into a kind of icy cement that not only seals the capstone and its faults and fractures, but also solidifies the CO_2 *in situ* within the injection zone.[18]

Third, OCCS benefits from the substantial storage and safety advantage of being able to remove and relocate pore space salines into ambient ocean salines because the salines are chemically very similar. Therefore, the benthic setting of OCCS provides risk reduction opportunities. The Environmental Protection Agency (EPA) has already approved such saline relocations for offshore gas projects.[19] Thus there is less likelihood of excessive pressure leading to escaping CO_2 and at the same time storage capacity can be increased.[20]

Fourth, OCCS benefits from the circumstances of seabed leaks being naturally contained in a way that terrestrial CCS lacks for its leaks at ground level. Leaks of CO_2 at deep benthic levels naturally pool as a liquid or congeal into hydrates,[21] both of which might be recoverable for mitigation purposes – something incredibly unlikely for airborne leaks from terrestrial CCS.[22]

Fifth, OCCS is located offshore away from human communities that might otherwise be in harm's way under terrestrial CCS plans, and thus the offshore aspect itself provides certain advantages over onshore CCS options.[23] Sixth, given that most of the expected OCCS zones would lie in the exclusive economic zones (EEZs) beyond territorial seas, the governance of those projects would face fewer levels of overlapping governance and might be more readily and efficiently regulated by central or federal authorities without overlapping concerns of local governance.[24]

---

17 House et al. (2006), 12291.

18 Koide et al. (1997), S253–258. House et al. (2006), 12292–4. Li, Q. et al. (2009), 504–507.

19 Schrag (2009), 1658–9.

20 Schrag (2009), 1659.

21 Li, Q. et al. (2009), 503. House et al. (2006), 12291.

22 See Koide et al. (1997), S255, for a finding that in certain conditions, the volumes of benthically released CO_2 might be safely dispersed in the water column.

23 Schrag (2009), 1659.

24 While the international legal characterization of the injected carbon dioxide might remain unclear in certain circumstances, there are emerging norms of permissible offshore CCS, as reflected in Annex I of the London Protocol and in OSPAR Decision 2007/2 (see section 4.4 below).

Thus OCCS potentially presents the benefits of terrestrial CCS with fewer of the risks and hazards. If CCS were to be seen as a desirable "second best" technological option until those carbon-free and renewable energy sources become available, then OCCS is arguably a "better second best."

2.2 UNFCCC's CDM on OCCS: The Need for Regulations

The Clean Development Mechanism (CDM) of the Kyoto Protocol provides financial opportunities for countries listed in Annex I of the United Nations Framework Convention on Climate Change (UNFCCC) to support investment in emission reduction projects in non-Annex I countries whilst making baseline emission offsets available to those Annex I countries.[25] China has long been a key recipient of CDM funding;[26] the potential to include CCS projects within CDM financial tools would be of substantial benefit to supporting CCS projects in China.

While the CDM did not originally include CCS activities, it has been updated to include CCS activities under certain circumstances. Decision 10/CMP.7 ("the Decision")[27] enabled certain CCS projects to be included within the financial toolsets supported by the UNFCCC's CDM. Importantly, the Decision requires the provision and enforcement of particular regulatory frameworks by a host if the CDM benefits are to be made available for CCS projects.

The Decision established a reference definition for includable acts of CCS; the definition requires the sources of carbon emissions to be anthropogenic and that the storage is in an "underground geological storage site."[28] It defined such geological storage sites to require the presence of both a cap rock system and an underlying injection formation.[29] These

---

[25] Kyoto Protocol to the United Nations Framework Convention on Climate Change, opened for signature March 16, 1998, 2303 UNTS 148 [hereinafter Kyoto Protocol] (entered into force February 16, 2005), at Article 12. United Nations Framework Convention on Climate Change, May 9, 1992, 1771 UNTS 107 [hereinafter UNFCCC], at Annex I. See also "Clean Development Mechanism (CDM)," United Nations Framework Convention on Climate Change. Available at http://unfccc.int/kyoto_protocol/mechanisms/clean_development_mechanism/items/2718.php.

[26] Lecocq & Ambrosi (2007), 141–2.

[27] Decision 10/CMP.7: Modalities and procedures for carbon dioxide capture and storage in geological formations as clean development mechanism project activities. Available at http://unfccc.int/resource/docs/2011/cmp7/eng/10a02.pdf#page=13 [hereinafter Decision 10/CMP.7].

[28] Decision 10/CMP.7. Annex A(1)(a).

[29] Decision 10/CMP.7. Annex A(1)(b).

two definitions provide effective exclusion to a variety of offshore CCS options, such as injection into bathic water columns or under mud layers *sans* geological capstone. However, it did not ban all forms of offshore CCS; therefore, those methods that include some form of a cap rock containment system should qualify. It does define what forms of liability should be associated with CDM-coordinated CCS projects.[30] Liability governance is to be regulated by the host state and the particular means and rules governing the liabilities of a particular CCS project must be explicated in the project design document prior to the approval of the project.[31]

The Decision prescribes that the Executive Board of the CDM should undertake measures to establish documentation to guide the selection of CCS sites, of risk and safety assessments, and of environmental and socio-economic impact assessments.[32]

The Decision also details the requirements incumbent on parties wishing to host CCS activities within the CDM framework, but who are not included within Annex I to the UNFCCC; the People's Republic of China is not listed within Annex I.[33] Penultimate of those requirements is the requirement to establish "laws or regulations" which achieve a list of specific measures.[34] Those measures include regulations to address site selection and development, to define the property rights associated with CCS projects, to provide remedies and redress for injuries resultant from those projects, and to provide liability arrangements for those projects.[35] The Decision requires that the geological storage sites comply with the implemented regulations.[36]

Of note, the Decision forbids CDM-coordinated offshore projects from being established in international waters.[37] While the coordination of the term "international waters" is left unresolved vis-à-vis the United Nations Convention on the Law of the Sea (UNCLOS) term of "high seas," it is clear that the Decision contemplates and endorses CDM-coordinated offshore CCS projects within some notion of jurisdictional waters. The Decision also

---

30 Decision 10/CMP.7. Annex A(1)(j).

31 See Decision 10/CMP.7. Annex F(8)(e) and Decision 10/CMP.7. Annex Appendix B(5)(22).

32 Decision 10/CMP.7. Annex C(4)(b), (c) and (d).

33 UNFCCC, List of Annex I Parties to the Convention. Available at http://unfccc.int/parties_and_observers/parties/annex_i/items/2774.php.

34 Decision 10/CMP.7. Annex F(8).

35 Decision 10/CMP.7. Annex F(8)(a), (b), (c), (d), and (e). The liability arrangements are also referred to in Decision 10/CMP.7. Annex G(10)(f) and at (11)(c).

36 Decision 10/CMP.7. Annex Appendix B(1)(1).

37 Decision 10/CMP.7. Annex Appendix B(1)(2).

requires that geological sites only be permitted if there is "no significant risk of seepage, no significant environmental or health risks exist."[38] Thus, if China seeks to implement offshore CCS, then it must do so within its own waters and at sites that pose no foreseeable risks of "significant damages."[39]

In conclusion, the Decision enables hosts to avail themselves of CDM financing for certain offshore CCS projects, if the host provides a set of laws and regulations to ensure the attainment of certain measures. In order to qualify its CCS projects under the CDM regime, China will need to have in place regulations that qualify under Decision 10/CMP.7. Thus the question becomes, "does China have adequate CCS regulatory measures in place?" In the next section, the answer is revealed to be "not yet."

2.3 China's Existing Measures on Regulating CCS and OCCS

China is preparing to implement CCS strategies; it has made both domestic and international commitments to ensure that it can limit and reduce its greenhouse gas emissions. The People's Republic of China is a signatory to both the UNFCCC and to its Kyoto Protocol.[40] In 2012 the PRC communicated to the UNFCCC that China would include the development of CCS as part of its efforts to achieve sustainable development and to mitigate greenhouse gas emissions.[41] China's 12th Five-Year Plan set a path for clean development and its 12th Five-Year Work Plan on Controlling GHG Emissions (2011–2015) required the development of CCS research and projects.[42] In 2015 China delivered its Intended Nationally Determined Contributions (INDCs) to the UN's UNFCCC Secretariat, which included commitment to additional CCS capacity.[43]

However, currently China has "no specific national regulations for CCUS projects in China."[44] The development of laws and regulations for CCS within China could benefit from earlier enactments in related areas

---

[38] Decision 10/CMP.7. Annex Appendix B(1)(1).

[39] With additional reference to Decision 10/CMP.7. Annex A(1)(j).

[40] Lui et al. (2014), 6904. See also the UNFCCC list of signatories; UNFCCC, "Status of Ratification of the Convention." Available at http://unfccc.int/essential_background/convention/status_of_ratification/items/2631.php.

[41] Lui et al. (2014), 6904.

[42] Lui et al. (2014), 6905.

[43] The language on CCS technologies can be found on page 9, at section 2(10): "加强对节能降耗、可再生能源和先进核能、 碳捕集利用和封存等低碳技术的研发 和 产业化示范, 推广利用 二氧化碳驱油、驱煤层气技术." (Underscoring added to highlight the terms for CCS.) Available at http://www4.unfccc.int/submissions/indc/Submission%20Pages/submissions.aspx.

[44] Lui et al. (2014), 6906.

of law. China's Law on Environmental Impact Assessments (EIAs)[45] requires that EIAs must be submitted during the feasibility study phase of project planning.[46] In addition, the new Environmental Protection Law came into force as of January 2015.[47]

A variety of ministries and other organs have coordinated to begin the development of CCS and OCCS regulations. In 2013 the Ministry of Science and Technology (MoST) published a "Special Plan on Carbon Capture, Utilization, and Storage."[48] The Special Plan refers to goals of environmental impact assessments and of risk controls as foundation issues to be addressed.[49]

The National Development and Reform Commission (NDRC) is the agency responsible for energy and climate change policy.[50] In 2013 it issued the "Notice on Promoting Carbon Capture, Utilization, and Storage Pilot and Demonstration."[51] That policy advised local governments to administer pilot projects according to then-newly issued guidelines.[52] The policy also called for the development and formulation of standards, engineering codes, and regulations for facility safety and environmental protection.[53] It also calls for a deepening of international coordination and cooperation.[54]

In October 2013, the Ministry of Environmental Protection (MEP) issued the "Notice on Strengthening the Environmental Protection of

---

45 See《中华人民共和国环境影响评价法》已由中华人民共和国第九届全国人民代表大会常务委员会第三十次会议于2002年10月28日.

46 Lui et al. (2014). A variety of pre-existing standards under that law might well apply to CCS project EIAs, such as the Technical Guidelines on (i) Environmental Risk Assessment (HJ/T 169-2004), (ii) EIA on Atmosphere (HJ 2.2-2008), (iii) EIA on Groundwater (HJ 19-2011), and (iv) EIA on Ecological Impact (HJ 19 2011). Lui et al. (2014), 6096. Also potentially applicable guidelines might include those for land-based oil and gas operations (HJ/T349-2007). Lui et al. (2014), 6907.

47 Lui et al. (2014), 6906. See 《中华人民共和国环境保护法》 已由 中华人民共和国第十二届全国人民代表大会常务委员会第八次会议于 2014年4月24日 修订通过，现将修订后的"中华人民共和国环境保护法."

48 Lui et al. (2014), 6905.

49 Lui et al. (2014), 6905.

50 Lui et al. (2014), 6905.

51 Lui et al. (2014), 6905.

52 Lui et al. (2014), 6905.

53 Lui et al. (2014), 6905.

54 Lui et al. (2014), 6905. It is worth noting that since 2012, China has served as Co-Secretary, with Canada, on the development of the ISO's new standards for CCS operations, that of "ISO/TC 265 Carbon dioxide capture, transportation, and geological storage." See http://www.iso.org/iso/iso_technical_committee?commid=648607.

Pilot and Demonstration Projects for Carbon Capture, Utilization, and Storage." The Notice provided a wide range of requirements aimed "at all environmental authorities, enterprises, and industries."[55] It is reported that the MEP is coordinating efforts to draft environmental protection requirements and standards for CCS and OCCS projects.[56] The regulatory goal is said to "provide a scientific basis for formulating CCUS environmental management systems suitable for China."[57]

One important motive for development of CCS regulations, including OCCS regulations, is to assist in qualifying Chinese CCS projects for financing under the UNFCCC's CDM.[58] Also, the establishment of CCS regulations would enable China to receive GHG emission reduction credits (CERs) for future successes with their CCS systems.[59]

In order to achieve all of those goals, China will need regulations that meet international standards; but it will also need regulations that are suitable for China's legal institutions.

3. OPTIMAL USES OF PUBLIC AND PRIVATE REGULATION

The question which type of regulation would be optimal for regulating risky activities has been addressed in the law and economics literature. That literature, on the one hand, shows that public *ex ante* regulation of uncertain risks may have advantages, especially when compared to *ex post* liability rules (section 3.1). However, public regulation may also have particular limits, as a result of which it cannot be used alone and should be combined with liability rules (section 3.2). Moreover, in some cases the information and cost advantage of the operators may be such that private regulation could be preferred (section 3.3). This section seeks to explore those findings in illumination of the potential strategies available to policy makers within China.[60] It will be

---

55 Lui et al. (2014), 6906.

56 Lui et al. (2014), 6906.

57 Lui et al. (2014), 6907. As part of the effort to develop a deeper scientific foundation, China's Geological Survey's Center for Hydro-Geology and Environmental Geology has undertaken research on a water well that pierced a natural carbon-rich water reservoir and became a model of a venting event. Lui et al. (2014), 6909.

58 Lui et al. (2014), 6905. See the discussion on the CDM's decision on CCS and of the required legal and regulatory measures in section 2.2.

59 Lui et al. (2014), 6909.

60 While this section will be tailored to the issues attending the development of a regulatory framework for offshore CCS within China's marine jurisdiction, the overall discussion follows the arguments raised in chapter 6 of Faure & Partain

concluded that it is optimal for China to seek a smart combination of public and private regulation as well as liability rules (section 3.4).

3.1 On Regulations

While it might appear unnecessary to question the need for regulation, as regulations are commonly found in legal systems around the globe, it is useful to examine why, from a public interest perspective, a government might find the issuance and enforcement of regulations to be preferable to the alternatives, such as dispute resolution via rules of civil liability. First, we turn to a discussion of when regulations would be expected to be more robust than other options, and then we turn to when other options might simply be defective. In both cases we find a positive role for regulations and the standards that they provide.

A first issue of concern is *what* might be governed – the act leading to injury or the damages resulting from injury. Regulations can provide a means of control over both activity-in-progress and over injuries resulting from risky activities.[61] This is preferable in many cases to the tool of civil liabilities, which respond primarily to injuries-in-fact. Thus the use of regulations enables a governing party to interact and control acts of risky behavior prior to the injury occurring. Given that the operations of offshore CCS are going to occur in the near future, whereas the risks of latent injuries could stretch on for centuries, it will be critical to be able to govern the risky acts at the time they are undertaken, or preferably in advance of their being undertaken.[62] Neither option would be available without regulatory authority; thus the development of offshore CCS should be anticipated by the prior development of regulations.

A second issue of concern is *when* rules or standards ought to intervene, either before the incident of harm or after the incident of harm. This is known as the *ex ante* versus *ex post* question.[63] It is obviously tricky to enforce or recommend rules and standards that do not yet exist, but that is the case in the application of civil liability rules. Civil liability rules are determined in court cases responding to injuries-in-fact, and as such cannot render rules and standards until after the period ideal for monitoring risky behavior.[64] Liability can set standards, but typically the

---

(2017). Additional discussions and deeper foundations of the regulatory theories discussed here are provided in that chapter.

61 Faure & Weishaar (2012), 404, citing Bergkamp (2000).

62 Adelman & Duncan (2011), 22.

63 Faure & Weishaar (2012), 404, citing Bergkamp (2000).

64 See Van den Bergh & Visscher (2008), 29.

standards created through court decisions have a prospective character, that is they prescribe the behavior that is required from operators in the future; liability rules typically are not retrospective. Control of risky behavior obviously requires standards to be in place prior to the onset of any such behavior. Regulations enable such an approach.[65] Rules and standards can be developed in advance of the need for the regulations and brought to the public awareness as part of both education and governance of future events of the now-regulated risky activity. In the circumstances of offshore CCS, it will be very important to establish clear standards for who can undertake those risks, how those CCS activities would be undertaken, and to what extent positive and negative incentives could be brought to promote efficient modes of offshore CCS activity. That will necessitate *ex ante* setting of standards by regulation.[66]

A third issue of concern relates to *who* should determine the new rules and standards. The standards emerging from civil liability are either determined by a judge (when a so-called negligence or fault regime is applied) or by the operators themselves (when strict liability applies). Strict liability has the advantage of shifting the social costs of the activity to the operator, but the disadvantage is that the optimal techniques for preventing harm will remain the private information of the operator. The duty of care, determined by the court within the application of the negligence rule, will in principle inform the public at large and operators of the applicable standard. However, access to the information provided through case law may be difficult and, moreover, judges may not always be in the best position to determine efficient care standards, especially with respect to complicated technologies like CCS. Regulations can be deliberately assembled and drafted by civil servants, by scientists, by politicians, by members of the public, or by combinations of all of the above.[67] Regulations, both public and private, can be made public in character so that standards are well known before decisions on risky activities are made. The potential impacts of offshore CCS operations are multiple and socially complex; the standards to govern those operations need to be inclusive of many genres of expertise and from diverse interest holders. Such an approach favors the development of regulations.

The above discussion has provided circumstances wherein regulations would be expected to be more robust than rules of civil liability; but those scenarios assumed functioning liability systems. This is not always the case;

---

65 Van den Bergh & Visscher (2008), 29.

66 Adelman & Duncan (2011), 22.

67 See Stigler (1961), 231. See also Schwartz & Wilde (1979), 630 and Mackaay (1980).

rules of civil liabilities can fail to be efficient in certain scenarios.[68] Standards based on rules of civil liability are not expected to be efficiently determined if the litigation is undertaken by parties with substantial asymmetries in information.[69] A second source of dysfunction is when the tortfeasor is in a state of insolvency or is otherwise insensitive to the judgments of the court.[70] A third source is when the lawsuit necessary to render judgment is unlikely to come forward;[71] there can be no judgment and no creation or enforcement of standards if the court never comes to session. Such lack of adjudication can occur when injuries are difficult to detect (perhaps they accumulate over a long period of time), when there is low expectation of enforcement, or when there are low probabilities of the judgments being enforced.[72]

Might offshore operators have asymmetrical access to the geological, geophysical, and ecological measurements that might be critical to understanding risk and avoidance?[73] Yes, it would be only reasonable to assume so. Might it be possible that some operators might be or become insolvent, or otherwise judgment-proof, when the storage site activities result in injuries to third parties? Yes, it would be only reasonable to assume some operators might be insolvent or otherwise unavailable at that date. Might victims of offshore CCS injuries be unaware or have difficulties in properly identifying the source of their injuries?[74] Yes, that appears to be a potential problem given the environmental complexity of offshore CCS and the temporal range of risk exposure given the long-term storage of the CO_2. Might it be difficult to provide enforcement and enforce judgments?[75] Again, considering the unique aspects of offshore CCS and the long-term latency of its liabilities, yes, it is reasonable to foresee that regulations might well be a robust solution in these circumstances.

It is in precisely the above scenarios that rules and standards laid down in regulations are necessary to fill the governance void. Civil agencies could assist to collect disparately possessed aspects of relevant information from the offshore CCS activities to produce public reports that could rebalance the knowledge asymmetries.[76] That data set could then be used in direct governance of those offshore CCS activities by regulators, or it could be

68 See Shavell (1984), 357.
69 Shavell (1984), 357.
70 Shavell (1984), 357.
71 Shavell (1984), 357.
72 Klass & Wilson (2008), 159. See also Gerard & Wilson (2009), 1099.
73 Shavell (1984), 359.
74 See Shavell (1984), 363 and Landes & Posner (1984), 417.
75 Hylton (2001), 529.
76 Hylton (2008), 156.

shared with private litigants at risk from CCS-related injuries, to improve the function of civil liability. Regulators could act to intervene in risky behavior demonstrated by offshore operators prior to the onset of insolvency, or could engage in punitive measures that retain their efficacy against an insolvent tortfeasor – if caught in the present time, operators could face loss of license or prison time, thus obviating the problem of insolvency.[77] Regulators could ensure that violations of offshore CCS standards result in detection of transgressions, the carriage of enforcement, and the surety of enforced judgments, as regulators can be provided with budgets, time, and powers not routinely available to individual members of the general public.[78]

Indeed, the very circumstances of offshore CCS operations – that they are very technologically complex, that they occur remote and are obscured from potential victims, and that the costs of addressing these issues is substantial and beyond individualized perspectives – bears witness to the argument that public regulations could enable more robust governance than merely the use of rules of civil liability.

3.2 Potential Problems of Pure Public Regulatory Frameworks

However, while it is clear that regulations will often be a robust governance strategy, there are foreseeable scenarios within which public regulations could fall short of optimality. In such conditions, private regulation or even self-governance might be more robust. This section explores these governance concepts.

Public regulations could fail to be robust under certain circumstances. First, public regulation has historically tended to focus on avoiding or punishing "bad acts" instead of focusing on optimal pathways. To focus on "bad acts" is to address only half of the Calabresian maxim to reduce the net costs of injuries and the social costs of avoiding the injuries, and this incomplete approach results in inefficient policy.[79] Generally, public regulations may not be able to capture all potential risks related to CCS.

Second, public regulation can also bear high administrative costs. These relate not only to the costs of drafting the standards in regulations, but also to the costs of monitoring and enforcement of those standards. The drafting costs could result from information asymmetries or problems of

---

77 Shavell (1986), 43.

78 Hylton (2001), 518–19.

79 There are many potential citations, but perhaps one of the pithiest is found in Calabresi (1975), 656: "*in terms of the goal of minimizing accident and accident prevention costs.* For short, I shall call this goal 'optimal deterrence [of accidents]'." [Italics in original text.]

information assembly – some problems require localized and/or specialized knowledge to solve them, which may lay beyond the grasp of the public regulator. There is hence a danger that the administrative costs of regulation would outweigh the benefits.

Third, public regulations generally entail the establishment of a jurisdiction-wide set of standards to be applied equally to all parties. However, the governance of risky activities is often best approached from a mode of decentralization, as different actors may possess different levels of technology or skill, which could affect the efficient paths to prevention and precaution for each. Thus, if each were allowed to pursue their own unique yet efficient options for safety, then the resultant net social welfare would be greater.[80] Application of a general rule would deny each their most efficient strategy and also likely result in greater injuries and thus reduced welfare.[81]

Fourth, the generation of standards via public regulation can engage many diverse subsets of the public, as well as experts and civil servants. But that is in itself a process of high transaction costs, and given limited budgets, limited manpower, and the competition from other regulatory goals and needs, it is a process that usually is undertaken infrequently or intermittently.[82] Also, we have so far assumed that regulation would always be drafted in the public interest. However, efforts to draft regulations can become entangled in lobbying efforts or lobby capture. Private interest may hence dictate the contents of regulations. Thus, public regulations tend to become ossified or "sticky"; the result is inflexible standards that do not continue to be efficient as circumstances continue to evolve and change.[83]

Given the above four concerns, if they were to manifest themselves, then purely public regulation of offshore CCS activities could fail to render efficient incentives on precaution and prevention, and thus fail to achieve robust policy results. That is not to say that public regulation should not be undertaken, but rather that it might need buttressing and reinforcement under certain circumstances to attain more robust results.

There are reasons for worrying that purely public regulation might not be sufficient for China's CCS governance strategy. There have yet been few occurrences of "bad acts" in the CCS industry as it is still in its infancy; however, historical experiences from subterranean methane storage and of well blow-outs from both methane wells and carbon dioxide wells have

---

80 Glachant (1998), 182.
81 See Faure (2012), 281.
82 See Shavell (1976).
83 See Arthur (1989), 116.

elucidated what might be foreseeable injuries from such bad acts, and as such, regulators will be seeking to contain the risks from those specific harms.

Second, given the sophisticated technological character of offshore CCS operations, it is foreseeable that knowledge asymmetries are likely to be present, at least in the early years of the industry. Knowledge from experience must be accumulated, raw scientific learning will need to be transmitted and conveyed in publications and at conferences, and it will take time to become certain of which scientific and engineering results are reliable and promotable as forms of "best practices." In the interim, regulators and other public bodies may find it challenging to keep up with those operators and researchers close to the field activities.

Third, CCS is a technology built on a mountain of patents, in alignment with the broader upstream energy industry. Each operator will bring unique technologies to its storage operations; patents both protect and exclude the use of technologies, and as such, each operator may be facing technologically distinguishable safety agendas. In that foreseeable scenario, common public regulation would deny each operator its own efficient pathway to optimal safety decisions.

And finally, given the broad range of stakeholders facing the development of offshore CCS facilities, there would be many foreseeable scenarios wherein regulators and the drafting of regulations might be exposed to substantial risks of lobby capture. Thus, given the complex circumstances of offshore CCS facilities, optimal governance may require a toolset beyond the traditional public regulatory approach.

3.3 On Private Regulatory Efforts and Self-Governance

Private regulation is the mechanism wherein one private party agrees to be monitored and policed by a second private party. Private regulation can operate in the absence of public regulation or in a complementary space to public regulation. Its argument of efficiency is predicated on the assumption that those actors closest to the generation of materially relevant information on the risky activity, and thus those with the lowest costs of acquiring that information, might be the most efficient setters of standards for that risky activity.[84] And legally, the state itself could enable or support that private governance function.[85]

This could be the relationship of a public corporation accepting the

[84] Ogus (2010), *passim*.
[85] Ogus & Carbonara (2012), 232.

financial audit results of a public accounting agency, for example Coca-Cola accepting the audit results of PwC, or in the relationship of joint investors who designate one investor as project operator of full surveillance of the other investors, as is routine in Joint Operating Agreements (JOAs) in the energy sector.[86] Another common instance of such arrangements is found in the insurance markets, where the insured party agrees to monitor and circumscribe its behavior in order to obtain favorable insurance rates and premiums.[87] All of these examples demonstrate the potential for private parties to establish and enforce forms of private regulation amongst themselves.

There are specific scenarios wherein private regulation might be more robust than public regulations. First, when a high degree of uncertainty remains regarding the means to efficiently achieve precautionary and preventative goals, then private actors close to the activity may learn more quickly than public regulators and may be capable of reacting more quickly to newly obtained information and to adjust and update standards accordingly.[88] Second, when an industry is undergoing rapid knowledge acquisition and regulations need to be adjusted quickly and efficiently, then private regulation may enable those actors closest to the cutting edge of developments to update and adjust the standards in a more efficient manner.[89] Third, when there is a possibility that public regulation may be subject to forces of corruption or coercion, private regulatory efforts may then be more efficient.[90] Fourth, when the interests of the risk-taker and the adjacent communities are aligned, then private regulation may be robust.[91] Fifth, the transaction costs of private regulation are generally observed to be lower than those of public regulations. Private industrial actors may be able to organize quickly and with fewer impediments of bureaucracy;[92] as such, the costs of adapting to technological changes would be expected to be lower for private regulatory efforts.[93]

Given that offshore CCS is a nascent technology and that it will remain in a state of rapid technological advancement in the immediate future,

---

[86] Gunningham et al. (1999), 214 and 216.

[87] Gunningham et al. (1999), 217.

[88] Ogus & Carbonara (2012), 234, citing Grajzl & Murrell (2007).

[89] Miller (1984). See also Ogus (1995), 98.

[90] Ogus & Carbonara (2012), 235, citing Glaeser & Schleifer (2003), and to Nunez (2010).

[91] Ogus & Carbonara (2012), 234, citing Grajzl & Murrell (2007).

[92] See Miller (1984). But take note: this is not to say that large industrial actors have no internal bureaucracies, more that such actors retain sufficient autonomy of action to be able to bypass those problems when profitable.

[93] Van den Bergh (2008), 794.

standards will need to be updated on a quick and routine basis, contrary to the mode of public regulations. Also, translating the privately obtained data into publicly discoursed data for developing public regulations could lose critical time and delay the roll-out of improved regulations; thus private regulation of offshore CCS might be the more robust option. Further, the economics of large financial projects and the human temptations of public regulators have often been a concern for regulatory efficacy; this is no less the case for large environmental projects such as China's potential offshore CCS sites. Yet private insurance companies or non-operator joint investors may have sufficient clout and capital to more effectively resist or prevent such distortion and to impose robust private regulations on CCS operators.[94] It is less clear that the interests of offshore CCS operators and adjacent communities will be well aligned, but as Dan Farber recently suggested, perhaps such operators could be required to live in those communities and thus reinforce those incentives, and in such a case, perhaps the operator may indeed self-regulate to prevent harm to itself and thus protect the community at the same time.[95] And finally, it is foreseeable that the industrial group of operators, their insurers, and other vested parties may well be able to cost-effectively and rapidly develop and advance private regulations that may exceed the efforts of public regulators to design efficient standards for offshore CCS operations.

Thus, given the reasons presented above, it would be robust for China to pursue the benefits of private and self-regulation in the advancement of its CCS policy development.

3.4 Conclusion – Use Both Public and Private Regulation in Coordination

It has been demonstrated that both public and private means of regulation could be effectively brought to bear on the development of China's offshore CCS strategies. Obviously the operators involved in CCS may, within the particular Chinese context, often be (wholly or partially) state-owned. In that sense one could hold that the distinction between public and private regulation becomes blurred. However, when referring to private regulation, we not only target regulation by and from operators, but also from international (standardization) organizations or international agencies.[96] And as the implementation of private regulation need not preclude the

---

[94] For more information on the role of insurers as private regulators, see Ben-Shahar & Logue (2012).

[95] Farber (2015).

[96] These existing private regulatory frameworks will be further discussed in section 5.

operation of public regulation, and as private regulation can be leveraged to improve on the performance of public regulation, it is suggested that China pursues a governance strategy that jointly implements both public and private means of regulation over offshore CCS activities.

In the following section it will be shown that while there are multiple public regulatory frameworks for CCS for China's regulators to build upon, private regulatory frameworks remain few and mostly works-in-progress. However, pathways for China to advance the potential of private regulation of OCCS will be discussed. Thus it is foreseeable that China could readily benefit from the efficient implementation and integration of public and private regulation of OCCS activities.

4. EXISTING PUBLIC REGULATORY FRAMEWORKS FOR OCCS

An efficient regulator might like to ask whether there are pre-existing regulations for offshore CCS activities that could be used as models. And, yes, there are existing offshore CCS regulations and models of CCS offshore regulations to draw from.

There are multiple instances of public regulatory frameworks that govern a variety of concerns related to OCCS activities. It would appear that there are several tiers of such regulations, depending on the amount of discretion, or subsidiarity, left to lower bodies or states to provide more locally fitted regulatory content. For the purposes of this chapter, they are entitled Tier I, Tier II, Tier III, and Tier IV approaches to public regulatory frameworks, as they move from more centralized and unified to decentralized and incomplete.

4.1 Tier I Regulatory Frameworks

Tier I represents regulatory frameworks that are unilateral and singular within a domestic setting. Specific domestic enactments, as presented in the UK and in Norway, are examples of those framework types.

The Petroleum Act of 1998 provides for the governance of submarine pipelines and of the oil and gas industry within the UK;[97] as such it is closely related to the regulation of OCCS.[98] The Petroleum Act enables

---

[97] Milligan (2014), 167.

[98] Of particular note, the regulation of OCCS *sans* EOR-related activities is governed under the Energy Act 2008, but EOR-related CCS (and OCCS)

the Department of Energy and Climate Change (DECC) to issue licenses for offshore enhanced oil recovery (EOR)-related CO_2 injection projects.[99]

The Climate Change Act of 2008 "sought to tie in present and future UK governments into legally binding emission targets."[100] These commitments are to be met with the implementation of 5-year carbon budgets.[101] The Act also formally introduced the Committee on Climate Change (CCC); the CCC was created as an independent body to advise the government on desirable carbon budget goals and cost-effective means of attaining those goals.[102] As a part of these goals, the UK planned to budget £1 billion for the development of commercially deployable OCCS by the 2020s.[103]

The UK enacted the Energy Act of 2008, to provide for licensing of CCS activities, which was subsequently updated by the Carbon Dioxide (Licensing) Regulations 2010 and the Carbon Dioxide (Closure of Licensing) Regulations 2011.[104] The Energy Act of 2008 enables the regulation of OCCS within the UK's territorial seas and within its Gas Importation and Storage Zone.[105] Depending on the zone concerned, the operating licenses can be obtained from either the Secretary of State for the DECC or from the Scottish Ministers, as appropriate.[106] These authorities are authorized by the Act to issue regulations on OCCS and related matters.[107] Both have issued regulations on OCCS;[108] these

---

would be governed by the Petroleum Act, in coordination: Milligan (2014), 166–7.

99 Milligan (2014), 168.

100 Lee (2009), 141.

101 Lee (2009), 141.

102 Lee (2009), 142.

103 Milligan (2014), 162. That "billion" is understood in the American sense of a billion, £1,000,000,000.

104 See Havercroft & Macrory (2014), 11. In turn, it is worth noting that the UK system was guided by the developments under the London Protocol and OSPAR. See Milligan (2014), 165.

105 Milligan (2014), 166.

106 Milligan (2014), 166 and 168. In addition, the Crown Estate Commissioners may grant leases for certain OCCS projects under the Energy Act. Milligan (2014), 168.

107 Milligan (2014), 166.

108 Milligan (2014), 166. UK regulations, excepting those covering Scotland, include The Storage of Carbon Dioxide (Licensing) Regulations 2010, The Storage of Carbon Dioxide (Termination of Licenses) Regulations 2011, The Storage of Carbon Dioxide (Licensing) Regulations 2011, The Storage of Carbon Dioxide (Amendment of the Energy Act 2008) Regulations 2011, The Storage of Carbon Dioxide (Access to Infrastructure) Regulations 2011, and The Storage of Carbon Dioxide (Inspections) Regulations 2012. Milligan (2014), 166 at footnotes 64, 65, 66, 67, and 71. The Scottish regulations are The Environmental Liability

regulations conform with the regulatory requirements set out by the EU CCS Directive.[109]

The Norwegian approach is primarily intended to amend two pre-existing regulatory regimes already regulating offshore oil and gas activities.[110] Norway has chosen to extend its existing petroleum regime to include CCS activities, as opposed to creating a separate CCS-specific tranche of regulations.[111] The bulk of CCS transportation and monitoring activities are regulated under the Petroleum Act and its affiliated regulations.[112] The Pollution Control Act and its regulations oversee allowing CO_2 injection activities and the composition requirements for the fluidized CO_2 stream.[113] Were greenfield sites to be sought for offshore CCS, in lieu of brownfield depleted petroleum reserves, then the Norwegian Ministry of Petroleum and Energy has advised that new legislation would be required to enable that activity.[114]

The Japanese have pursued a similar approach to Norway, except that instead of relying on a non-existent petroleum regime, Japan expanded its Marine Pollution Prevention Act to enable the regulation of OCCS activities, as overseen by the Japanese Ministry of the Environment.[115]

4.2 Tier II Regulatory Frameworks

Tier II represents regulatory frameworks that, while legally binding on other states or units, are binding primarily in a guiding and standard-setting sense. To better provide carbon sinks and to reduce greenhouse gas emissions under the Kyoto Protocol, and with the evolution of the London Protocol and the Convention for the Protection of the Marine Environment of the North-East Atlantic (OSPAR) to address CCS activities, the EU adopted its Directive on the Geological Storage of Carbon Dioxide ("CCS Directive").[116] The CCS Directive provides

---

Amendment Regulations (2011) and The Energy Act 2008 (Storage of Carbon Dioxide) Regulations (2011). Milligan (2014), 166 at footnotes 69 and 70.

109 Milligan (2014), 166–7.

110 Gravdahl Agerup (2014), 2 and 5.

111 Gravdahl Agerup (2014), 5.

112 Gravdahl Agerup (2014), 5.

113 Gravdahl Agerup (2014), 5.

114 Gravdahl Agerup (2014), 7.

115 Stanley & McCoy (2014), 6 and 7.

116 Directive 2009/31/EC of the European Parliament and of the Council of April 23, 2009 on the geological storage of carbon dioxide and amending Council Directive 85/337/EEC, European Parliament and Council Directives 2000/60/EC, 2001/80/EC, 2004/35/EC, 2006/12/EC, 2008/1/EC and Regulation (EC) No

binding guidance to EU Member States on how they need to implement their own domestic regulations on CCS activities, yet leaves each Member State some flexibility in the means and measures undertaken to achieve compliance with the CCS Directive.

The CCS Directive closely coordinates with the requirements of Decision 10/CMP.7. Recall that this is the Decision that details under which particular conditions certain CCS projects can be included within the Clean Development Mechanism (CDM).[117] The Directive addresses the selection of storage sites and exploration permits.[118] The Directive does not explicitly address property rights; it does, however, address the need for exclusivity of storage permits to exclude other actors and other activities from the storage zones. Moreover, public access to the registry of those permits must be provided.[119] As for liability, remedies, and redress of injuries, the Directive provides for both pre- and post-closure time periods.[120] Additionally, the Directive requires that financial security and financial mechanisms are set up to provide capital for the previously discussed liability, remedies, and redress of injuries.[121]

Thus, broadly speaking, the CCS Directive provides ample governance to fulfill the requirements of Decision 10/CMP.7 whilst retaining substantial subsidiarity for local regulations to provide additional regulatory details.

4.3 Tier III Regulatory Frameworks

Tier III represents governmental policy without binding effect to coordinate or standardize localized regulatory efforts. This is often followed by enactment of specific regulations.

The Australian Regulatory Guiding Principles for Carbon Dioxide and Geological Storage are an instance of this type of framework.[122] The Guiding Principles led to the adoption of the federal Offshore Petroleum

---

1013/2006; OJ L 140, June 5, 2009, 114–135 [hereinafter CCS Directive]. For reference to the need for reduced emissions and additional sinks, see CCS Directive, Prolog (1), (4), and (5). For reference to the activities updating the London Protocol and the OSPAR Convention, see CCS Directive, Prolog (13) and (14), respectively. See also CCS Directive, Ch. 1, Art. 1, Sec. 1.

117 See section 2.2.

118 CCS Directive, Arts 4, 5, and 6, and in greater detail at Annex I.

119 CCS Directive, Arts 6, 8, 9, and 25.

120 CCS Directive, Art. 9, Sec. 6, 7, and 9; at Art. 16; at Art. 17, Sec. 2, and at Art. 18.

121 CCS Directive, Arts 19 and 20.

122 Ministerial Council on Mineral and Petroleum Resources (MCMPR), (2005).

Amendment (Greenhouse Gas Storage) Act of 2008 for Australian federal waters. Also, the State of Victoria was able to build on the Guidelines to develop its Victorian Greenhouse Gas Geological Sequestration Act 2008 (No. 61 of 2008), which was followed by the Offshore Petroleum and Greenhouse Gas Storage Act (2010). Secondary regulations have built on these statutes: namely the Greenhouse Gas Geological Sequestration Regulations 2009 and the Offshore Petroleum and Greenhouse Gas Storage Regulations 2011.[123]

Similarly, the Interstate Oil & Gas Compact Commission, which includes both American and Canadian member states, has provided model statutes and model general rules and regulations for its member states to use as a template in the development of their own CCS regulatory efforts. These models have, to differing extents and in alternative forms, been adopted in Alberta, British Columbia, California, Indiana, Michigan, Montana, New Mexico, New York, North Dakota, Nova Scotia, Oklahoma, Saskatchewan, and Texas. [124]

4.4 Tier IV Regulatory Frameworks

Tier IV represents incomplete or fragmentary regulatory structures. The United States remains without official CCS regulatory guidance at the federal level, except for specific regulations on the function and impact of injection wells to affect underground water quality; most other regulatory measures have been left to the local states to address. Similarly, the London Protocol, within its 2012 Specific Guidelines for the Assessment of Carbon Dioxide for Disposal into Sub-Seabed Geological Formations, provides regulatory guidance on the types of suitable injectant fluids, on suitable storage sites, and on other closely related environmental assessment measures, but lacks any reference to liability governance or on remedies and compensation for injuries, amongst other missing topics. These Tier IV frameworks are reviewed below.

4.4.1 London Convention, Protocol, and Annex I

The 1972 Convention on the Prevention of Marine Pollution by Dumping of Wastes (London Convention) was originally drafted to better enable the protection of the ocean from the dumping of wastes at sea.[125] Changes in time and technology, and an effort to update the

---

[123] See Havercroft & Macrory (2014), 9 to 10.
[124] See Interstate Oil & Gas Compact Commission (2008).
[125] Lee (2009), 137.

Convention, are reflected in the development of the London Protocol, which expands and modernizes the original Convention.[126] One of the most important differences between the two agreements is that while the Convention was primarily limited to activities "at sea," the Protocol has been expanded to include activities at sea, on the seabed, and underneath in the sub-seabed and subsoils.[127] Additionally, the Convention originally targeted the elimination of waste dumping at sea, whereas the Protocol takes a precautionary approach to the elimination of pollution more generally.[128]

The London Convention prohibits the dumping of "wastes and other matters" at sea.[129] "Dumping" is defined under the Convention to include "any deliberate disposal at sea of wastes or other matter from vessels, aircraft, platforms, or other man-made structures at sea."[130]

However, the linguistic focus of the Convention is "at sea" and not in the earth or geological zones thereunder.[131] Also, to the extent that "disposal" is associated with the extraction of crude oil, natural gas, or other offshore minerals, then the Convention does not apply.[132] Thus, Norway's OCCS experiment at Sleipner, which is associated with hydrocarbon recovery, was deemed not to be affected by the disposal and waste rules of the Convention.[133]

The Convention currently has 152 Contracting States.[134] These Contracting States represent "99.20% of the gross tonnage of the world's merchant fleet." [135] Thus, the London Convention carries much gravitas in international law.

The 1996 Protocol defined dumping as "any storage of wastes or other

---

[126] Lee (2009), 137.

[127] Lee (2009), 137–8.

[128] Purdy (2006), 24.

[129] Weeks (2007), 257. Annex I to the Convention provides a listing of the recognized "wastes and other matters." Weeks (2007), 257. There is also a list of materials that may be disposed of at sea within Annex II. Weeks (2007), 257.

[130] 1972 Convention on the Prevention of Marine Pollution by Dumping of Wastes and Other Matter, 1046 UNTS 120; ATS 1985 No 16; 11 ILM 1294 [hereinafter London Convention], Art. III.1(a)(i). Weeks (2007), 258.

[131] Weeks (2007), 258.

[132] London Convention, Art. III.1(c). Weeks (2007), 258.

[133] Weeks (2007), 258.

[134] IMO, Status of Multilateral Conventions and Instruments in Respect of which the International Maritime Organization or its Secretary-General Performs Depositary or Other Functions (International Maritime Organization (April 10, 2015), 105 [hereinafter IMO 2015].

[135] IMO 2015.

matter in the seabed or subsoil thereof from vessels, aircraft, platforms, or other man-made structures at sea."[136] And as Milligan pointed out, "'wastes and other matter' are broadly defined as 'material and substance of any kind, form, or description'."[137] The Protocol therefore generally forbids the dumping of wastes at sea, on the seabed, or in the subsoil of the seabed.[138] Thus, if CO_2 were considered "other matter" and if it were to be placed in or under the seabed per the technology design of OCCS, then it might be characterized as "dumping" and thus potentially prohibited under the Protocol. Additionally, the Protocol requires the application of a "precautionary approach to environmental protection from dumping of wastes."[139]

However, the Protocol does contain an Annex I, which enables certain items to be excluded from consideration as "waste or other matter."[140] If certain items are permitted under the conditions established within Annex II, then those items can be stored at sea, on the seabed, or in the subsoil of the seabed.[141]

As of November 2006, Annex I was amended to enable the sequestration of CO_2.[142] When CO_2, not mixed with other wastes, is injected into sub-seabed geological formations, then those volumes of CO_2 are excluded from consideration as waste.[143]

> Carbon dioxide streams referred to in paragraph 1.8 may only be considered for dumping, if:
> (1) disposal is into a sub-seabed geological formation; and
> (2) they consist overwhelmingly of carbon dioxide. They may contain incidental associated substances derived from the source material and the capture and sequestration processes used; and
> (3) no wastes or other matter are added for the purpose of disposing of those wastes or other matter.[144]

It is important to note that the modifications for the enabling of OCCS projects did nothing to lessen the precautionary requirements otherwise generally applying to the whole of the Protocol.[145]

---

136 Milligan (2014), 164; citing London Protocol Art. 1(4.1)(3).
137 Milligan (2014), 164; citing London Protocol Art. 1(8).
138 Milligan (2014), 164.
139 Weeks (2007), 259.
140 Milligan (2014), 164.
141 Milligan (2014), 164.
142 Milligan (2014), 164–5.
143 Lee (2009), 138; Milligan (2014), 164–5; Weeks (2007), 260.
144 Protocol Amendment, Annex I. See also Weeks (2007), 260–61.
145 Weeks (2007), 261.

Officially, 80 countries are current Contracting States to the Protocol, but five countries with strong interests in OCCS remain only Signatories.[146] As of April 10, 2015, the United States[147] and the Nordic countries of Denmark, Finland, Norway, and Sweden remained only Signatories to the Protocol.[148] Nevertheless, as even the US has adopted domestic laws strongly in alignment with the Protocol, the majority of the world's merchant fleets are governed under the Protocol and its norms as extensions of the previous Convention.[149] Thus, under certain conditions the offshore sequestration of CO_2 in most countries with potential OCCS needs would be regulated under the London Protocol and the London Convention.

4.4.2 OSPAR on OCCS

The 1992 Convention for the Protection of the Marine Environment of the North-East Atlantic (OSPAR) protects the "maritime area," which includes the water column, the seabed, and the sub-seabed and subsoils.[150]

OSPAR has recognized the dangers of ocean acidification and of the chemical impacts on oceanic waters from excess amounts of atmospheric CO_2.[151] OSPAR requires that all parties "take all possible

---

[146] IMO 2015, 158.

[147] The US is listed both as a Signatory and as a Contracting State. IMO 2015, "Status of Multilateral Conventions," at 158 and 159, respectively. The United States was once expected to become a Contracting Party, and for that reason it is listed as one "subject to ratification." However, that did not and has not occurred. The US's National Oceanic and Atmospheric Administration (NOAA) provides the history: "*The United States participated extensively in the Protocol's development and signed the Protocol on March 31, 1998.* The Protocol was submitted to the Senate for its advice and consent to ratification on September 4, 2007. Subsequently, *the Senate Foreign Relations Committee favorably reported the Protocol* with one understanding and two declarations, and as set forth in a report dated September 11, 2008, *recommended the full Senate give its consent to ratification. That has yet to happen.* The Bush Administration submitted proposed implementing legislation along with a section-by-section analysis in 2007. No action was taken on the proposed legislation during the 110th Congress." NOAA, "Marine Pollution: Ocean Dumping." (Italics added.) Available at http://www.gc.noaa.gov/gcil_mp_ocean_dumping.html.

[148] IMO 2015, 158.

[149] The reported number is "95.23% of the gross tonnage of the world's merchant fleet." IMO 2015, 159.

[150] Lee (2009), 138; Milligan (2014), 165.

[151] Lee (2009), 138. See OSPAR Commission (2006). Available at http://www.ospar.org/documents?v=7049.

steps to prevent or eliminate pollution."[152] Similarly, OSPAR requires all parties to "conserve the marine ecosystems" by taking the necessary actions and measures against anthropogenic threats to those ecosystems.[153] Thus, under OSPAR, if the implementation of OCCS could be characterized as a possible step or measure that could reduce the anthropogenic threats to the oceans posed by increased levels of atmospheric CO_2, then there might be an obligation to implement OCCS.

Originally, in parallel to the UNCLOS frameworks, OSPAR allowed CO_2 injection *if and only if* those OCCS activities were in co-implementation with oil or gas extraction activities.[154] In 2004 OSPAR was extended and clarified to allow for the subterranean sequestration of CO_2 in maritime areas.[155] In 2007 OSPAR amended Annexes II and III to the Convention to enable the development of OCCS so long as the storage was in geological formations.[156] A key requirement is that the injected CO_2 fluids be placed in sub-soil geological formations for permanent sequestration while simultaneously presenting no significant adverse risks to human life or health or to the environment.[157] Thus, OCCS would be allowed under the amendment, but other forms of marine sequestration, such as water-column placement or sea fertilization, are not endorsed by the amendment.

OSPAR has provided guidelines for the management of the risks from OCCS projects.[158] First, there are dual requirements that permitting procedures should (1) "ensure the avoidance of significant adverse effects on the marine environment," and (2) target the "permanent containment of CO_2 streams in geological formations."[159] Further, within the Decision

---

152 Milligan (2014), 165. 1992 Convention for the Protection of the Marine Environment of the North-East Atlantic, 2354 UNTS 67; 32 ILM 1069 (1993) [hereinafter OSPAR], Art. 2(1)(a).

153 Milligan (2014), 165. OSPAR Art. 2(1)(a).

154 Lee (2009), 138.

155 Lee (2009), 138.

156 Milligan (2014), 165. OSPAR Decision 2007/1 to Prohibit the Storage of Carbon Dioxide Streams in the Water Column or on the Sea-bed (June 25–29, 2007) [hereinafter OSPAR Decision 2007/1].

157 Milligan (2014), 165, citing OSPAR Art. 3(2)(f)(iv).

158 Lee (2009), 138. OSPAR Decision 2007/2 on the Storage of Carbon Dioxide Streams in Geological Formations (June 25–29, 2007) [hereinafter OSPAR Decision 2007/2], sec. 3.1. "Any authorisation or regulation shall be in accordance with the *OSPAR Guidelines for Risk Assessment and Management of Storage of CO_2 Streams in Geological Formations*, as updated from time to time." (Italics added.)

159 OSPAR Decision 2007/2, sec. 3.2.

itself, there is a listing of requirements that any regulatory framework should address:

1. "a description of the operation, including injection rates";[160]
2. "the planned types, amounts and sources of the CO_2 streams, including incidental associated substances, to be stored in the geological formation"; [161]
3. "the location of the injection facility"; [162]
4. "characteristics of the geological formations";[163]
5. "the methods of transport of the CO_2 stream";[164]
6. "a risk management plan that includes:
   a. monitoring and reporting requirements;
   b. mitigation and remediation options *including* the pre-closure phases; and
   c. a requirement for a site closure plan, including a description of post-closure monitoring and mitigation and remediation options; monitoring shall continue until there is confirmation that the probability of any future adverse environmental effects has been reduced to an insignificant level."[165]

Not all carbon sequestration would relieve and protect the ocean, as OSPAR has also decided to prohibit water-column-based carbon sequestration technologies:[166]

> The placement of carbon dioxide streams in the water column or on the seabed is prohibited, unless it results from normal operations as described in Article 1(g)(i) of the Convention or is for a purpose other than the mere disposal thereof as described in Article 1(g)(ii) of the Convention and is in accordance with the relevant provisions of the Convention.[167]

This was primarily because:

> [C]arbon dioxide storage in the water column or on the sea-bed is not a sustainable storage option, is likely to result in harm to living resources and marine

[160] OSPAR Decision 2007/2, sec. 3.2(1).
[161] OSPAR Decision 2007/2, sec. 3.2(2).
[162] OSPAR Decision 2007/2, sec. 3.2(3).
[163] OSPAR Decision 2007/2, sec. 3.2(4).
[164] OSPAR Decision 2007/2, sec. 3.2(5).
[165] OSPAR Decision 2007/2, sec. 3.2(6).
[166] OSPAR Decision 2007/1.
[167] OSPAR Decision 2007/1.

> ecosystems and is thus neither a viable solution with regard to mitigating climate change nor compatible with the aims of the Convention.[168]

Thus, not unlike the London Convention and Protocol, OSPAR has evolved over time to allow and to regulate offshore CCS activities. While the London Convention and Protocol focused on vessel-related activities, OSPAR takes its paradigmatic perspective from oceanic and marine protection. The conventions operate in a complementary sense, and potentially suggest a means for tracking two simultaneous but coordinated frameworks, that of guiding and guarding the activity of human operators and that of protecting and stewarding oceanic ecologies.

5. EXISTING PRIVATE REGULATORY FRAMEWORKS FOR OCCS

In contrast to the various examples of public regulatory frameworks for CCS activities, there are few private models. The two leading models are the International Organization for Standardization (ISO) draft standards for CCS activities (section 5.1) and the International Energy Agency (IEA)'s Model Framework (section 5.2).

Both sets of standards are intended as models, rather than as any form of public regulation or any form of agreed-to regulation under private contract. But they both provide insight into how such standards could emerge, and do provide models that private parties could adopt or implement via private contract. For example, China could require, via public regulation, that insurance companies providing policies to CCS operators ensure that the operators are in compliance with the norms detailed within either set of standards.

5.1 ISO Technical Committee 265 on CCS Standards

In 2011 the ISO created a Technical Committee charged with setting a range of technical standards for the advancement of the CCS industry.[169] There are currently over a dozen CCS standards in development within the Committee.[170] For CCS facilities, the draft standards include a wide array of topics central to OCCS activities:

---

168 OSPAR Decision 2007/1.

169 Global CCS Institute (2013).

170 See ISO (undated a), "Standards and projects under the direct responsibility of ISO/TC 265 Secretariat."

> onshore, offshore, storage in depleted hydrocarbon reservoirs, saline aquifers, other storage options, site selection, site characterisation, risk assessment, risk management (including consequences of monitoring results), wells (requirements for new wells and long-term safety of old wells), procedures and conditions for closure, storage leakage avoidance and remediation, post-closure requirements, storage monitoring, equipment and materials, composition and concentration of CO_2 streams, and HSE.[171]

What must be emphasized for the purposes of China's potential to integrate private regulations into its own regulatory framework, is that China is already a leading presence on the drafting of this set of CCS standards as Co-Secretary to the Committee.[172] Meetings of the Committee have been held in Beijing, on the Beijing campus of the China University of Petroleum.[173] Thus, in this case, not only could China adopt these private standards, but it could also play a leading role in setting such standards.

5.2 IEA Model Regulatory Framework

The International Energy Agency (IEA) published its Model Regulatory Framework for CCS activities in 2010.[174] The Framework provides both model language and in-depth explanations of the need for and purpose(s) of each section of the Framework.

Site selection for storage sites is addressed at § 6.4. The Framework not only provides model text language, but also provides a listing of technical concerns that would need a review akin to an environmental impact assessment.[175] Property right issues related to CCS activities are addressed at § 3.2. The Framework details a range of rights issues from immovable property assignments in the stored gas, of surface infrastructure, of the ownership of the sub-surface pore space, and of the associated intellectual property rights necessary to operate the technology involved in CCS activities.[176] Liability and compensation concerns are addressed in several parts of the Framework. Corrective and remediation measures are addressed in § 6.8, operator's liability prior to closure in § 6.10, and the

171 Global CCS Institute (2013).

172 See ISO (undated b), "ISO/TC 265 Carbon Dioxide Capture, Transportation, and Geological Storage."

173 See ANSI News and Publications (2013).

174 IEA (2010).

175 IEA (2010), 70 and 72.

176 IEA (2010), 26, 27, and 28.

transfer of post-closure liabilities in § 6.11.[177] As the Framework covers the requirements of Decision 10/CMP.7 as well as many other relevant regulatory concerns for CCS activities, it is a strong model for China to recommend to private parties for adoption.

6. SUMMARY AND CONCLUSIONS

China has multiple goals: to strengthen and grow its economy whilst simultaneously reducing greenhouse gas emissions. While green energy technologies are emerging, and China is a leading actor in that field, the urgency to contain carbon emissions presses for a near-term means to eliminate and prevent emissions.

One of the primary methods to achieve the goal of reducing greenhouse gas emissions from fossil fuel-combusting plants is the cluster of technologies called carbon capture and storage. But CCS faces a variety of complex legal issues, from environmental to financial concerns. China needs to develop a regulatory framework that could address a broad range of CCS-related concerns. Additionally, China could benefit from certain financial opportunities if its CCS projects could be coordinated with the CDM under the Kyoto Protocol.

We argue that China could efficiently draft CCS regulations that jointly implement both public and private regulations. A range of public regulatory models were evaluated and then categorized into four classes of regulations based on differing levels of vertical control and grants of subsidiarity to local governmental units. Non-governmental agencies were found to be drafting private standards to address a range of activities and legal issues related to CCS activities. In addition, it was found that China is already well engaged in international efforts to draft non-governmental standards.

Therefore, China is already well positioned to make efficient use of both public and private regulations to govern offshore CCS activities. Further, as many of the public and private regulatory frameworks evaluated were found to sufficiently address the regulatory requirements of Decision 10/CMP.7, China's use of those regulatory frameworks would facilitate the enabling of CDM financing tools for Chinese OCCS projects. In addition, we equally held that regulation, both public and private, may have its limits in fully capturing the risks related to CCS. For that reason, private enforcement, more particularly through

---

177 IEA (2010), 89, 91, and at 100, respectively.

liability rules, may remain an important supplementary tool for providing additional incentives for prevention of accidents – for example, where regulation may have become outdated or is inefficient as a result of regulatory capture. However, for private enforcement and liability rules to be able to play this supplementary role effectively, important steps in improving the functioning of the courts within China still have to be taken.

REFERENCES

Adelman, D.A. and I.J. Duncan (2011), "The Limits of Liability in Promoting Safe Geologic Sequestration of CO_2," 22 *Duke Environmental Law & Policy Forum* 1.

ANSI News and Publications (2013), "ISO TC 265 Establishes Working Group on Carbon Dioxide Storage through Enhanced Oil Recovery," December 12. Available at https://www.ansi.org/news_publications/news_story.aspx?menuid=7&articleid=3587e363-e401-4557-b7bd-17d7e1ad50a6.

Arthur, W.B. (1989), "Competing Technologies, Increasing Returns, and Lock-In by Historical Events," 99 *Economic Journal* 116.

Ben-Shahar, O. and K.D. Logue (2012), "Outsourcing Regulation: How Insurance Reduces Moral Hazard," 111 *Michigan Law Review* 197.

Bergkamp, L. (2000), "The Proper Scope of Joint and Several Liability," 6 *Tijdschrift voor Milieuaansprakelijkheid* 154.

Calabresi, Guido (1975), "Optimal Deterrence and Accidents: To Fleming James, Jr.," Faculty Scholarship Series, Paper 1981.

Convention on the Prevention of Marine Pollution by Dumping of Wastes and Other Matter of 1972, 1046 UNTS 120; ATS 1985 No 16; 11 ILM 1294 (London Convention).

Convention for the Protection of the Marine Environment of the North-East Atlantic of 1992, 2354 UNTS 67; 32 ILM 1069 (1993) (OSPAR).

Dahowski, R.T., X. Li, C.L. Davidson, N. Wei, J.J. Dooley and R.H. Gentile (2009), "A Preliminary Cost Curve Assessment of Carbon Capture and Storage Potential in China," 1 *Energy Procedia* 2849.

Decision 10/CMP.7: Modalities and procedures for carbon dioxide capture and storage in geological formations as clean development mechanism project activities. Available at http://unfccc.int/resource/docs/2011/cmp7/eng/10a02.pdf#page=13.

Directive 2009/31/EC of the European Parliament and of the Council of April 23, 2009 on the geological storage of carbon dioxide and amending Council Directive 85/337/EEC, European Parliament and Council Directives 2000/60/EC, 2001/80/EC, 2004/35/EC, 2006/12/EC, 2008/1/EC and Regulation (EC) No 1013/2006; OJ L 140, 5.6.2009.

Farber, Dan (2015), "Addressing Externalities: A Modest Proposal – How to Make Health and Safety a Personal Priority for Industry Officials," *Legal Planet*, University of California at Berkeley, October 19. Available at http://legal-planet.org/2015/10/19/addressing-externalities-a-modest-proposal/.

Faure, Michael G. (2012), "Designing Incentives Regulation for the Environment," in: *Global Environmental Commons: Analytical and Political Challenges in*

Building Governance Mechanisms (Eric Brousseau, Tom Dedeurwaerdere, Pierre-André Jouvet and Marc Willinger (eds), Oxford University Press).

Faure, Michael G. and Roy A. Partain (2017), *Carbon Capture and Storage: Efficient Legal Policies for Risk Governance and Compensation* (Boston, MA: MIT Press).

Faure, Michael G. and S.E. Weishaar (2012), "The role of environmental taxation: economics and the law," in: *Handbook of Research on Environmental Taxation*, 399 (Janet E. Milne and Mikael Skou Andersen (eds), Cheltenham: Edward Elgar).

Gerard, D. and E.J. Wilson (2009), "Environmental Bonds and the Challenge of Long-Term Carbon Sequestration," 90(2) *Journal of Environmental Management* 1097.

Glachant, M. (1998), "The Use of Regulatory Mechanism Design in Environmental Policy: A Theoretical Critique," in: *Sustainability and Firms: Technological Change and the Changing Regulatory Environment*, 179 (Sylvie Faucheux, John M. Gowdy and Isabelle Nicolai (eds), Cheltenham: Edward Elgar).

Glaeser, Edward L. and Andrei Shleifer (2003), "The Rise of the Regulatory State," 41(2) *Journal of Economic Literature* 401.

Global CCS Institute (2013), "Developing International Standards for CCS," March 4. Available at http://www.globalccsinstitute.com/insights/authors/markbonner/2013/03/04/developing-international-standards-ccs.

Grajzl, Peter and Peter Murrell (2007), "Allocating Lawmaking Powers: Self-Regulation vs Government Regulation," 35 *Journal of Comparative Economics* 520.

Gravdahl Agerup, Mette Karine, Assistant Director General (2014), "Norway: Legal and Regulatory CCS Framework," Norwegian Ministry of Petroleum and Energy, 6th IEA International CCS Regulatory Network Meeting.

Gunningham, N., M. Phillipson and P. Grabosky (1999), "Harnessing Third Parties as Surrogate Regulators, Achieving Environmental Outcomes by Alternative Means," 8 *Business Strategy and the Environment* 211.

Havercroft, Ian and Richard Macrory (2014), *Legal Liability and Carbon Capture and Storage: A Comparative Perspective* (Global CCS Institute, University College London: Faculty of Law).

House, Kurt Zenz, Daniel P. Schrag, Charles F. Harvey and Klaus S. Lackner (2006), "Permanent Carbon Dioxide Storage in Deep-Sea Sediments," 103(33) *Applied Physical Sciences* 12291.

Huang, Ying, Hong-Xu Guo, Cui-Ping Lao and Dai-Qing Zhao (2014), "Study of a Roadmap for Carbon Capture and Storage Development in Guangdong Province China," 35(9) *International Journal of Sustainable Energy* 858.

Hylton, Keith N. (2001), "When Should We Prefer Tort Law to Environmental Regulation?," 41 *Washburn Law Journal* 515.

Hylton, Keith N. (2008), "A Positive Theory of Strict Liability," 4(1) *Review of Law & Economics* 153.

IEA (2010), Carbon Capture and Storage: Model Regulatory Framework (2010).

IMO (2015), Status of Multilateral Conventions and Instruments in Respect of which the International Maritime Organization or its Secretary-General Performs Depositary or Other Functions (April 10, 2015).

Interstate Oil & Gas Compact Commission (2008), "CO_2 Storage: A Legal and Regulatory Guide for States," May 28. Available at http://www.ieaghg.org/docs/Finance2/3 Final presentation IEA NY 5-28-08.pdf.

ISO (undated a), "Standards and projects under the direct responsibility of ISO/TC 265 Secretariat," Store, Standards Catalog. Available at http://www.iso.org/iso/home/store/catalogue_tc/catalogue_tc_browse.htm?commid=648607&development=on.

ISO (undated b), "ISO/TC 265 Carbon Dioxide Capture, Transportation, and Geological Storage," Standards Development, Technical Committees. Available at http://www.iso.org/iso/iso_technical_committee?commid=648607.

Klass, Alexandra B. and Elizabeth J. Wilson (2008), "Climate Change and Carbon Sequestration: Assessing a Liability Regime for Long-Term Storage of Carbon Dioxide," 58 *Emory Law Journal* 103.

Koide, H., Y. Shindo, Y. Tazaki, M. Iijima, K. Ito, N. Kimura and K. Omata (1997), "Deep Sub-Seabed Disposal of CO_2 – The Most Protective Storage," 38(Suppl.) *Energy Conversion and Management* S253.

Kyoto Protocol to the United Nations Framework Convention on Climate Change, opened for signature March 16, 1998, 2303 UNTS 148 (Kyoto Protocol) (entered into force February 16, 2005).

Landes, W.M. and R.A. Posner (1984), "Tort Law as a Regulatory Regime for Catastrophic Personal Injuries," 13 *Journal of Legal Studies* 417.

Lecocq, Franck and Philippe Ambrosi (2007), "The Clean Development Mechanism: History, Status, and Prospects," 1 *Review of Environmental Economic Policy* 134.

Lee, Robert G. (2009), "Sub-Seabed Carbon Sequestration: Building the Legal Platform," 30 *Liverpool Law Review* 131.

Li, Qi, Zhishen Wu and Xioachun Li (2009), "Prediction of CO_2 Leakage during Sequestration into Marine Sedimentary Strata," 50 *Energy Conversion and Management* 503.

Li, X.C., N. Wei, Z.M. Fang, Q. Li, R.T. Dahowski and C.L. Davidson (2009), "CO_2 Point Emission and Geological Storage Capacity in China," 1 *Energy Procedia* 2793.

Li, X.C., N. Wei, Z.M. Fang, Q. Li, R.T. Dahowski and C.L. Davidson (2011), "Early Opportunities of Carbon Capture and Storage in China," 4 *Energy Procedia* 6029.

Liu, Hengwei and Kelly Sims Gallagher (2009), "Driving Carbon Capture and Storage Forward in China," 1 *Energy Procedia* 3877.

Lui, Lan-Cui, Gregory Leamon, Qi Li and Bofeng Cai (2014), "Development Towards Environmental Regulation of CCUS Projects in China," 63 *Energy Procedia* 6903.

Mackaay, E. (1980), *Economics of Information and Law* (Groupe de recherche en consommation).

Miller, J.C. III (1984), "The FTC and Voluntary Standards: Maximizing the Net Benefits of Self-Regulation," 4 *Cato Journal* 897.

Milligan, Ben (2014), "Planning for Offshore CO_2 Storage: Law and Policy in the United Kingdom," 48 *Marine Policy* 162.

Ministerial Council on Mineral and Petroleum Resources (MCMPR) (2005), Carbon Dioxide Capture and Geological Storage Australian Regulatory Guiding Principles.

Nunez, Javier (2010), "Can Self Regulation Work? A Story of Corruption, Impunity and Cover Up," 31 *Journal of Regulation Economics* 209.

Ogus, Anthony I. (1995), "Rethinking Self-Regulation," 15 *Oxford Journal of Legal Studies* 97.

Ogus, Anthony (2010), "The Paradoxes of Legal Paternalism and How to Resolve Them," 30(1) *Legal Studies* 61.
Ogus, Anthony and Emanuela Carbonara (2012), "Self-Regulation," in: *Encyclopedia of Law & Economics, Volume 7: Production of Legal Rules* (Gerrit De Geest and Francesco Parisi (eds), Cheltenham: Edward Elgar).
OSPAR Commission (2006), "Effects on the Marine Environment of Ocean Acidification Resulting from Elevated Levels of CO_2 in the Atmosphere" (Biodiversity Series). Available at http://www.ospar.org/documents/dbase/publications/p00285/p00285_ocean%20acidification.pdf.
OSPAR Decision 2007/1 to Prohibit the Storage of Carbon Dioxide Streams in the Water Column or on the Sea-bed (June 25–29, 2007).
OSPAR Decision 2007/2 on the Storage of Carbon Dioxide Streams in Geological Formations (June 25–29, 2007).
Purdy, Ray (2006), "The Legal Implications of Carbon Capture and Storage under the Sea," 7(1) *Sustainable Development Law & Policy* 22.
Schrag, Daniel P. (2009), "Storage of Carbon Dioxide in Offshore Sediments," 325 *Science* 1658.
Schwartz, A. and L. Wilde (1979), "Intervening in Markets on the Basis of Imperfect Information: A Legal and Economic Analysis," 127 *University of Pennsylvania Law Review* 630.
Shavell, Steven (1976), "Sharing Risks of Deferred Payment," 84(1) *Journal of Political Economics* 161.
Shavell, Steven M. (1984), "Liability for Harm versus Regulation of Safety," 13 *Journal Legal Studies* 357.
Shavell, Steven M. (1986), "The Judgment Proof Problem," 6 *International Review of Law & Economics* 43.
Stanley, Tristan and Sean McCoy (2014), 6th IEA International CCS Regulatory Network Meeting: Taking Stock of Progress and Identifying Next Steps (International Energy Agency).
Stigler, George J. (1961), "The Economics of Information," 69(3) *Journal of Political Economics* 213.
United Nations Framework Convention on Climate Change, May 9, 1992, 1771 UNTS 107.
Van den Bergh, R. (2008), "De Maatschappelijke Wenselijkheid van Gedragscodes Vanuit Rechtseconomisch Perspectief," 6772 *Weekblad voor Privaatrecht, Notariaat en Registratie* 792.
Van den Bergh, R. and L.T. Visscher (2008), "Optimal Enforcement of Safety Law," in: *Mitigating Risk in the Context of Safety and Security. How Relevant is a Rational Approach?*, 29 (R.V. de Mulder (ed.), Rotterdam: Erasmus University Rotterdam).
Weeks, Ann Brewster (2007), "Sub-Seabed Carbon Dioxide Sequestration as a Climate Mitigation Option for the Eastern United States: A Preliminary Assessment of Technology and Law," 12(2) *Ocean & Coastal Law Journal* 245.
Zhou, Di, Zhongxian Zhao, Jie Liao and Zhen Sun (2011), "A Preliminary Assessment on CO_2 Storage Capacity in the Pearl River Mouth Basin Offshore Guangdong China," 5 *International Journal of Greenhouse Gas Control* 308.

9. Does the environmental Kuznets curve hold for China? An empirical examination

Binwei Gui, Michael G. Faure and Guangdong Xu*

1. INTRODUCTION

In recent decades China has experienced remarkable economic growth during which it has enjoyed an average annual growth rate of approximately 10 per cent. As a result of this unprecedented and miraculous growth, China's economy has expanded impressively and is now the second largest economy in the world (with a nominal GDP of US$10.36 trillion in 2014), behind only the United States. China is currently the world's largest exporter, largest manufacturer, largest holder of foreign exchange reserves and second-largest destination of foreign direct investment (FDI).[1] Concurrently, living standards have increased across the board in China, and hundreds of millions of people have been raised out of absolute poverty as China has moved into the ranks of upper-middle-income economies. According to Brandt et al.,[2] 'three and a half decades of reform have produced a genuine leap forward in the size of China's economy and the prosperity of its citizens'.

China's growth miracle, however, has not been without costs. Certain economic, political and social problems, including corruption, inequality, financial inefficiency and other economic distortions, have arisen to threaten China's economic sustainability and social stability.[3] Environmental

* This chapter is supported by the Program for Young Innovative Research Teams of the China University of Political Science and Law (project number 16CXTD 09).

[1] World Bank and the Development Research Center of the State Council of China (2013).

[2] See Brandt, Ma and Rawski (2014), 102.

[3] See, for example, Allen, Qian and Qian (2005); Pei (2006); Hsieh and Klenow (2009); Knight (2014); Perry (2014).

pollution is another serious challenge faced by the Chinese government and Chinese society. For example, according to the 2010 Global Burden of Disease (GBD) report, outdoor air pollution contributed to 1.2 million deaths and 25 million healthy years of life lost in China in 2010. In fact, its environmental pollution is so severe that Elizabeth Economy[4] describes China as 'an environmental disaster'. Similarly, Gilley[5] concludes that 'China's environmental sub-system may have reached a point of near-collapse'.

What is the relationship between China's economic growth and its environmental challenges? Is economic growth a determinant of environmental pollution and is the so-called environmental Kuznets curve (EKC) hypothesis therefore relevant to understanding contemporary China? Stemming from the seminal works of Grossman and Krueger,[6] the EKC hypothesis suggests that pollution follows an inverted U-shaped relationship with income growth: when income is at a relatively low level, pollution increases with economic growth, but this correlation pattern becomes inverse after the income level reaches a certain threshold, beyond which the pollution trend becomes negative as the economy continues to grow. In other words, environmental pollution might be an inevitable by-product of economic growth, at least during the early stages of such growth.

The EKC hypothesis has been confirmed by several studies that focus on China. For example, using Chinese provincial data over the 1985–2005 period, Song et al.[7] find that there is a long-run co-integrating relationship between per capita emissions of three pollutants (wastewater emission, waste gas emission and solid waste generated) and per capita GDP, and that all three pollutant emissions exhibit an inverse U-shaped relationship with economic growth (i.e., as the economy grows, waste gas, wastewater and solid wastes first increase and then decline after each passes a certain respective threshold turning point). Similar conclusions have been reached in the previous literature.[8] Nonetheless, there is some disagreement regarding this subject. For example, in a more recent study, Yang et al.[9] show that the EKC hypothesis 'cannot be considered valid' for any of the seven emission indicators used by their study (including CO_2, SO_2, industry dust, industry gas, industry smoke, industry SO_2, and

4 Economy (2007), 39.

5 Gilley (2012), 225.

6 See Grossman and Krueger (1991, 1995).

7 Song, Zheng and Tong (2008).

8 See, for example, Brajer, Mead and Xiao (2008); Diao et al. (2009); He (2009).

9 Yang, He and Chen (2015), 54.

industry wastewater emissions) and therefore argue that their finding 'confirms the fragility of the EKC hypothesis for the Chinese case'. More generally, Brajer et al.[10] conduct a review of Chinese studies published in international journals until 2009 that describes a general picture of the EKC literature related to China as 'quite varied' and 'much like the blind men describing the elephant by touch'; moreover, 'each of these studies presents an incomplete picture of China's true overall EKC relationship'. In summary, there are 'large divergences in the conclusions about the validity of the EKC hypothesis for China'.[11]

This chapter will contribute to this debate by testing the applicability of the EKC hypothesis to the case of China. In addition, we will explore the role of institutions[12] in shaping the connection between income and pollution in China, and we will pay special attention to the heterogeneity in EKC patterns among China's different regions, the channels through which institutions may influence pollution control and environmental quality, and the effects of the economic structure and pollution abatement measures on pollution levels. The remainder of this chapter is organized as follows. Section 2 offers background information on China's environmental status quo. Section 3 presents a literature review of the EKC hypothesis. Section 4 examines the applicability of the EKC hypothesis to China and the role of institutions in shaping the income and pollution nexus. Finally, we conclude in section 5.

2. CHINA'S ENVIRONMENTAL POLLUTION

Seven types of environmental problems were highlighted in the Asian Development Bank report: water pollution and water availability, air quality, solid waste management, natural disasters, land degradation, deteriorating biodiversity and inadequate forestry resources.[13] In comparison with other types of environmental problem, air pollution seems to have attracted the most attention both domestically and internationally, particularly after the winter of 2013 when nationwide smog descended upon China, which was described as 'one of the worst environmental

---

[10] Brajer, Mead and Xiao (2011), 385.

[11] Yang, He and Chen (2015), 42.

[12] We use a broader definition of institution here, referring not only to law and regulations, but also to their enforcement characteristics. Therefore the incentives and constraints faced by judges and regulatory agencies are also relevant.

[13] Zhang and Crooks (2012).

disasters in history'.[14] This event led to the coining of a new word to describe China's disastrous air quality: 'airpocalypse'.[15]

Air pollution is prevalent in most Chinese cities. The Asian Development Bank reports that less than 1 per cent of the 500 largest cities in China meet the air quality standards recommended by the World Health Organization, and seven of China's cities are among the ten most polluted cities in the world.[16] Air pollutants (such as $PM_{2.5}$, PM_{10}, and Total Suspended Particles (TSP))[17] are detrimental and can be lethal to human health. For example, Ebenstein et al.[18] examine the relationship between income, pollution and mortality in China from 1991 to 2012 and estimate that a 100 μg/m^3 increase in PM_{10} exposure is associated with a decline in life expectancy of 1.5 years at birth and 2.3 years by the age of five. These authors further show that this negative association is driven by elevated cardiorespiratory mortality rates. Northern China suffers more from air pollution than southern China because of China's special winter heating policy, which was designed specifically for northern China. China's heating systems are primarily coal-based and technically inefficient, which means that incomplete combustion of coal in these boilers leads to severe air pollution. Chen et al.[19] show that life expectancies are approximately 5.5 years lower in the north because of an increased incidence of cardiorespiratory mortality, and that the 500 million residents of northern China experienced a loss of more than 2.5 billion life years during the 1990s because of the winter heating policy.

Air pollution also means economic costs. Chen and He[20] report that more than 371,000 residents of China lost their lives in 2007 as a result of excessive emissions of $PM_{2.5}$, PM_{10}, and ozone pollutants; the

---

14 Wang (2015), 108.

15 See, for example, 'Chinese struggle through "airpocalypse" smog', available at http://www.theguardian.com/world/2013/feb/16/chinese-struggle-through-airpocalypse-smog (accessed 15 June 2013). Two entries related to this event can also be found in Wikipedia: '2013 Eastern China smog' (https://en.wikipedia.org/wiki/2013_Eastern_China_smog) and '2013 Northeastern China smog' (https://en.wikipedia.org/wiki/2013_Northeastern_China_smog) (both accessed 21 March 2017).

16 Zhang and Crooks (2012).

17 $PM_{2.5}$ are particles with a diameter of 2.5 micrometres or less. PM_{10} have an aerodynamic diameter between 2.5 and 10 micrometres. TSP consists of particles with a diameter of 100 micrometres or less and therefore includes both PM_{10} and $PM_{2.5}$.

18 Ebenstein et al. (2015).

19 Chen et al. (2013a).

20 Chen and He (2014).

corresponding health costs (the sum of medical expenses and loss of wages caused by illness and premature death) totalled 618.052 billion CNY, and approximately 87 per cent of that figure resulted from excess $PM_{2.5}$ concentrations. Similarly, Matus et al.[21] show that as the result of PM_{10} and ozone-related pollution, Chinese welfare costs (the sum of net wages lost as a result of pollution and losses in leisure time value) increased from US$ 22 billion in 1975 to US$ 112 billion in 2005. These authors further estimate that the damage to human health from air pollution in China measured between 6 per cent and 9 per cent of China's GDP between 1995 and 2005.

Water pollution in China is even more challenging than air pollution. For example, according to one 2012 report, 'up to 40 per cent of China's rivers were seriously polluted' and '20 per cent were so polluted their water quality was rated too toxic even to come into contact with'.[22] The 2013 State of the Environment Report Review issued by the Ministry of Environmental Protection (MEP) shows that although the overall water quality in the river basins has improved since 2009, the water quality of several main rivers – including the Yellow River, the Songhua River and the Hai River – has continued to deteriorate.[23] The same report also shows that 11.5 per cent of Chinese lakes were heavily polluted, 1.6 per cent were moderately polluted and 26.2 per cent were lightly polluted, as measured in 2013. As a consequence of pollution, nearly half of the 634 Chinese rivers, lakes and reservoirs tested in 2011 failed to meet drinking standards during all or part of the year.[24] The quality of groundwater in China is also poor. It is estimated that the supply of drinking water for 70 per cent of the total population – and more than 95 per cent of the rural population – comes from groundwater.[25] Unfortunately, 90 per cent of China's shallow groundwater is polluted, and an alarming 37 per cent is so foul that it cannot even be treated for use as drinking water.[26]

Water pollution in turn leads to serious health problems. For example, Ebenstein[27] finds that a single grade of deterioration in water quality – based on a six-grade scale – increases the death rate due to digestive cancer (including oesophageal, stomach and liver cancer) by 9.7 per cent. As digestive cancers are responsible for nearly one million (980,000) deaths

---

21 Matus et al. (2012).
22 Economy (2013).
23 China Water Risk (2014).
24 Tao and Xin (2014).
25 Lu et al. (2008).
26 Qiu (2011).
27 Ebenstein (2012).

in China per annum, almost 93,000 deaths could be avoided annually by improving China's water by one grade. Moreover, digestive cancer is not the only health problem associated with water pollution. Recent studies of water pollution have confirmed its impact on health in terms of increased rates of colorectal cancer, mental health problems, oxidative damage, DNA migration and cytotoxicity.[28] Health-related damage resulting from water pollution is particularly severe in rural areas. Liu[29] reports that there are 459 so-called 'cancer villages' that have cancer rates that are significantly higher than normal. Most such villages are clustered near rivers with the lowest grade of pollution on the government's six-grade scale, and some of these villages have cancer rates that are 30 times higher than national averages.

Air pollution and water pollution are just part of the big picture. China continues to suffer from other types of environmental degradation, such as soil pollution, desertification, biodiversity loss and local climatic change.[30] Therefore, it may not be surprising to find that China has received alarmingly low scores on several existing comprehensive measures of environmental systems. For example, when China is evaluated using the Environmental Performance Index (EPI), which 'ranks how well countries perform on high-priority environmental issues in two broad policy areas – protection of human health from environmental harm and protection of ecosystems', its overall score is 43 out of 100, placing it 118th out of 178 countries in 2014.[31] Similarly, another measure, the Global Climate Risk Index (GDRI), which analyses retrospective economic and human losses from extreme weather (storms, floods, heat waves, etc.), places China among the 20 nations most vulnerable to climate change because of its current environmental degradation.[32] As a nation, China is also considered to have one of the highest negative environmental impacts under the Environmental Impact Index developed by Bradshaw, Giam and Sodhi.[33]

Ten years have passed since Pan Yue, the vice minister of the State

---

28 Lu et al. (2008).

29 Liu (2010).

30 See Economy (2007); Zhang and Crooks (2012).

31 See http://sedac.ciesin.columbia.edu/data/collection/epi (accessed 29 March 2017). The EPI scores country performance in nine areas consisting of 20 indicators. It is a joint project between the Yale Center for Environmental Law and Policy (YCELP) and the Center for International Earth Science Information Network (CIESIN) at Columbia University, in collaboration with the Samuel Family Foundation and the World Economic Forum.

32 See http://germanwatch.org/en/download/10333.pdf (accessed 18 June 2015).

33 Bradshaw, Giam and Sodhi (2010).

Environmental Protection Administration (SEPA, which became the MEP in 2008), warned that the Chinese miracle 'will end soon because the environment can no longer keep pace'.[34] Nonetheless, the state of China's environment does not seem to have improved. What can explain the coexistence of a rapidly growing economy and a severely deteriorating environmental system in China? Does China's experience conform to the pattern described by the EKC hypothesis, and economic growth is not translating into environmental improvement simply because China remains in the left part of the EKC? If so, when will China reach the turning point of the EKC? Will this process occur spontaneously or be driven by certain fundamental institutional reforms? We explore these questions in the following sections.

3. THE EKC HYPOTHESIS: A BRIEF LITERATURE REVIEW

The environmental Kuznets curve is named after Noble Prize Winner Simon Kuznets, who wrote about the relationship between a country's income inequality and income levels.[35] Since the 1980s scholars have also applied this concept to environmental pollution, establishing an empirical relationship between measures of environmental quality and national income.[36] According to the literature, there is an inverted U-shaped relationship as a result of which, in the early phases of economic development, increased economic development leads to greater environmental degradation, whereas after a certain turning point has passed, increased economic development leads to environmental improvements.

There are a few reasons offered for why pollution levels may decrease as income levels rise.[37] One explanation is that, at higher income levels, the nature of industry may shift away from polluting heavy industry and towards more environmentally friendly service industries. Higher income levels would also tend to foster technological progress, thus leading to more efficient use of energy and materials and environmental improvements.[38]

---

34 See 'Spiegel interview with China's Deputy Minister of the Environment: "The Chinese Miracle Will End Soon"', available at: http://www.spiegel.de/international/spiegel/spiegel-interview-with-china-s-deputy-minister-of-the-environment-the-chinese-miracle-will-end-soon-a-345694.html (accessed 13 July 2015).

35 Kuznets (1955).

36 Grossman and Krueger (1991, 1995).

37 For an overview, see Strand (2002).

38 Porter and Van der Linde (1995).

Similarly, as welfare levels rise, citizens' demands for environmental protection strengthen.[39]

In particular, certain studies have attempted to analyse in more detail the precise channels through which income may influence pollution levels. One study argues that there is no direct relationship between income levels and environmental degradation, but that the channel through which increased income affects environmental quality is education.[40] Specifically, increased investment in education leads to a higher demand for environmental quality. Others point to the importance of trade patterns. One study points to the fact that improvements in environmental quality at higher levels of per capita income can (at least partly) be explained by the tendency of developed countries to import manufactured goods from less-developed countries, thus leading to a relocation of pollution-intensive industries from developed to developing countries.[41] Similarly, Stern has argued that the EKC is largely the result of the effects of trade on the distribution of polluting industries.[42]

Certain studies have also emphasized the importance of regulation; in other words, the stringency of environmental laws – and their enforcement – as a channel through which wealth and increased environmental quality are connected. Arrow et al. argue that 'in most cases where emissions have declined with rising income, the reductions have been due to local institutional reforms such as environmental legislation and market-based incentives to reduce environmental impacts'.[43] Dasgupta et al. argue that the reason that pollution decreases as income levels rise is that richer countries regulate pollution more strictly than poorer countries and pollution levels decrease as a result.[44] The latter result has also been confirmed by Esty and Porter, who show that not only the structure but also the enforcement of environmental regulations has a strong impact on environmental performance.[45]

However, it is fair to say that the EKC hypothesis still faces serious challenges. In the words of Yang et al.:

> since the seminal work of Grossman and Krueger (1994), the EKC hypothesis has been one of the most hotly debated issues in environmental economics-related

39 Arrow et al. (1995).
40 Barros, Mendonça and Nogueira (2002).
41 Nahman and Antrobus (2005).
42 Stern, Common and Barbier (1996); Stern and Common (2001).
43 Arrow et al. (1995), 520.
44 Dasgupta et al. (2002).
45 Esty and Porter (2005).

> research. Although over 200 empirical studies have been published in international peer-reviewed journals, there appears to be more controversy than consensus regarding the validity of this hypothesis.[46]

In general, the previous literature has indicated several incoherencies in EKC-related empirical studies.[47] The first incoherence is that between empirical results based on cross-country static experience and theoretically assumed single-country dynamic processes. Second, there is incoherence between the importance of the topics for developing countries and the significantly less frequent participation of developing countries in the most representative cross-country EKC studies. Finally, there is incoherence between the original reduced-form pollution-income nexus, which implicitly assumes an automatic decoupling tendency between growth and pollution after reaching a threshold point, and the ever-growing curiosity in determining certain 'structural' factors that concretely contribute to a downward trend in pollution.

As we have shown in the introduction, the debate regarding the EKC in China has also been particularly intense. Yang et al. report that there are more than 413 published papers on topics related to the EKC in China in English or Chinese.[48] Excluding the 45 literature surveys, the other 368 studies are essentially empirical studies using various statistical data from China. These authors further report that 'similar to the international level literature, there are also large divergences in the conclusions about the validity of the EKC hypothesis for China'. Moreover, Brajer et al.[49] conclude that 'previous EKC studies on China seem to be akin to the proverbial story of the blind men and the elephant: each individual pollution measure and estimation specification seems to find its own relationship'.

4. POLLUTION, INCOME AND INSTITUTIONS IN CHINA: AN EMPIRICAL EXAMINATION

4.1 Does China Follow the EKC? A Tentative Analysis

In this section four indicators that are frequently used in the literature, that is industrial waste gas, SO_2, CO_2 and wastewater, will be used to

46 Yang, He and Chen (2015), 41.
47 Yang, He and Chen (2015).
48 Yang, He and Chen (2015), 42.
49 Brajer, Mead and Xiao (2011), 395.

Table 9.1 Descriptive statistics of the pollution and income variables

Variables	Definition	mean	median	s.d.	min	max	obs.
Ind_Waste_Gas	Industrial waste gas per capita (10,000 m^3/person)	2.86	2.14	2.6	0.41	25.79	510
SO_2	SO_2 emission per capita (ton/10,000 persons)	191.03	154.3	121.88	22.92	644.72	480
CO_2	CO_2 emission per capita (ton/10,000 persons)	4.81	4.07	2.85	1.03	16.93	480
Waste_Water	Wastewater per capita (ton/person)	41.41	37.59	20.3	13.88	142.11	480
GDP_pc	GDP per capita (10,000 CNY/person)	2.42	1.85	1.78	0.41	9.76	510

Source: *China Statistical Yearbook* and *China Environment Statistical Yearbook*.

proxy for China's environmental quality.[50] Gross Domestic Product (GDP) per capita (at a constant 2013 price level) is employed as the explanatory variable to test the EKC hypothesis. The data span the period from 1977 to 2013, covering China's 30 provinces (excluding Tibet). Descriptive statistics on pollution and income variables are shown in Table 9.1.

The regression equation that is used to test the EKC relationship is as follows:

$$\log(P) = \beta_0 + \beta_1 \log(Y) + \beta_2 \log(Y)^2 + \varepsilon$$

where P is the pollution level and Y is GDP per capita. In running a regression, if a regression coefficient is not significant, the insignificant coefficient will be discarded and the regression analysis will be performed again. The regression results are illustrated in Figures 9.1 to 9.4 (Figure 9.1 for industrial waste gas, Figure 9.2 for SO_2, Figure 9.3 for CO_2, and Figure 9.4 for wastewater). The regression equations are situated at the top of these figures, and y* represents the threshold turning point if there

50 We use industrial waste gas, SO_2 and CO_2 rather than $PM_{2.5}$ or PM_{10} in our study because the latter two are city-based and therefore not suitable for our study that focuses on regional heterogeneity in environmental conditions.

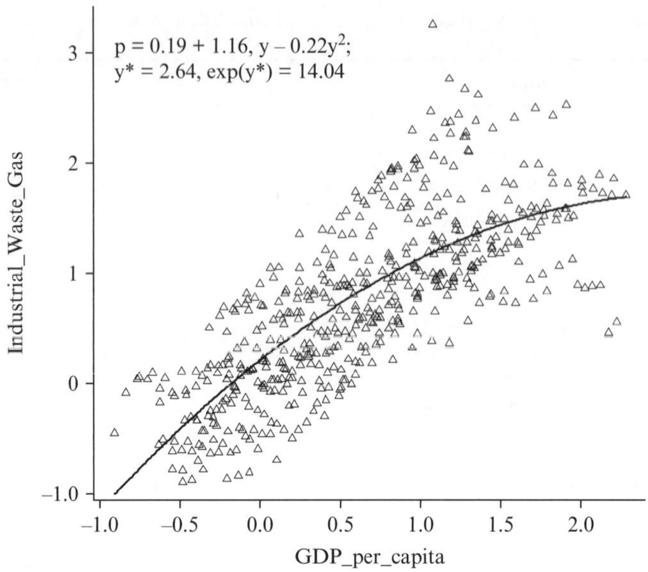

Figure 9.1 EKC for industrial waste gas

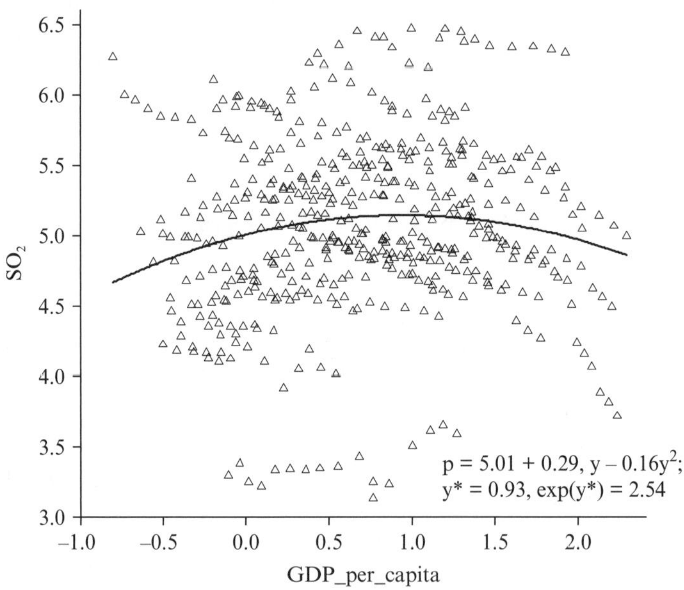

Figure 9.2 EKC for SO_2

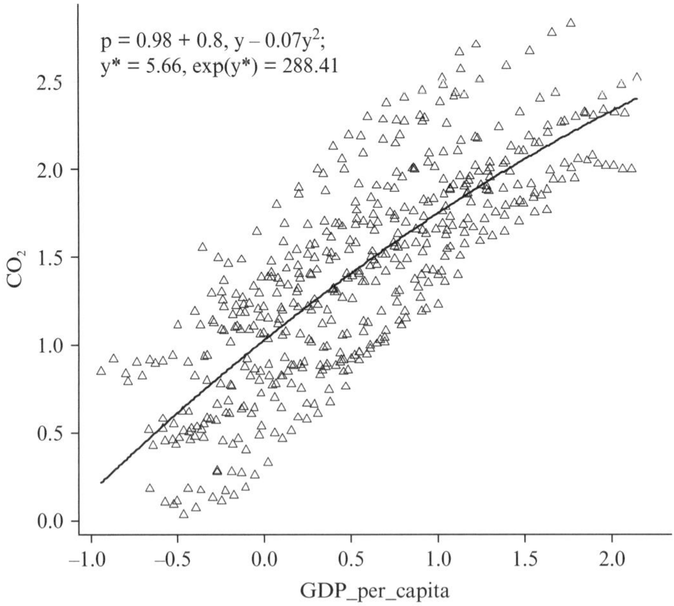

Figure 9.3 EKC for CO_2

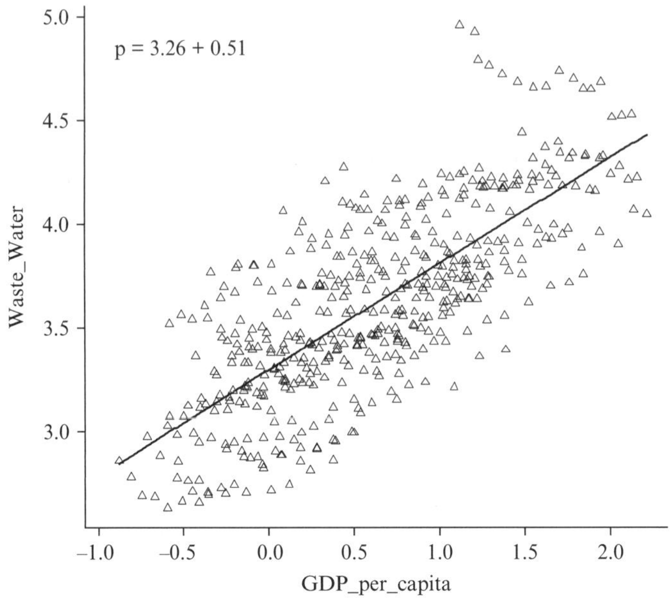

Figure 9.4 EKC for wastewater

is an inverted U-shaped pollution curve (EKC). In addition, because the regression is performed using logarithmic transformation, the value of the turning point is reverted to the original value (unit: 10,000 CNY/person) through exponentiation (exp).

As shown in Figures 9.1 and 9.2, there is a clear inverted U-shaped trend for industrial waste gas and SO_2, with the turning points at CNY 140,400 and 25,400, respectively. In 2013 the average GDP per capita in China was CNY 41,800, which means that the turning point for SO_2 was reached in most regions. For industrial waste gas, it will take an average of 14.8 years for China to reach the turning point with per capita income increasing at a rate of 7 per cent. For CO_2 (Figure 9.3), we find only a weak inverted U-shaped trend: whereas the growth rate of CO_2 emissions has gradually slowed as income per capita increases, the threshold turning point, which is at CNY 2,880,000, is far beyond the current per capita income level of China. More specifically, even for Beijing, the region with the highest economic growth rate among all Chinese provinces, it will take 50 years for the city to reach the CO_2 turning point. For water pollution (Figure 9.4), we find a linear relationship between GDP per capita and wastewater emissions.

4.2 Different EKC Patterns in Different Regions

Given the diversity in economic and social development among China's different regions, it is not unreasonable to assume that these regions may follow different EKC patterns. To examine possible heterogeneity in EKC patterns among China's different regions, we extended the above EKC regression equation by including the individual effects (a_i). In other words, we assumed that the equations differ only in intercepts, but not in either the shapes or the turning points of the curves. The extended EKC equation is as follows:

$$\log(P_{it}) = \beta_0 + \beta_1 \log(Y_{it}) + \beta_2 \log(Y_{it})^2 + a_i + \varepsilon_{it}$$

A fixed effect model is used to estimate the probable heterogeneous EKC curves, and the results are reported in Table 9.2.

The F-statistics suggest that individual effects are significant at the 1 per cent level, which means that different regions do not follow the same EKC trend. Our hypothesis is therefore supported.

Furthermore, heterogeneous EKC among regions may differ not only in intercepts but also in the shape of the curves and turning points. Certain explanatory variables, such as institutions, must be introduced to explore the latter differences. Institutions may influence the relationship between income and pollution in several ways. For example, it may be argued that people will

Table 9.2 EKC model showing the individual effects

	Ind_Waste_Gas	SO_2	CO_2	Waste_Water
log(y)	1.301***	0.435***	0.85***	0.372***
	(0.03)	(0.04)	(0.018)	(0.021)
log(y)^2	–0.152***	–0.246***	–0.05***	–0.04***
	(0.02)	(0.025)	(0.012)	(0.013)
adj. R2	0.84	0.194	0.86	0.586
F statistics	89.565***	95.182***	144.316***	78.896***
obs.	510	480	480	480

Notes: The numbers in parentheses represent standard errors. '***' indicates 1% level of significance.

demand higher environmental quality as per capita incomes rise, and environmental regulation will be strengthened and pollution problems will be addressed in response. We may therefore find an EKC relationship between income and pollution. However, whether and how environmental authorities react is determined by the political institutions that shape bureaucrats' incentives, collect and allocate information, and balance different social goals. Similarly, if a strong government sticks to pro-industry economic policies and prevents the economy from evolving into a service-based growth pattern, higher income will translate into lower environmental quality levels, and we may therefore face a linear relationship between income and pollution. In summary, we can argue that, at a given income level, the better the institutional quality (a responsible and responsive government, an impartial and dependent judicial system, professional and competent regulatory agencies, etc.), the more effective pollution control will be.

Two types of indicators, that is doing business indicators and the ratio of foreign direct investment to GDP (FDI), are chosen to proxy for China's institutional quality. The doing business indicators are derived from *Doing Business in China 2008*.[51] *Doing Business* is an annual report issued by the World Bank that 'provides objective measures of business regulations and their enforcement across 189 economies and selected cities at the subnational and regional level'.[52] We use *Doing Business in China*

[51] The report is available at: http://www.doingbusiness.org/~/media/WBG/DoingBusiness/Documents/Subnational-Reports/DB08-Sub-China.pdf (accessed 29 March 2017).

[52] See 'About Doing Business', available at: http://www.doingbusiness.org/about-us (accessed 28 November 2015).

Table 9.3 Doing business indicators of different regions in China, 2008

region	start	register	credit	contract	region	start	register	credit	contract
Anhui	0.32	0.48	0.57	0.52	Jiangsu	0.96	0.81	0.97	0.93
Beijing	0.85	0.61	0.76	0.78	Jiangxi	0.43	0.44	0.24	0.66
Chongqing	0.57	0.67	0.38	0.79	Jilin	0.65	0.67	0.31	0.53
Fujian	0.84	0.85	0.98	0.7	Liaoning	0.75	0.51	0.55	0.75
Gansu	0.28	0.17	0.16	0.43	Ningxia	0.33	0.49	0.19	0.69
Guangdong	0.91	0.87	0.9	0.97	Qinghai	0.36	0.44	0.29	0.46
Guangxi	0.28	0.12	0.12	0.6	Shaanxi	0.34	0.64	0.17	0.8
Guizhou	0.19	0.21	0.22	0.54	Shandong	0.91	0.82	0.81	0.8
Hainan	0.6	0.36	0.4	0.72	Shanghai	0.86	0.97	0.81	0.87
Hebei	0.57	0.43	0.69	0.67	Shanxi	0.46	0.33	0.6	0.62
Heilongjiang	0.54	0.51	0.67	0.6	Sichuan	0.48	0.61	0.67	0.55
Henan	0.6	0.3	0.48	0.64	Tianjin	0.79	0.78	0.78	0.8
Hubei	0.58	0.35	0.6	0.63	Xinjiang	0.59	0.53	0.22	0.59
Hunan	0.41	0.36	0.31	0.51	Yunnan	0.36	0.37	0.28	0.45
Inner-Mongolia	0.62	0.47	0.52	0.61	Zhejiang	0.97	0.77	0.74	0.89

Source: World Bank *Doing Business in China 2008*; the data in this table = 1 – World Bank's original data.

2008 because it is the only doing business report in China that measures institutional quality at the regional – rather than the national – level. The indicators cover four areas of business regulation and their enforcement: starting a business, registering property, getting credit (creating and registering collateral) and enforcing contracts. The FDI reflects the openness of a region, and a more open region may also have a more business-friendly institutional environment because foreign enterprises may require an institutional environment that is similar to that found in their homeland, or because these enterprises may bring new ideas and practices to open areas.[53] The descriptive statistics of the doing business indicators and the FDI indicator are presented in Tables 9.3 and 9.4.

[53] Certainly, the relationship between FDI and pollution is still a highly debated issue. The 'pollution haven' hypothesis argues that there is a possibility that multinational firms, particularly those engaged in highly polluting activities, may relocate to countries with weaker environmental standards. Therefore, we may find a negative relationship between FDI inflows and environmental quality. See, for example, Smarzynska and Wei (2001). In a recent study, Zugravu-Soilita finds that the effects of FDI on pollution are dependent on certain institutional factors, such as the stringency of environmental regulation. See Natalia Zugravu-Soilita (2015).

Table 9.4 Descriptive statistics of the institutional variables

Variable	Definition	mean	median	s.d.	min	max	obs.
start	Starting a business	0.58	0.58	0.22	0.19	0.97	30
register	Registering property	0.53	0.5	0.22	0.12	0.97	30
credit	Obtaining credit	0.51	0.54	0.26	0.12	0.98	30
contract	Enforcing contracts	0.67	0.65	0.14	0.43	0.97	30
FDI	FDI per capita	0.06	0.03	0.08	0.01	0.75	480

Source: World Bank *Doing Business in China 2008* and *China Statistical Yearbook*.

As Tables 9.3 and 9.4 show, there are remarkable differences in institutional quality among Chinese regions. On average, regions in eastern China, such as Guangdong, Jiangsu and Shanghai, have much higher scores in terms of the doing business indicators than those in western China, such as Gansu, Guangxi and Guizhou.

Following Panayotou,[54] we construct a regression equation that includes an interaction term to measure the impact of the institutional variables on the EKC relationship:

$$\begin{aligned}\log(P) &= \beta_0 + \beta_1 \log(Y) + \beta_2 \log(Y)^2 + \alpha_1 I + \alpha_2 I \log(Y) + \varepsilon \\ &= (\beta_0 + \alpha_1 I) + (\beta_1 + \alpha_2 I)\log(Y) + \beta_2 \log(Y)^2 + \varepsilon\end{aligned}$$

where P, Y and I are the pollution level, GDP per capita and the institutional variables, respectively. We predict that the institutional variables may influence both the shapes and turning points of the curves: when $\beta_2 < 0$, the lower α_1 is, the lower the horizontal position of the curve; and the lower α_2 is, the lower the turning point of the curve. In other words, the lower α_1 and α_2 are, the more positive the effect of institutional variables on pollution control. The regression results are reported in Table 9.5.

As shown in Tables 9.5(a)–(c), with respect to industrial waste gas, SO_2 and CO_2, the coefficients of the doing business indicators (which can be argued to proxy for government efficiency) and FDI are consistent with our predictions, that is the better the institutional quality in a region, the more effective the region's pollution control, and the lower both the horizontal position and the turning point of EKC in the region. However, we find a counterintuitive result for wastewater: the higher score that a region obtains for institutional quality, the more wastewater discharge can be found in that region. We presume that this finding results from the

54 Panayotou (1997).

Table 9.5(a) The effect of institutional variables on EKC: I-industrial waste gas

inst	start		register		credit		contract		FDI	
log(y)	1.47***	1.379***	1.238***	1.321***	1.38***	1.38***	1.436***	1.293***	1.25***	1.252***
	(0.087)	(0.061)	(0.081)	(0.062)	(0.078)	(0.078)	(0.166)	(0.063)	(0.072)	(0.071)
log(y)^2	–0.138**	–0.202***	–0.253***	–0.202***	–0.108**	–0.108**	–0.17***	–0.201***	–0.239***	–0.235***
	(0.057)	(0.037)	(0.049)	(0.038)	(0.051)	(0.051)	(0.051)	(0.039)	(0.047)	(0.043)
I	–1.136***	–1.343***	–1.39***	–1.199***	–0.472***	–0.472***	–1.404***	–1.591***	–2.337***	–2.271***
	(0.175)	(0.103)	(0.159)	(0.105)	(0.14)	(0.14)	(0.26)	(0.164)	(0.439)	(0.276)
I*log(y)	–0.301	–	0.281	–	–0.451***	–0.451***	–0.27	–	0.102	–
	(0.206)	–	(0.174)	–	(0.165)	(0.165)	(0.292)	–	(0.522)	–
adj. R2	0.69	0.689	0.671	0.67	0.642	0.642	0.65	0.65	0.622	0.622
obs.	510	510	510	510	510	510	510	510	480	480

Table 9.5(b) The effect of institutional variables on EKC: II-SO_2

inst	start		register		credit		contract		FDI	
log(y)	0.305**	0.432***	0.204*	0.204*	0.388***	0.376***	0.792***	0.841***	0.297***	0.297***
	(0.128)	(0.095)	(0.12)	(0.12)	(0.11)	(0.093)	(0.237)	(0.223)	(0.088)	(0.088)
log(y)^2	–0.245***	–0.144***	–0.24***	–0.24***	–0.125*	–0.136**	–0.046	–	–0.227***	–0.227***
	(0.087)	(0.055)	(0.074)	(0.074)	(0.072)	(0.055)	(0.074)	–	(0.057)	(0.057)
I	–1.158***	–0.823***	–0.63***	–0.63***	–0.604***	–0.639***	0.498	0.618*	–4.543***	–4.543***
	(0.271)	(0.15)	(0.242)	(0.242)	(0.201)	(0.121)	(0.387)	(0.335)	(0.536)	(0.536)
I*log(y)	0.459	–	0.469*	0.469*	–0.05	–	–0.942**	–1.113***	2.517***	2.517***
	(0.309)	–	(0.259)	(0.259)	(0.23)	–	(0.422)	(0.32)	(0.637)	(0.637)
adj. R2	0.074	0.072	0.026	0.026	0.066	0.068	0.023	0.024	0.168	0.168
obs.	480	480	480	480	480	480	480	480	480	480

Table 9.5(c) The effect of institutional variables on EKC: III-CO_2

inst	start		register		credit		contract		FDI	
log(y)	0.992***	1***	0.905***	0.881***	0.986***	0.99***	0.935***	0.911***	0.856***	0.856***
	(0.074)	(0.072)	(0.067)	(0.05)	(0.063)	(0.062)	(0.132)	(0.048)	(0.053)	(0.053)
log(y)^2	–0.022	–	–0.051	–0.065**	0.027	–	–0.054	–0.059*	–0.112***	–0.112***
	(0.049)	–	(0.042)	(0.032)	(0.041)	–	(0.04)	(0.03)	(0.036)	(0.036)
I	–0.579***	–0.541***	–0.471***	–0.52***	–0.145	–0.177*	–1.123***	–1.152***	–2.095***	–2.095***
	(0.14)	(0.11)	(0.126)	(0.086)	(0.106)	(0.094)	(0.192)	(0.125)	(0.321)	(0.321)
I*log(y)	–0.195	–0.257**	–0.078	–	–0.435***	–0.377***	–0.045	–	0.856**	0.856**
	(0.176)	(0.11)	(0.146)	–	(0.134)	(0.102)	(0.23)	–	(0.399)	(0.399)
adj. R2	0.676	0.676	0.655	0.655	0.66	0.66	0.685	0.686	0.669	0.669
obs.	480	480	480	480	480	480	480	480	450	450

Table 9.5(d) The effect of institutional variables on EKC: IV-wastewater

inst	start		register		credit		contract		FDI	
log(y)	0.34***	0.382***	0.282***	0.256***	0.386***	0.386***	0.236**	0.236**	0.468***	0.468***
	(0.058)	(0.023)	(0.053)	(0.05)	(0.052)	(0.052)	(0.1)	(0.1)	(0.041)	(0.041)
log(y)^2	–0.066*	–	–0.121***	–0.143***	–0.082**	–0.082**	–0.06*	–0.06*	–0.072***	–0.072***
	(0.04)	–	(0.033)	(0.029)	(0.034)	(0.034)	(0.031)	(0.031)	(0.027)	(0.027)
I	0.506***	0.673***	0.145	–	0.179*	0.179*	0.954***	0.954***	0.506**	0.506**
	(0.124)	(0.068)	(0.108)	–	(0.095)	(0.095)	(0.164)	(0.164)	(0.254)	(0.254)
I*log(y)	0.232	–	0.576***	0.697***	0.319***	0.319***	0.346*	0.346*	1.551***	1.551***
	(0.141)	–	(0.115)	(0.073)	(0.109)	(0.109)	(0.178)	(0.178)	(0.302)	(0.302)
adj. R2	0.636	0.635	0.632	0.632	0.608	0.608	0.67	0.67	0.646	0.646
obs.	480	480	480	480	480	480	480	480	480	480

Notes: Numbers in parentheses are standard errors. '***', '**' and '*' indicate 1%, 5% and 10% levels of significance, respectively. For each regression model, we report two types of results: the first consists of the initial regression results with all the explanatory variables included, and the second consists of the results with standardized regression coefficients.

difference in domestic wastewater discharge in different regions, that is the eastern regions of China – which have higher scores on institutional quality, on average – have larger populations and more abundant water resources than the central and western regions of the country, which generally have weaker institutional environments, and therefore suffer from a higher level of domestic wastewater discharge.

4.3 How Do Income and Institutions Influence Pollution? Examining the Channels

Having confirmed the positive effects of institutional quality on pollution control, we now turn to the specific channels through which both income and institutions influence environmental quality. Theoretically, three channels through which income may influence pollution have been identified: the scale effect, the composition (structure) effect and the abatement effect.[55] The scale effect means that with the expansion of economic scale, pollution levels will increase, because increased economic activity results in increased levels of resource use and waste. The composition of economic activity influences environmental quality because different sectors of the economy have different pollution intensities. Compared with agriculture or services, industry (particularly manufacturing) tends to be more pollution-intensive. Therefore, with the evolution of an economy from an agricultural base to an industry base and then to a service base, the pollution level may first increase and then decrease. Finally, the abatement of pollution is driven by demand and supply factors, both of which are influenced by income. On the demand side, at high levels of income, people are more concerned with environmental quality than they are at low income levels. On the supply side, economic growth leads to higher incomes and higher public expenditure on pollution abatement, which low-income countries cannot afford.

We focus on the effects of institutional quality on pollution control via the composition channel and abatement channel because pollution problems can be addressed only through these two channels. By contrast, the scale effect indicates deteriorating environmental quality.

We first examine the composition effect, that is we study whether income and institutions contribute to pollution abatement by means of economic structural transformation. Obviously, if the share of industry in GDP decreases with income growth and institutional improvement, then the environmental challenges faced by an economy may be mitigated. The regression equation is as follows:

---

[55] Panayotou (1997); Brock and Taylor (2005).

$$S = \beta_0 + \beta_1\log(Y) + \beta_2\log(Y)^2 + \beta_3 I + \varepsilon$$

where S is economic structure (proxied by the share of industry in GDP), Y is GDP per capita, and I is the institutional variable. Because there may be an interaction effect between income levels and economic structure, we use a one- or two-period lag of income level as instrumental variables to perform the regression. Moreover, because the doing business indicators are static variables, we use a panel model with random individual effects and report the regression results in Table 9.6.

The results show that there is an apparent inverted U-shaped relationship between income level and the economic structure, that is as income increases, the share of industry in GDP first increases and then decreases. However, the general impact of institutions on the economic structure is not significant. Whereas certain indicators (e.g., start, contract) have a weak negative impact on the share of industry in GDP, other indicators (e.g., register, credit, FDI) have a weak positive impact. In other words, the influence of institutional quality on the economic structure is mixed: on the one hand, better institutions may decrease the importance of industry in economic growth by accelerating structural transformation; on the other hand, better institutions may increase the share of industry in GDP by attracting more manufacturing firms to invest in regions characterized by better institutional environments.

We now turn to the abatement effect. The regression equation is as follows:

$$A = \beta_0 + \beta_1\log(Y) + \beta_2\log(P) + \beta_3 I + \varepsilon$$

where A represents pollution abatement measures, Y denotes GDP per capita, P is the pollution level, and I represents the institutional variables. In this study, we focus on three pollution abatement measures, that is the number of facilities used for waste gas treatment, the volume of investment in waste gas treatment and the number of facilities for wastewater treatment. When we study the effects on the number of facilities for waste gas treatment and the volume of investment in waste gas treatment, we use the indicator of industrial waste gas to proxy for the pollution level; in analysing the influence on the number of facilities used for wastewater treatment, we use the indicator for wastewater. Because there may be an interaction effect between pollution abatement measures and the pollution level, we use a one- or two-period lag of the pollution level as instrumental variables in the regression. Again, because the doing business indicators are static variables, we use a panel model with random individual effects and report the regression results in Tables 9.7(a)–(c).

Table 9.6 Effects of income level and institutions on economic structure

inst	start		register		credit		contract		FDI	
log(y)	0.078***	0.078***	0.078***	0.078***	0.078***	0.078***	0.078***	0.078***	0.078***	0.078***
	(0.007)	(0.007)	(0.007)	(0.007)	(0.007)	(0.007)	(0.007)	(0.007)	(0.007)	(0.007)
log(y)^2	–0.023***	–0.024***	–0.024***	–0.024***	–0.024***	–0.024***	–0.023***	–0.024***	–0.024***	–0.024***
	(0.004)	(0.004)	(0.004)	(0.004)	(0.004)	(0.004)	(0.004)	(0.004)	(0.004)	(0.004)
I	–0.015	–	0.016	–	0.029	–	–0.037	–	0.011	–
	(0.053)	–	(0.054)	–	(0.044)	–	(0.084)	–	(0.037)	–
adj. R2	0.303	0.303	0.302	0.303	0.302	0.303	0.303	0.303	0.297	0.303
obs.	450	450	450	450	450	450	450	450	450	450

Notes: Numbers in parentheses are standard errors. '***', '**' and '*' indicate 1%, 5% and 10% levels of significance, respectively.

Table 9.7(a) The effects of income level and institutions on pollution abatement measures: I-the number of facilities for waste gas treatment

inst	start		register		credit		contract		FDI	
log(y)	–0.366***	–0.366***	–0.338***	–0.338***	–0.314***	–0.314***	–0.323***	–0.323***	–0.223***	–0.234***
	(0.062)	(0.062)	(0.061)	(0.061)	(0.06)	(0.06)	(0.06)	(0.06)	(0.056)	(0.057)
P	0.59***	0.59***	0.57***	0.57***	0.55***	0.55***	0.558***	0.558***	0.484***	0.489***
	(0.053)	(0.053)	(0.052)	(0.052)	(0.051)	(0.051)	(0.052)	(0.052)	(0.048)	(0.049)
I	1.248***	1.248***	1.104***	1.104***	0.827***	0.827***	1.537***	1.537***	0.216	–
	(0.188)	(0.188)	(0.193)	(0.193)	(0.158)	(0.158)	(0.291)	(0.291)	(0.171)	–
adj. R2	0.507	0.507	0.5	0.5	0.5	0.5	0.498	0.498	0.486	0.486
obs.	450	450	450	450	450	450	450	450	450	450

Table 9.7(b) *The effects of income level and institutions on pollution abatement measures: II-the volume of investment in waste gas treatment*

inst	start		register		credit		contract		FDI	
log(y)	0.19	–	0.163	–	0.142	–	0.249	–	0.31**	0.31**
	(0.199)	–	(0.192)	–	(0.182)	–	(0.185)	–	(0.142)	(0.142)
P	0.946***	1.098***	0.966***	1.098***	0.981***	1.098***	0.904***	1.098***	0.837***	0.837***
	(0.166)	(0.056)	(0.162)	(0.056)	(0.154)	(0.056)	(0.156)	(0.056)	(0.125)	(0.125)
I	0.1	–	0.252	–	0.345	–	–0.323	–	–2.314***	–2.314***
	(0.458)	–	(0.456)	–	(0.36)	–	(0.664)	–	(0.615)	(0.615)
adj. R2	0.457	0.451	0.457	0.451	0.457	0.451	0.459	0.451	0.483	0.483
obs.	450	450	450	450	450	450	450	450	450	450

Table 9.7(c) *The effects of income level and institutions on pollution abatement measures: III-the number of facilities for wastewater treatment*

inst	start		register		credit		contract		FDI	
log(y)	–0.002	–	0	–	0	–	0.006	–	0.001	–
	(0.039)	–	(0.039)	–	(0.038)	–	(0.039)	–	(0.039)	–
P	0.493***	0.5***	0.485***	0.5***	0.484***	0.484***	0.463***	0.475***	0.5***	0.5***
	(0.102)	(0.051)	(0.101)	(0.051)	(0.1)	(0.051)	(0.101)	(0.052)	(0.1)	(0.051)
I	0.338	–	0.529	–	0.517*	0.517*	1.083**	1.071**	0.225	–
	(0.333)	–	(0.332)	–	(0.271)	(0.267)	(0.48)	(0.468)	(0.2)	–
adj. R2	0.205	0.204	0.209	0.204	0.211	0.212	0.215	0.215	0.205	0.204
obs.	420	420	420	420	420	420	420	420	420	420

Notes: Numbers in parentheses are standard errors. '***', **' and '*' indicate 1%, 5% and 10% levels of significance, respectively.

The results show that pollution abatement measures are mainly affected by the pollution level, whereas the effects of income level and institutional quality are not significant. The effects of income level and institutional quality are negligible for the volume of investment in waste gas treatment and the number of facilities for wastewater treatment. With respect to the number of facilities for waste gas treatment, the influence of income level on the pollution abatement measures is negative, although both income level and institutional quality show a significant impact, which conflicts with the theoretical prediction.

A puzzle emerges at this juncture. In section 4.2 our results show that institutional quality exerts a significant positive impact on pollution control. However, our findings here indicate that institutional quality influences neither the economic structure nor pollution abatement measures (the two main channels through which institutions may significantly influence the pollution level in the conventional literature). Thus, through which channels do institutions affect the pollution level? We explore a 'three-effect model' (scale, composition and abatement) to determine whether there is another channel through which institutional quality may influence the pollution level.

4.4 The Three-effect Model and its Augmented Version

A basic three-effect model can be written as follows:

$$\log(P) = \beta_0 + \beta_1 \log(Y) + \beta_2 S + \beta_3 \log(A) + \varepsilon$$

where P is the pollution level, Y is the economic scale (proxied by GDP per capita), S indicates the economic structure (measured by the share of industry in GDP-second), and A represents the abatement effect (proxied by the number of facilities for waste gas treatment – facilities gas, the volume of investment in waste gas treatment – investment gas, and the number of facilities for wastewater treatment – facilities water). As there may be an interaction effect between pollution abatement measures and the pollution level, we use a one- or two-period lag of pollution abatement measures as instrumental variables to perform the regression. Once again, we use a panel model with random individual effects and report the regression results in Table 9.8.

The results are surprising. The pollution abatement measures increase rather than decrease pollution, that is introduction of a greater number of pollution abatement measures is related to higher pollution levels. We believe that this finding may be connected to data manipulation in China's pollution abatement measures. Our results are based on Chinese

Table 9.8 Three-effect model

	Industrial Waste Gas		SO_2		CO_2		Wastewater	
log(y)	0.811***	0.81***	–0.188***	–0.149***	0.717***	0.742***	0.272***	0.276***
	(0.053)	(0.048)	(0.066)	(0.056)	(0.029)	(0.015)	(0.032)	(0.014)
Second	1.327***	1.288***	1.311***	1.346***	0.699***	0.714***	0.015	–
	(0.29)	(0.288)	(0.349)	(0.35)	(0.17)	(0.161)	(0.168)	–
facilities gas	0.444***	0.445***	0.147	–	0.014	–	0.008	–
	(0.118)	(0.085)	(0.152)	–	(0.082)	–	(0.078)	–
investment gas	0.076*	0.08**	0.112**	0.105**	0.039*	–	0.006	–
	(0.041)	(0.038)	(0.049)	(0.049)	(0.023)	–	(0.024)	–
facilities water	–0.013	–	0.186	0.279**	0.091	0.236***	0.308***	0.344***
	(0.136)	–	(0.183)	(0.13)	(0.096)	(0.055)	(0.096)	(0.052)
adj. R2	0.854	0.858	0.192	0.184	0.907	0.918	0.64	0.643
obs.	420	420	420	420	390	390	420	420

Notes: Numbers in parentheses are standard errors. '***', '**' and '*' indicate 1%, 5% and 10% levels of significance, respectively.

official statistics, which are dubious, at least according to several studies. In certain cities officials are known to have manipulated pollution data to meet regulatory targets.[56] We believe this manipulation may have also occurred in the fields of pollution abatement measures, particularly since the beginning of the 11th Five Year Plan (2006), when environmental targets became important criteria for the first time in cadre promotion decisions. Thus, the facilities for pollution abatement may be invested to 'create numbers' to appease the central government; therefore, there will be more investment in pollution abatement in more polluted areas, leading to a positive correlation between abatement measures and the pollution level.

Although the real operational outcomes of these facilities are unverifiable, we surmise that these outcomes may be different in different regions of China. More specifically, in regions characterized by high institutional quality, the government may be more serious about its responsibilities regarding public good provision (including environmental protection), it may monitor the operation of pollution abatement facilities more strictly, and it may therefore address pollution problems more effectively. This hypothesis will be tested below.

We introduce an interaction term between institutional quality and pollution abatement measures to the three-effect model and obtain an augmented three-effect model as follows:

$$\log(P) = \beta_0 + \beta_1\log(Y) + \beta_2 S + \beta_3\log(A) + \beta_4 I + \beta_5 I^*\log(A) + \varepsilon$$

We report the regression results below in Tables 9.9(a)–(d).

Our predictions are supported by the regression results.[57] The institutional indicators and the interaction term between institutional quality

---

56 Chen et al. (2013b); Ghanema and Zhang (2014).

57 Our conclusion should be read with caution. The proxy we use for institutional quality, particularly the doing business indicators, mainly focus on business regulation. Our story is based on the assumption that these indicators can be used to measure the overall institutional environment of a region accurately and that a region that obtains a higher score on such indicators may also perform well in other areas, such as environmental regulation. We believe that this assumption is not unreasonable, and our empirical results indeed confirm the prediction derived from such assumption. Nevertheless, there is a possibility that the quality of business regulation of a region is irrelevant to the performance of that region in providing other public services, such as environmental regulation. If so, the findings presented by this study may need certain other explanations, or resort to other channels through which these doing business indicators may influence the pollution level of different regions.

Table 9.9(a) *The augmented three-effect model: I-industrial waste gas*

inst	start		register		credit		contract		FDI	
log(y)	0.857***	0.814***	0.85***	0.882***	0.876***	0.9***	0.899***	0.897***	0.773***	0.77***
	(0.048)	(0.053)	(0.045)	(0.031)	(0.046)	(0.029)	(0.086)	(0.035)	(0.058)	(0.063)
Second	0.477	–	0.755**	0.832***	0.857**	0.997***	0.488	–	1.255***	1.291***
	(0.373)	–	(0.351)	(0.305)	(0.336)	(0.283)	(0.521)	–	(0.29)	(0.289)
facilities gas	2.045***	2.361***	1.57**	1.612***	1.367***	0.976***	4.887**	2.944***	0.507***	0.454***
	(0.713)	(0.359)	(0.795)	(0.376)	(0.446)	(0.209)	(2.457)	(0.713)	(0.158)	(0.085)
investment gas	0.095	0.079*	0.085	–	–0.005	–	–0.987	–	0.09	0.122**
	(0.259)	(0.042)	(0.204)	–	(0.143)	–	(1.198)	–	(0.071)	(0.057)
facilities water	–0.771	–0.948**	0.21	0.25**	–0.283	0.209*	0.518	0.268**	0.072	–
	(0.908)	(0.403)	(0.583)	(0.117)	(0.574)	(0.118)	(1.415)	(0.126)	(0.201)	–
I	0.152	–	–0.818	–1.173***	–0.46	–0.998***	–4.818	–1.716***	–0.728	–
	(1.604)	–	(1.039)	(0.29)	(1.008)	(0.224)	(4.771)	(0.476)	(1.507)	–
I*(facilities gas)	–2.488**	–2.941***	–1.966	–2.089***	–1.573**	–1.032***	–6.243*	–3.582***	–0.715	–
	(1.065)	(0.483)	(1.241)	(0.564)	(0.68)	(0.275)	(3.397)	(0.957)	(1)	–
I*(investment gas)	–0.117	–	–0.12	–	0.037	–	1.387	–	–0.415	–0.613**
	(0.381)	–	(0.315)	–	(0.22)	–	(1.657)	–	(0.432)	(0.285)
I*(facilities water)	1.352	1.554***	–0.081	–	0.589	–	–0.42	–	–0.184	–
	(1.332)	(0.562)	(0.867)	–	(0.848)	–	(1.967)	–	(1.452)	–
adj. R2	0.848	0.838	0.856	0.878	0.854	0.881	0.785	0.863	0.85	0.856
obs.	420	420	420	420	420	420	420	420	420	420

Table 9.9(b) The augmented three-effect model: II-SO_2

inst	start		register		credit		contract		FDI	
log(y)	–0.124**	–0.155***	–0.147**	–0.174***	–0.136**	–0.147***	–0.023	–	–0.15**	–0.147**
	(0.063)	(0.043)	(0.06)	(0.045)	(0.058)	(0.04)	(0.196)	–	(0.074)	(0.057)
Second	0.844*	1.147***	0.928*	1.237***	1.118***	1.226***	0.17	–	1.411***	1.506***
	(0.491)	(0.395)	(0.473)	(0.402)	(0.426)	(0.367)	(1.097)	–	(0.351)	(0.348)
facilities gas	1.869**	0.976**	1.715	1.327***	1.292**	0.908***	9.34*	2.539***	0.087	–
	(0.947)	(0.391)	(1.108)	(0.506)	(0.566)	(0.247)	(5.223)	(0.818)	(0.201)	–
investment gas	–0.388	–	–0.219	–	–0.147	–	–3.625	–	0.101	0.14***
	(0.338)	–	(0.269)	–	(0.181)	–	(2.707)	–	(0.086)	(0.046)
facilities water	0.086	–	0.26	–	–0.111	–	1.598	–	0.157	–
	(1.201)	–	(0.796)	–	(0.729)	–	(3.048)	–	(0.269)	–
I	–1.914	–0.62*	–1.12	–	–0.983	–0.633**	–12.652	–	0.652	1.075***
	(2.11)	(0.372)	(1.398)	–	(1.279)	(0.302)	(10.79)	–	(1.91)	(0.402)
I*(facilities gas)	–2.52*	–1.221**	–2.47	–1.717**	–1.82**	–1.235***	–12.518*	–3.336***	0.932	–
	(1.411)	(0.557)	(1.719)	(0.773)	(0.862)	(0.37)	(7.235)	(1.155)	(1.214)	–
I*(investment gas)	0.709	–	0.469	–	0.375	–	5.144	–	–0.152	–
	(0.497)	–	(0.416)	–	(0.278)	–	(3.743)	–	(0.531)	–
I*(facilities water)	0.201	–	–0.121	–	0.456	–	–1.725	–	0.091	–
	(1.765)	–	(1.182)	–	(1.077)	–	(4.217)	–	(1.881)	–
adj. R2	0.129	0.214	0.124	0.178	0.172	0.225	0.023	0.149	0.194	0.171
obs.	420	420	420	420	420	420	420	420	420	420

Table 9.9(c) *The augmented three-effect model: III-CO_2*

inst	start		register		credit		contract		FDI	
log(y)	0.711***	0.727***	0.714***	0.742***	0.711***	0.721***	0.712***	0.742***	0.731***	0.727***
	(0.024)	(0.021)	(0.022)	(0.015)	(0.023)	(0.015)	(0.025)	(0.015)	(0.033)	(0.021)
Second	0.544**	0.679***	0.703***	0.703***	0.646***	0.708***	0.617**	0.714***	0.753***	0.656***
	(0.226)	(0.154)	(0.211)	(0.161)	(0.211)	(0.156)	(0.253)	(0.161)	(0.174)	(0.158)
facilities gas	0.341	–	–0.024	–	0.281	–	0.101	–	–0.043	–
	(0.42)	–	(0.471)	–	(0.268)	–	(1.125)	–	(0.103)	–
investment gas	0.097	0.039*	0.041	–	0.004	–	0.089	–	0.046	0.039*
	(0.133)	(0.02)	(0.103)	–	(0.08)	–	(0.413)	–	(0.038)	(0.021)
facilities water	–0.429	–	0.106	0.25***	–0.088	0.207***	0.094	0.236***	0.082	0.103*
	(0.527)	–	(0.322)	(0.055)	(0.343)	(0.056)	(0.567)	(0.055)	(0.138)	(0.06)
I	0.042	–	–0.697	–0.795***	–0.477	–0.764***	–1.009	–	0.033	–
	(0.915)	–	(0.568)	(0.278)	(0.611)	(0.21)	(1.588)	–	(0.892)	–
I*(facilities gas)	–0.412	–	0.154	–	–0.323	–	–0.065	–	0.924*	–
	(0.621)	–	(0.726)	–	(0.399)	–	(1.542)	–	(0.528)	–
I*(investment gas)	–0.079	–	–0.002	–	0.065	–	–0.068	–	–0.085	–
	(0.195)	–	(0.159)	–	(0.122)	–	(0.573)	–	(0.22)	–
I*(facilities water)	0.734	–	–0.083	–	0.216	–	–0.04	–	–0.61	–0.585***
	(0.782)	–	(0.479)	–	(0.509)	–	(0.797)	–	(0.956)	(0.195)
adj. R2	0.898	0.919	0.902	0.916	0.898	0.918	0.903	0.918	0.901	0.914
obs.	390	390	390	390	390	390	390	390	390	390

Table 9.9(d) *The augmented three-effect model: IV-Wastewater*

inst	start		register		credit		contract		FDI	
log(y)	0.239***	0.239***	0.258***	0.267***	0.263***	0.262***	0.233***	0.279***	0.257***	0.264***
	(0.028)	(0.022)	(0.028)	(0.017)	(0.029)	(0.017)	(0.039)	(0.028)	(0.036)	(0.018)
Second	–0.019	–	0.015	–	0.012	–	0.102	–	0.059	–
	(0.225)	–	(0.221)	–	(0.212)	–	(0.325)	–	(0.169)	–
facilities gas	–0.01	–	0.034	–	–0.107	–	–0.282	–	0.014	–
	(0.438)	–	(0.534)	–	(0.292)	–	(1.534)	–	(0.099)	–
investment gas	0.047	–	0.02	–	–0.005	–	0.37	0.041**	0.006	–
	(0.151)	–	(0.122)	–	(0.089)	–	(0.581)	(0.021)	(0.042)	–
facilities water	0.848	1.133***	0.793**	0.968***	0.831**	0.84***	0.883	–	0.378***	0.418***
	(0.548)	(0.279)	(0.375)	(0.231)	(0.385)	(0.174)	(0.767)	–	(0.136)	(0.08)
I	0.148	–	0.033	–	–0.399	–	1.651	1.429***	–1.346	–1.28**
	(0.958)	–	(0.652)	–	(0.664)	–	(2.22)	(0.302)	(0.941)	(0.557)
I*(facilities gas)	0.109	–	–0.019	–	0.221	–	0.457	–	0.386	–
	(0.65)	–	(0.824)	–	(0.44)	–	(2.107)	–	(0.587)	–
I*(investment gas)	–0.049	–	–0.012	–	0.025	–	–0.497	–	0.034	–
	(0.222)	–	(0.189)	–	(0.136)	–	(0.804)	–	(0.257)	–
I*(facilities water)	–1.061	–1.421***	–0.991*	–1.181***	–1.056*	–0.985***	–1.099	–	–1.656*	–1.659***
	(0.808)	(0.4)	(0.556)	(0.349)	(0.568)	(0.255)	(1.079)	–	(0.936)	(0.574)
adj. R2	0.626	0.591	0.624	0.603	0.605	0.607	0.612	0.651	0.635	0.637
obs.	420	420	420	420	420	420	420	420	420	420

Notes: Numbers in parentheses are standard errors. '***', '**' and '*' indicate 1%, 5% and 10% levels of significance, respectively. For each regression model, we report two types of results: the first is the initial regression results with all the explanatory variables included, and the second is the results with standardized regression coefficients.

and the pollution abatement measures all have negative signs, indicating that institutional quality does indeed matter for pollution control, but this channel operates by improving the operational performance of pollution abatement measures, rather than by increasing a region's pollution control investment, such as more investment into the facilities for waste gas treatment. Without a sound institutional infrastructure, such as professional and competent regulatory agencies, more investment in pollution control will not automatically translate into better environmental quality. Polluting enterprises may install pollution abatement facilities to comply with legal or regulatory requirements, but without continuous monitoring, independent legal enforcement and strict punishment for law-breakers, the profit motivation will push these enterprises to attempt to minimize the operational costs of these facilities. In other words, pollution abatement facilities will be idle or underemployed and thus have little effect on pollution control.

5. CONCLUSION

China's economic miracle has been achieved with severe environmental costs, such as substantial air and water pollution, which have been shown to be detrimental (and even life-threatening) to the health of China's citizens. It is natural to argue that environmental pollution is an inevitable by-product of China's extraordinary economic growth, rapid industrialization and large-scale urbanization. More pollution is generated as more factories are established, as more coal is burned to produce electricity, and as more private cars are produced, sold and used for commuting and recreational purposes. The so-called environmental Kuznets curve (EKC), which claims that there is a universal nexus of income and pollution, thus seems relevant for elucidating China's present circumstances.

We test the applicability of the EKC to China in this chapter and find that at least for certain pollution indicators, such as industrial waste gas and SO_2, there is indeed an inverted U-shaped trend that conforms to the prediction of the EKC. Certainly, economic growth is neither the only nor the most important driving force behind China's environmental degradation. Pollution can be reduced by technological innovations, by adjustments in resource pricing and environmental services, and by legal and policy interventions. Whether and to what extent these strategies will be adopted, in turn, depends on certain institutional factors. We therefore inject such institutional indicators into our analysis and find that these institutional variables to a large extent account for the heterogeneity in EKC patterns in China's different regions, and that regions with better institutional quality enjoy preferable EKC patterns (lower positions and lower turning points).

We further show that the channel through which institutional quality may impact the environment is different from that predicted by conventional theory. Our study shows that institutional indicators affect the pollution level through the operational outcomes of pollution abatement measures rather than by affecting structural transformation or the volume of pollution abatement facilities. In other words, without a sound institutional framework, investments in pollution control will have no real effect on pollution abatement, which is similar to a 'law in a book' that will never be translated into a 'law in action', without effective implementation and enforcement of the relevant law.

REFERENCES

Allen, Franklin, Jun Qian and Meijun Qian (2005), 'Law, Finance, and Economic Growth in China', 77 *Journal of Financial Economics* 57.

Arrow, Kenneth, Bert Bolin, Robert Costanza, Partha Dasgupta, Carl Folke, C.S. Holling, Bengt-Owe Jansson, Simon Levin, Karl-Goran Maler, Charles Perrings and David Pimentel (1995), 'Economic Growth, Carrying Capacity, and the Environment', 268 *Science* 520.

Barros, Fabio Granja e, Augusto F. Mendonça and Jorge M. Nogueira, 'Poverty and Environmental Degradation: The Kuznets Environmental Curve for the Brazilian Case', Department of Economics, University of Brasilia, Working Paper 267, December 2002, available at http://www.ceemaunb.com/jmn/publicacoes/InequalityandEKC.pdf (accessed 20 March 2017).

Bradshaw, Corey J.A., Xingli Giam and Navjot S. Sodhi (2010), 'Evaluating the Relative Environmental Impact of Countries', 5 *PLoS ONE* e10440.

Brajer, Victor, Robert W. Mead and Feng Xiao (2008), 'Health Benefits of Tunneling through the Chinese Environmental Kuznets Curve (EKC)', 66 *Ecological Economics* 674.

Brajer, Victor, Robert W. Mead and Feng Xiao (2011), 'Searching for an Environmental Kuznets Curve in China's Air Pollution', 22 *China Economic Review* 383.

Brandt, Loren, Debin Ma and Thomas G. Rawski (2014), 'From Divergence to Convergence: Reevaluating the History Behind China's Economic Boom', 52 *Journal of Economic Literature* 45.

Brock, William A. and M. Scott Taylor (2005), 'Economic Growth and the Environment: A Review of Theory and Empirics', in Philippe Aghion and Steven Durlauf (eds), *Handbook of Economic Growth* (Volume 1B) (Elsevier, Amsterdam).

Chen, Su-Mei and Ling-Yun He (2014), 'Welfare Loss of China's Air Pollution: How to Make Personal Vehicle Transportation Policy', 31 *China Economic Review* 106.

Chen, Yuyu, Avraham Ebenstein, Michael Greenstone and Hongbin Li (2013a), 'Evidence on the Impact of Sustained Exposure to Air Pollution on Life

Expectancy from China's Huai River Policy', 110 *Proceedings of the National Academy of Sciences of the United States of America* 12936.

Chen, Yuyu, Ginger Zhe Jin, Naresh Kumar and Guang Shi (2013b), 'Gaming in Air Pollution Data? Lessons from China', NBER Working Paper No. 18729, available at http://www.nber.org/papers/w18729 (accessed 3 July 2015).

China Water Risk (2014), '2013 State of Environment Report Review', 9 July, available at http://chinawaterrisk.org/resources/analysis-reviews/2013-state-of-environment-report-review/ (accessed 11 July 2015).

Dasgupta, Susmita, Benoit Laplante, Hua Wang and David Wheeler (2002), 'Confronting the Environmental Kuznets Curve', 16 (1) *Journal of Economic Perspectives* 147.

Diao, X.D., S.X. Zeng, C.M. Tam and Vivian W.Y. Tam (2009), 'EKC Analysis for Studying Economic Growth and Environmental Quality: A Case Study in China', 17 *Journal of Cleaner Production* 541.

Ebenstein, Avraham (2012), 'The Consequences of Industrialization: Evidence from Water Pollution and Digestive Cancers in China', 94 *Review of Economics and Statistics* 186.

Ebenstein, Avraham, Maoyong Fan, Michael Greenstone, Guojun He, Peng Yin and Maigeng Zhou (2015), 'Growth, Pollution, and Life Expectancy: China from 1991–2012', 105 *American Economic Review* 226.

Economy, Elizabeth (2007), 'The Great Leap Backward? The Costs of China's Environmental Crisis', 86 *Foreign Affairs* 38.

Economy, Elizabeth (2013), 'China's Water Pollution Crisis', The Diplomat, 22 January, available at: http://thediplomat.com/2013/01/forget-air-pollution-chinas-has-a-water-problem/ (accessed 11 July 2015).

Esty, Daniel C. and Michael E. Porter (2005), 'National Environmental Performance: An Empirical Analysis of Policy Results and Determinants', 10 (4) *Environment and Development Economics* 391.

Ghanema, Dalia and Junjie Zhang (2014), '"Effortless Perfection": Do Chinese Cities Manipulate Air Pollution Data?' 68 (2) *Journal of Environmental Economics and Management* 203.

Gilley, Bruce (2012), 'Comparing National Sustainability in China and India', in Xiaoming Huang, Alex C. Tan and Sekhar Bandyopadhyay (eds), *China, India and the End of Development Models* (Palgrave Macmillan, Basingstoke).

Grossman, Gene M. and Alan B. Krueger (1991), *Environmental Impacts of a North American Free Trade Agreement* (NBER Working Paper No. 3914).

Grossman, Gene M. and Alan B. Krueger (1995), 'Economic Growth and the Environment', 110 *Quarterly Journal of Economics* 353.

He, Jie (2009), 'China's Industrial SO_2 Emissions and Its Economic Determinants: EKC's Reduced vs. Structural Model and the Role of International Trade', 14 *Environment and Development Economics* 227.

Hsieh, Chang-Tai and Peter J. Klenow (2009), 'Misallocation and Manufacturing TFP in China and India', 124 *Quarterly Journal of Economics* 1403.

Knight, John (2014), 'Inequality in China: An Overview', 29 *World Bank Research Observer* 1.

Kuznets, Simon (1955), 'Economic Growth and Income Inequality', 45 *American Economic Review* 1.

Liu, Lee (2010), 'Made in China: Cancer Villages', 52 *Environment: Science and Policy for Sustainable Development* 8.

Lu, Wen-Qing Shao-Hua Xie, Wen-Shan Zhou, Shao-Hui Zhang and Ai-Lin Liu (2008), 'Water Pollution and Health Impact in China: A Mini Review', 2 *Open Environmental Sciences* 1.

Matus, Kira, Kyung-Min Nam, Noelle E. Selin, Lok N. Lamsal, John M. Reilly and Sergey Paltsev (2012), 'Health Damages from Air Pollution in China', 22 *Global Environmental Change* 55.

Nahman, Anton and Geoff Antrobus (2005), 'Trade and the Environmental Kuznets Curve: Is Southern Africa a Pollution Haven?' 73 (4) *South African Journal of Economics* 803.

Panayotou, Theodore (1997), 'Demystifying the Environmental Kuznets Curve: Turning a Black Box into a Policy Tool', 2 (4) *Environment and Development Economics* 465.

Pei, Minxin (2006), *China's Trapped Transition: The Limits of Developmental Autocracy* (Harvard University Press, Cambridge, MA).

Perry, Elizabeth J. (2014), 'Growing Pains: Challenges for a Rising China', 143 *Daedalus* 5.

Porter, Michael E. and Claas Van der Linde (1995), 'Toward a New Conception of the Environment–Competitiveness Relationship', 9 (4) *Journal of Economic Perspectives* 97.

Qiu, Jane (2011), 'China to Spend Billions Cleaning Up Groundwater', 334 *Science* 745.

Smarzynska, Beata K. and Shang-Jin Wei (2001), 'Pollution Havens and Foreign Direct Investment: Dirty Secret or Popular Myth?' NBER Working Paper No. 8465, available at http://www.nber.org/papers/w8465.pdf (accessed 20 March 2017).

Song, Tao, Tingguo Zheng and Lianjun Tong (2008), 'An Empirical Test of the Environmental Kuznets Curve in China: A Panel Cointegration Approach', 19 *China Economic Review* 381.

Stern, David I., Michael S. Common and Edward B. Barbier (1996), 'Economic Growth and Environmental Degradation: The Environmental Kuznets Curve and Sustainable Development', 24 (7) *World Development* 1151.

Stern, David I. and Michael S. Common (2001), 'Is there an Environmental Kuznets Curve for Sulfur?' 41 (2) *Journal of Environmental Economics and Management* 162.

Strand, Jon (2002), 'Environmental Kuznets Curves: Empirical Relationships between Environmental Quality and Economic Development', Memorandum No. 04/2002, Department of Economics, University of Oslo, available at http://www.sv.uio.no/econ/english/research/unpublished-works/working-papers/pdf-files/2002/Memo-04-2002.pdf (accessed 20 March 2017).

Tao, Tao and Kunlun Xin (2014), 'A Sustainable Plan for China's Drinking Water', 511 *Nature* 527.

Wang, Yuhua (2015), 'Politically Connected Polluters under Smog', 17 *Business and Politics* 97.

World Bank and the Development Research Center of the State Council of China (2013), *China 2030: Building a Modern, Harmonious, and Creative High-Income Society* (World Bank, Washington DC).

Yang, Haisheng, Jie He and Shaoling Chen (2015), 'The Fragility of the Environmental Kuznets Curve: Revisiting the Hypothesis with Chinese Data via an "Extreme Bound Analysis"', 109 *Ecological Economics* 41.

Zhang, Qingfeng and Robert Crooks (2012), *Toward an Environmentally*

Sustainable Future: Country Environmental Analysis of the People's Republic of China (Asian Development Bank, Mandaluyong City).

Zugravu-Soilita, Natalia (2015), 'How Does Foreign Direct Investment Affect Pollution? Toward a Better Understanding of the Direct and Conditional Effects', 66 (2) *Environmental and Resource Economics* 293, available at http://link.springer.com/article/10.1007%2Fs10640-015-9950-9 (accessed 20 March 2017).

10. Carbon labels: climate change regulation and legal risks and opportunities under WTO law

Stefan E. Weishaar and Ruohong Chen[1]

1. INTRODUCTION

The recently concluded Paris agreement entered into force on 4 November 2016. It incentivizes the signatory countries to implement their 'Nationally Determined Contributions' with a view to limiting global warming to 2 degrees Celsius above pre-industrial levels. The Paris Agreement (Article 6), which describes the mechanisms available to reach this goal, remains delightfully vague.

Legislators can therefore choose from a wide portfolio of instruments for addressing climate change and putting a price on greenhouse gas emissions. Putting a price on carbon entails that production costs increase vis-à-vis products from jurisdictions that do not put a price on carbon. Much research effort has been devoted to examining if a fall in the greenhouse gas (GHG) emissions within an Emissions Trading System (ETS) causes increases in GHG emissions abroad (carbon leakage), and if covered entities react to increased environmental costs by relocating to jurisdictions with lower environmental standards (pollution haven hypothesis).

Even though the overall finding of the literature is that carbon leakage does not arise at current allowance price levels, the fear of reduced competitiveness has led to the introduction of various policy measures designed to protect domestic industry.[2] A body of economic literature has examined the efficacy of several policy instruments including border

[1] This research is supported by BFSU Fundamental Research Funds for the Central Universities.

[2] In the case of the EU ETS for example, such measures include the granting of free emission allowances to energy-intensive and trade-exposed industries and the permission to grant state aid (subsidies).

tax adjustments[3] and carbon labels. Carbon labels are different from other trade measures since 'labels' are characterized as providing information about product properties to customers. They were originally introduced by UK supermarkets (Tesco and Marks & Spencer in 2007) and proliferated mainly as private sector standards, though there are also some carbon labels that are closely associated with governments (e.g. France's carbon footprint pilot programme, the UK's Carbon Reduction label or Japan's Carbon Footprint of Products System). Such carbon labels differ a lot in terms of their scope,[4] assessment methodology and comparability.[5]

Naturally, such protection measures have also received heightened interest from a World Trade Organization (WTO) perspective. In the recent years our understanding regarding the interpretation of Technical Barriers to Trade (TBT) advanced through a series of cases (*US–Tuna (II) Mexico*, *US–COOL*, *US–Clove*, *EC–Seal*). It is therefore timely to re-examine whether carbon labels could be used to address carbon leakage concerns and which risks and regulatory opportunities they pose from a WTO perspective. In particular, we are interested to see whether the WTO rules applicable to carbon labels are following law and economics insights, in the sense that these insights may guide States to select the most efficient labels.

This chapter is structured as follows. After this introduction we first present the object of carbon label regulation and select the various labels to be examined (section 2). Section 3 presents the law and economic insights regarding carbon labels and examines how the selected labels would be assessed from a law and economics perspective. Section 4 reviews the risks and opportunities presented by carbon labels under WTO rules, and pays particular attention to the necessity test. The second part of this section evaluates the selected carbon labels from the perspective of WTO rules and in particular the necessity test. The final section offers comparative and concluding remarks on the law and economics and the WTO assessment of carbon labels, and culminates in policy advice.

---

3 Kuik and Hofkes (2010).

4 One can, for example, distinguish between transport labels that focus on distance travelled or a life cycle analysis ('from cradle to grave').

5 On the methodological challenges, see for example Ernst and Young (2011).

2. OBJECT OF REGULATION AND CARBON LABEL SELECTION

The objects of regulation by carbon labels are the various greenhouse gas emissions such as carbon dioxide, methane, nitrous oxide and so on. They can be converted to an equivalent of 1 ton of CO_2, and are generally described as non-localized pollutants because the actual location of the emission is not relevant. From an environmental perspective it is the overall concentration of greenhouse gases in the atmosphere that is decisive, not where on the globe they were emitted. Emissions of greenhouse gases can stem from process and production methods.

Greenhouse gas emissions of (consumer) products stem from various sources: they can come from the carbon content of the product's inputs,[6] they are generated in the production process (so-called process emissions)[7] and are also associated with transportation. Emissions are generated at all levels of the value chain.

Since the amount of carbon that is released in the process of 'producing' a particular good is not visible as such in the product itself, and while elaborate certification, monitoring and enforcement mechanisms are required but difficult to safeguard, several types of labels have emerged at various levels of the value chain.

Starting from around 2008 several carbon label measures emerged. Based on the typology of Schaefer and Blanke,[8] we selected several typical carbon label measures according to their design and communication approach (see Table 10.1). In the course of this chapter we evaluate how they are assessed from a law and economics perspective and from a WTO perspective. With regard to the latter, we pay special attention to the TBT necessity test.

The Carbon Trust label is characterized by presenting a numeric greenhouse gas value. The Carbonfund label takes a carbon offset approach and offers companies the possibility to improve their environmental record by investing in carbon offset projects. The Indice Carbone of the French retailer Casino ranks the carbon footprint or CO_2 value of a particular product and standardizes it to a uniform mass unit of 100 g product based on the cradle-to-gate (B2B) assessment. This approach enables the consumer to make a fair comparison between similar products. The

6 Aluminium is an example of a product used in cars that uses vast amounts of energy in production; it is therefore carbon-intensive.

7 Around 30 per cent of the carbon content of cement, for example, is associated with the actual production process.

8 See Schaefer and Blanke (2014).

Table 10.1 Overview of selected carbon labels

	Label	Organization/ country	Approach	Standard	Feature	Method of verification	Method of accreditation of certifier
1	Single numeric CO_2 value	Carbon Trust, UK	No expiry date	PAS 2050	Different units/not comparable	Independent third-party	Operator accredits itself to certify
2	CO_2 value, Colour coded	Casino, French	No expiry date	Indice carbone	Instantly comparable	Self-verification (operator verifies the carbon footprints of own products, calculated by a consultant)	Not applicable (no use of certifier, but ADEME has validated the general methodology)
3	CO_2 Free labels	Carbonfund, USA	Carbon offset	PAS 2050/ISO 14044	Gold standard certificates	?	Third-party certifier
4	Only the best products are labelled within a product category	Climatop NPO, Switzerland	Limited to two years	ICA-ISO 14040	Only the best products within a 20% margin get the label	Independent third party (operator hires other company to peer review the carbon footprints it has calculated)	Operator selects the peer reviewer

Source: Schaefer and Blanke (2014), Guenther, Saunders and Tait (2012) and Bolwig and Gibbon (2009).

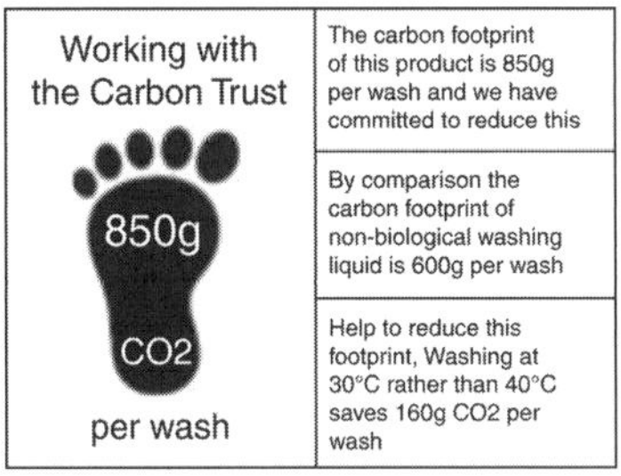

Figure 10.1 *Carbon Trust label*

Figure 10.2 *Carbonfund label*

Figure 10.3 *Climatop label*

Figure 10.4 *Casino Indice Carbone label*

Climatop label is based on a life cycle analysis study and is used by Migros (a Swiss retailer). This label bears no numeric value but is only awarded to the best products in a product category.

3. LAW AND ECONOMICS ANALYSIS

This section of the chapter first presents the law and economics analysis approach to carbon labels in general. Subsequently these insights are applied to the selected carbon labels.

3.1 Law and Economics and Carbon Labels

When examining carbon labels, one contemplates the use of public or private regulatory measures to address global warming. Regulatory measures here are conceptualized broadly as measures that intervene in the market. These measures can be either *public* or *private.*

Examinations from a regulatory law and economics perspective conventionally start with the question if *a regulatory intervention can be justified.* The underlying rationale for this premise is that regulatory measures should take efficiency considerations into account as well. This part of the text therefore briefly describes two views in the literature on economic regulation that help us understand the need for and the creation of regulation. First, a public interest approach, and then a private interest approach will be presented. While the public interest approach justifies regulation on the basis of so-called market failures, the private interest approach examines the potential dangers involved in the activities of market participants that strive for tailor-made regulation through lobbying (rent-seeking) and self-regulation.[9]

The public interest approach finds justification for regulatory interference with the market in the perceived shortcomings or failures of the markets. In the literature there are four market failures that prevent market forces from attaining an efficient outcome: (1) externalities, (2) problems with information asymmetry, (3) public goods and (4) market power. Each will be discussed in turn and applied to carbon labels.

Externalities are described by economists as costs or benefits affecting persons other than those taking action. Pollution is an example of a negative externality.[10] The market failure of externalities can be overcome

---

9 See Philipsen (2003), p. 23 ff.

10 See Cooter and Ulen (2004), p. 44 ff. for an economic analysis of externalities.

by internalizing the negative effects, that is by bringing the good into the market price mechanism. This can be achieved by levying adequate taxes for each level of usage of the underpriced good.[11] Taxes could be used for this purpose. Taxes in the Pigovian tradition, for example, would determine the value of social costs to be internalized – something that is inherently difficult to calculate. By contrast, taxes in the Baumol–Oates[12] tradition seek to circumvent the problem of setting an optimal tax rate and propose, as a second-best policy, a tax that would be set at levels to achieve environmental standards. Emissions trading systems are other means for putting a price on pollution. The existence of an externality as such does, however, not suffice to justify interventions in the market. The Coase theorem teaches us that in a market where transactions are costless (or very low), parties could 'internalize the externality' by means of bargaining.

In the case of carbon labels it is, however, expected that transaction costs are too high to allow for Coasian bargaining, particularly if a large number of (small) consumers are involved. Even when considering the situation where large wholesalers account for a significant part of the trade, transaction costs may still be too high. Given the substantial amount of information that is required to estimate the full carbon content of products, transaction costs may be too high to allow market actors to attain an efficient outcome. Coasian solutions may, however, be feasible for wholesalers if they are only targeted at particular products, if they are easy to measure or if they are only in connection with transportation. In those situations where transaction costs are too high, (mandatory) regulation can help to attain efficient outcomes – provided, of course, that the benefits associated with quality regulation are not outweighed by enforcement costs or distortions of competition.

It is worth mentioning, however, that carbon labels, albeit having – at least in part – an environmental objective, do not lead to an internalization of externalities as such. Internalization works in a rather indirect way. Carbon labels allow consumers to make an informed decision about their purchase and thereby enable producers to be rewarded for producing more environmentally friendly goods. From an environmental perspective an accurate representation of the carbon footprint of the product is desirable. This would point towards a carbon label that reflects the carbon content over the entire lifetime of the product (from cradle to grave), though this may conflict with other goals such as low administrative costs (see below).

---

[11] This is referred to as the 'Pigou tax'. See Pigou (1949), chapter 8.

[12] Baumol and Oates (1971).

Problems with information asymmetry between different economic actors can lead to devastating effects for the market. Akerlof describes how information asymmetry between buyers and sellers can lead to a situation in which the market could even break down because of deterioration in quality resulting from adverse selection.[13] Buyers suffer from an information disadvantage and take their estimate of the average quality of products sold as a basis for their willingness to pay. Under normal circumstances sellers, knowing very well the quality and value of their merchandise, are only willing to sell at such a price if their quality is average or below. Those sellers that do have a good product, by contrast, are unwilling to sell. Buyers will then adapt their expectations, and eventually a market suffering from information asymmetry may break down. Information asymmetry can be particularly grave if it occurs in contexts where judging the quality of goods and services *ex ante* is very difficult (experience goods) and where repeat interaction is not expected and reputation-building fails. This suggests that market intervention can be justified on the basis of information asymmetry problems, though it is worth mentioning that any interference with the market should be proportional to the expected benefits. The costs of correcting market failure through regulation should be smaller than the expected benefits from regulation. The most efficient regulatory mechanism should be chosen when taking into account the overall welfare effects for society, that is the sum of consumer surplus, producer surplus and deadweight loss.[14]

Given the large diversity of carbon labels, one can expect that information costs are high and consequently consumers are not informed about the requirements and quality safeguards of particular labels. In addition, since the carbon content does not affect the actual product and cannot be experienced during its use or consumption, we are dealing with a credence good, and consumers will therefore indeed suffer from information asymmetry. In such an environment where consumers cannot know the quality of the product even after purchase, the market may indeed break down as competing firms may introduce labels of their own without meeting high environmental standards (green-washing), and environmentally-minded companies find it too expensive to use high-quality labels. In order for carbon labels to work successfully in the market, quality control and a measure of regulation is required. Regulated schemes may also lead to a limitation of available labels and thereby contribute to transparency and consumer trust. This might point towards a mandatory framework for

[13] Akerlof (1970).

[14] Philipsen (2007), p. 116.

carbon labels. As will be discussed below, however, this is not risk-free and a careful balance between the costs and the benefits must be struck.

Public goods are goods or services that have very special properties: their consumption is non-diminishable and people cannot (easily) be excluded from enjoying them.[15] Goods that have high degrees of both properties are often referred to as pure public goods. A classic example of the first type is national defence. Despite the general demand for public goods, the market fails to provide them, since every potential customer has a strong incentive to benefit from the service without paying for it (free-riding). Consequently, such goods are frequently provided for through tax money. Private production does also exist, but takes the form of a donation or through the sale of important by-products to the public good.

A carbon label provides information to (potential) customers to enable them to make a better-informed decision. The information provided through the label has a public good character in the sense that it is non-diminishable and (potential) customers are not excluded from observing the label. The market failure free-riding associated with public goods does not, however, seem directly applicable to carbon labels, since in a strict sense the labels are not the product themselves. The market failure of public goods does not therefore seem to be applicable in the context of carbon labels.

Last but by no means least, the fourth kind of market failure is related to market power. *Market power* allows a monopoly, a monopsony or the ability of firms enjoying a position of market power (either individually or jointly) to maximize profits by increasing prices beyond competitive levels through restricting output.

In the context of carbon labels, market power is unlikely to play a role, provided that labels are accessible to all companies meeting the required standards and that the standards themselves are not set in such a way as to unduly discriminate against competitors.

While in the previous section justifications of governmental market interventions have been reviewed, it is worth mentioning that there are also areas of economics offering a different explanation as to why we see a lot of regulation around us. The public choice school of thought stresses the importance of interest groups in the formation of regulation. Public choice applies economic theories and methods to political behaviour[16] and is particularly interested in voters, politicians and self-interested

---

[15] For a short description see Cooter and Ulen (2004), p. 44 ff.

[16] Its founding fathers include Kenneth Arrow, James Buchanan, Gordon Tullock, Mancur Olson and William Niskanen.

government officials. Adherents of the public choice school of thought argue that market failure does not imply that governments should always intervene in the market, since there is the risk that government regulations create more costs to society than market failures.

Since this theory was originally developed in the context of democratic political systems, the export of its findings to other societies with a different organizational framework is not without problem. The concept of *rent-seeking*, however, is not closely related to collective (democratic) decision-making and hence is not limited to public choice theory. Rent-seeking is defined as an expenditure of scarce resources to capture an artificially created transfer.[17] Stigler first discussed the idea that it is the industry itself that demands regulation,[18] and that demand for regulation will be high if the benefits of restricting competition cannot be reached by the industry itself. According to Stigler's theory, which became known as the economic theory of regulation,[19] the industry would have an incentive to invest an amount equal to the expected utility of the benefit to be assigned by the State organ.[20] This benefit can, for example, take the form of a subsidy, or a (legal) monopoly right or the implementation of protectionist measures. Rent-seeking expenses do obviously significantly increase the costs to society of assigned monopoly rights or favours. And the social costs would even be higher if another interested party incurred expenses in lobbying the decision makers to resist the rent seekers.[21] Public choice does, however, recognize that large groups are not easily mobilized, and producers are more likely to take action as a small group, since they also stand to gain more.[22] Particularly where information costs are high and losses to individuals are limited, decision makers are more likely to yield to rent-seeking, since the parts of society that will suffer harm as a result are unlikely to resist.

Niskanen is generally considered the founder of the public choice literature on bureaucracy.[23] He assumed that bureaucrats have their own agenda, and that they are striving for power, prestige, payment and promotion. Given the information advantage bureaucrats have over the government, they are able to wisely exploit the electorate's demand for

---

17 Tollison (1982), p. 578. See also Chapter 1 of this book on regulatory capture.

18 Stigler (1971), p. 3.

19 For an extension of Stigler's ideas, see Pelzman (1976).

20 Posner (1975).

21 See Cullis and Jones (1998), p. 95.

22 Olson (1975).

23 Niskanen (1968, 1971).

their service to extract larger budgets from the government, and hence to create excessively large bureaus.

Peltzman[24] points out that a regulator can be 'captured' by the regulated industry if it does not have an independent source of information, but has to rely upon the regulated industry. The regulated industry can misinform the regulators in such a way as to induce them to accept price increases and so on. In this way industry regulation will become costly to society and inefficient. One way to address this is to link the profitability of companies to the capital installed and to offer them a 'fair rate of return'. The dilemma of regulating rates of return is, of course, that companies do have an incentive to overinvest and thus to waste resources (x-inefficiency).[25] The associated overcapitalization of course implies higher costs and higher prices for the company, and hence for society at large.[26]

When considering carbon labels, it is therefore important to be cautious as they can give rise to societal costs associated with inefficient regulation, such as rent-seeking costs, monopoly costs (regulatory capture), x-inefficiency in the regulated industry and a too-large regulatory body.

Another important consideration from a law and economics perspective is the costs of setting up and maintaining the regulatory measure. Preferably these costs should be low. In the context of carbon labels, such costs are associated with certification and monitoring in particular. Administrative costs can be expected to be lower for labels that only consider particular production inputs (such as energy usage, for example), or particular modes of transport (for example, air transport). Costs for labels that measure the carbon content from cradle to grave, however, require elaborate calculation methodologies and are believed to be very costly.

Besides administrative costs, there are also other efficiency considerations. *International trade* gives rise to strong societal benefits. Regulatory measures should therefore restrict trade as little as possible. Carbon labels do, however, have the potential to restrict trade (as will be elaborated upon in section 3). Measures that are non-mandatory may have a trade-restricting effect only if consumer preferences are such that they do not hold non-labelled products in high regard. Mandatory schemes, by contrast, can constitute barriers to trade by restricting market access by goods that do not meet the label requirements.

---

24 See Pelzman (1976).

25 Frank (1997), p. 414, refers to this in a rather intuitive way by calling it the 'gold plated water cooler effect'.

26 Averch and Johnson (1962).

The above examination of carbon labels offers complex insights that are pointing towards different directions. As for the question of the scope of a carbon label, it would be desirable to have a system that is as comprehensive as possible. Considerations of administrative costs and consumer considerations would point towards having a transparent and 'simple' scheme that could, for example, be based on production inputs or freight distance.

As for the question whether a carbon label system should be mandatory or not, the law and economics assessment offers different considerations as well. Considering the potential negative effects on trade and the danger of regulatory capture, rent-seeking and x-inefficiency, a non-mandatory system would be preferable. Yet given that carbon labels are credence goods and suffer from inherent information asymmetry, a market for carbon labels may not emerge in the absence of mandatory regulation that secures the monitoring and certification process and prevents green-washing. A careful weighing must be undertaken to balance the various points of consideration.

A law and economics assessment has also some insights to offer regarding the question whether regulation should be public or private. As a yardstick of who should take regulatory measures, law and economics scholars frequently look at who possesses superior information and who could effectively organize regulation.

Comparing the information that is available to the various actors, one can expect that companies will have better knowledge regarding their own line of business, while the government will have better information on multiple sectors. Similarly the government is expected to be better able to design (mandatory) compliance schemes for carbon labels as it can provide for effective legal enforcement across different sectors and along different levels of the supply chains. As presented above, government interference with the market can give rise to adverse effects such as regulatory capture, and so on, while private regulation will run into problems with green-washing.

3.2 Law and Economics on Carbon Labels: Application

After presenting the general law and economic insights on carbon labels, we will now apply them to the selected carbon labels. Each element identified above is taken in turn. Based on the assessment of the respective labels they are presented in a schematic fashion in Table 10.2.

3.2.1 Environment

From an environmental perspective, internalization of externalities provides the market failure justification from a law and economics perspective

Table 10.2 Law and economic assessment of carbon labels

	Casino Index	Carbon Trust	Climatop	Carbonfund
Environmental scope	++	++	++	+++
Information asymmetry	++	+	++	+++
Administrative burden	+/–	+/–	+/–	+/–
Public/private actors	+	+++	+	+++
International trade (same as Table 10.4)	+++	++	+	+
Overall	8	8	6	10

Note: The larger the number of plusses, the higher the degree of efficiency.

for regulation. The more complete the scope of emissions that are being brought within the sphere of a carbon label measure, the better from an environmental perspective.[27] It appears that on the basis of the ambition, there are few differences between the labels: they all seem to share a life cycle approach, and consequently the level of environmental ambition appears to be high for all the labels. Carbon Trust measures carbon life cycles of carbon footprints for an entire organization, product or industry. Casino's Carbon Index seems to be quite complete in capturing carbon emissions. It examines emissions from production stages, manufacturing, transport, packaging and distribution. Climatop captures emissions from a life cycle analysis that extends to all relevant emissions. Carbonfund goes a step further than the others in the sense that it also certifies carbon neutrality on the basis of carbon offsets in addition to offering a life cycle analysis. The latter label is therefore evaluated more positively.

3.2.2 Information asymmetry

The law and economics treatment discussed above indicated that there is a strong problem with information asymmetry concerning the carbon content of products, as consumers cannot ascertain what this is. The internalization of environmental externalities of carbon labels works in an indirect way, that is by influencing consumer buying behaviour. In this context, information issues (see below) are important. A high degree of transparency and comparability is therefore important. However, the labels differ strongly in terms of the information they afford to consumers. Stating numerical values (Carbon Trust) does not give consumers information on how one product compares to another. Casino's Carbon Index

[27] Of course there are also administrative costs that need to be considered.

offers some measure of information on this by offering a colour coding system. But still, consumers may not know by how much one product is more environmentally friendly than another. Similarly the Climatop label informs consumers that the product is among the top 20 per cent, but not by how much it is better than a competing product. The Carbonfund label also does not offer any information regarding the carbon content of the product – it does, however, enable consumers to avoid emissions, provided of course that the offset investments are indeed effective. It is worth mentioning that transparency and comparability is, however, not enough to safeguard against the negative effects of information asymmetry (such as green-washing). In order to do this, a measure of regulation – for example by government – would be necessary. All in all there is room for improvement for all labels, but since Carbontrust offers the least detailed information, it receives the lowest evaluation.

3.3.3 Administrative costs

It is suggested that administrative costs for labels that are based on easily measured inputs rather than a life cycle analysis will be lower. All labels examined are life cycle labels and are therefore assessed in a similar fashion.

3.3.4 Public and private actors

When it comes to deciding if public or private actors should be involved with carbon labels, law and economics suggests that there is a role for both types of actor. In all labels considered, private parties are involved, while public actors are not. Public actors can, however, help to reduce green-washing and may have or may be able to obtain superior information regarding other sectors and markets that is generally not available to a private party, who may only be able to negotiate obtaining information from its own suppliers. Regulators may also be better able to solicit the support of other governments and regulatory authorities in order to obtain better information for carbon labelling. Labels that have a stronger comparative focus will therefore benefit more from regulation. Consequently Carbon Index and Climatop have a lower evaluation than Carbonfund and Carbon Trust on this point.

3.3.5 International trade

The assessment of these carbon labels from an international trade perspective is facilitated by the fact that none of them is mandatory. Barriers to trade are thus assumed to be low, as a trade effect would only arise in the presence of strong consumer preferences. The assessment from a law and economics perspective is therefore essentially the same as from a WTO perspective (see Table 10.3 for the WTO assessment).

Table 10.3 Trade-restrictiveness of selected carbon label measures

		Compulsory third party certifier?	
		Yes	No
Access to market for products without label?	No	+++	++
	Yes	+	
		Climatop Carbonfund Carbon Trust	Indice Carbon

Note: The larger the number of plusses, the higher the degree of trade-restrictiveness.

4. CARBON LABELS UNDER WTO RULES

This section reviews the risks and opportunities of carbon labels under WTO rules and its adjudication. Subsequently, the section examines how the carbon labels presented in section 2 are evaluated under WTO rules. The assessment of the extent to which incentives under WTO rules follows law and economic insights will be made in the final section of this chapter.

WTO members may adopt various regulatory measures to address climate change. These include but are not limited to carbon tax, carbon footprint measurement, carbon label, carbon verification and certification, and so on. Unavoidably, such measures have an impact on international trade. WTO members who intend to implement carbon label measures should secure their compliance with WTO rules.

4.1 Applicability of the TBT to Npr-PPM Measures and its Relevance to Carbon Label

The relevant agreement for regulatory measures addressing climate change is the Technical Barriers to Trade Agreement (TBT). As far as the regulatory measures are addressing the carbon aspect of a product, the controversial issue of process and production methods (PPMs) arises.

PPM is normally understood as the way in which products are manufactured or processed and natural resources extracted or harvested. The WTO Agreement does not define PPM, nor does it explain the meaning of PPM in any other way. There is concern among developing countries in particular that PPMs might be abused for protectionist purposes. From the perspective of trade regulation, PPM measures are commonly divided into two categories: product-related and non-product-related, also known as incorporated and non-incorporated PPMs. Product-related

PPMs (pr-PPMs) are PPMs which leave a physical impact, that is traces in the final product. Non-product-related PPMs (npr-PPMs), which address production externalities, are linked to the non-physical aspects of a product and do not leave any traces in the final product. Developing countries would like to, in particular, keep npr-PPMs out of the WTO system, that is cases in which there is no way to distinguish how a final product was produced.

In the era of the General Agreement on Tariffs and Trade (GATT), making distinctions between products for regulatory purposes based on non-product-related characteristics, such as the production process, was viewed as illegal per se.[28] It has been a widely held belief that GATT does not permit national measures linked to aspects other than the physical characteristics of a product.[29]

However, some argue that such an approach is too stringent and it hinders governments from fulfilling their legitimate social policy goals. Viewing this from an environmental perspective, the denial of legality to PPM-related environmental measures under WTO law is seen as flawed.[30] Thus far the Dispute Settlement Body (DSB) has not eliminated the possibility of distinguishing products based on npr–PPMs. Given the fact that the second sentence of Annex 1.1 of the TBT includes explicit reference to label measures – 'It may also include or deal exclusively with terminology, symbols, packaging, marking or *labelling requirements* as they apply to a product, process or production method' – it is safe to conclude that both TBT rules and jurisprudence[31] reveal that the TBT applies to npr-PPMs, and therefore to all carbon label measures.

4.2 Mandatory/Voluntary Carbon Label Measures

The next question is, which articles of the TBT apply to carbon label measures. The TBT divides regulatory measures into technical regulations (which are mandatory) and standards (which are voluntary). Mandatory measures will be assessed according to TBT rules governing 'technical regulation' (mainly Article 2), while voluntary measures will be examined according to TBT provisions governing 'standard' (mainly Article 4 and Annex 3).

---

28 Hudec (1998).
29 Holzer (2014), p. 94.
30 Charnovitz (2002).
31 See Panel Report, *US–TUNA II (MEXICO)*, paras 7.78–7.79.

In *EC – Asbestos* and *EC – Sardines*,[32] the Appellate Body established a three-step test to determine if a measure is a technical regulation or a standard. Based on this test, a carbon label measure will fall under the scope of TBT 'technical regulation' if it (1) applies to an identifiable product or group of products, (2) lays down one or more characteristics of the product, and (3) is 'mandatory' in the sense that it is issued by a legislative body. This test was further developed in *US–Tuna II (Mexico)*, where American regulatory measures regarding a 'dolphin-safe' label on tuna products were challenged. In this case, the Appellate Body found that:

> Certain features exhibited by a measure may be common to both technical regulations falling within the scope of Article 2 of the TBT Agreement and, for example, standards falling under Article 4 of that Agreement. Both types of measures could, for instance, contain conditions that must be met in order to use a label. In both cases, those conditions could be 'compulsory' or 'binding' and 'enforceable'. Such characteristics, taken alone, cannot therefore be dispositive of the proper legal characterization of the measure under the TBT Agreement. Instead, it will be necessary to consider additional characteristics of the measure in order to determine the disciplines to which it is subject under that Agreement.[33]

Here the Appellate Body laid down four factors which will be used to distinguish mandatory technical regulation and voluntary standards. These are (1) whether the measure consists of a law or a regulation enacted by a WTO Member, (2) whether it prescribes or prohibits particular conduct, (3) whether it sets out specific requirements that constitute the sole means of addressing a particular matter, and (4) the nature of the matter addressed by the measure.

Based on this jurisprudence, if a carbon label measure is composed of legislative and regulatory acts of the State, especially if it sets out a single and legally mandated approach of carbon measurement and prohibits the usage of other similar labels, it will amount to a mandatory measure and will be regarded as technical regulation. And if that is the case, Article 2 of the TBT will apply and governs such carbon label measures. Otherwise it will be regarded as a voluntary measure and Article 4 and Annex 3 apply.

Among the selected carbon labels, the Indice Carbone of the French Casino Retailer, the Carbonfund label and the Climatop label are all private labels.[34] WTO agreements do not directly regulate measures

---

32 Appellate Body Report, *EC – Sardines*, para. 176, citing Appellate Body Report, *EC – Asbestos*, paras 66–70.

33 Appellate Body Report, *US–Tuna II (Mexico)*, para. 188.

34 Guenther, Saunders and Tait (2012).

carried out by private organs; currently the legitimacy of such private measures is a controversial topic that is far from being settled, and thus the legitimacy of such measures goes beyond the scope of this chapter. But if in the future the above-mentioned private carbon label measures are implemented by a public organ, as in the case of the Carbon Trust label, they may amount to mandatory measures if they are 'legislative and regulatory acts of the state' and if they 'set out a single and legally mandated approach' to carbon measurement and labelling. If this is the case, the labels will be assessed by TBT Article 2. In the following section we will focus on these potential mandatory carbon label measures and assess their compliance with TBT Article 2.

4.3 Discrimination against Foreign Like Products

As far as legitimacy of carbon labels is concerned, one of the most important analyses is whether foreign like products are discriminated against. TBT Article 2.1 provides that 'Members shall ensure that in respect of technical regulations, products imported from the territory of any Member shall be accorded treatment no less favourable than that accorded to like products of national origin and to like products originating in any other country'. Suppose a technical regulation grants different treatments to carbon-light and carbon-intensive products; does it breach the non-discriminatory principle of TBT Article 2.1? To answer this question, two issues have to be addressed. The first one is whether the carbon-light and carbon-intensive products are like products. The second issue is whether foreign carbon-intensive products are treated in an unfavourable way. If the answer to both questions is yes, then there might be a breach of TBT Article 2.1, unless such unfavourable treatment of foreign products amounts to a 'legitimate regulatory distinction'.

Whether carbon-light and carbon-intensive products are like products. Whether two products are like products has to be decided on a case-by-case basis. In *EC – Asbestos* the Appellate Body made it clear that four characteristics should be used to identify like products under GATT. These are (1) the physical properties of the products, (2) the extent to which the products are capable of serving the same or similar end-uses, (3) the extent to which consumers perceive and treat the products as alternative means of performing particular functions in order to satisfy a particular want or demand, and (4) the international classification of the products for tariff purposes.[35] In *US–Tuna II (Mexico)* the Panel interpreted the

[35] WT/DS135/AB/R, para. 101.

term 'like products' in TBT 2.1 in the same way as in GATT 3.4 and its related jurisprudence. Within these four criteria, the only one which may distinguish a carbon-light product from a carbon-intensive product is the third one, that is the extent to which consumers perceive and treat the products as alternative means of performing particular functions in order to satisfy a particular demand.

In this respect, *US–Tuna II (Mexico)* jurisprudence is highly relevant because it also involves npr-PPMs (the way tuna is harvested). In this case, Mexico claimed that the method of fishing and the geographic region in which the tuna were caught were unincorporated PPMs that were not relevant to the like products determination. The panel observed that:

> The information presented to the Panel does suggest that US consumers have certain preferences with respect to tuna products, based on their dolphin-safe status, and we do not exclude that such preferences may be relevant to an assessment of likeness. To the extent that consumer preferences, including preferences relating to the manner in which the product has been obtained, may have an impact on the competitive relationship between these products, we consider it a priori relevant to take them into consideration in an assessment of the likeness. However, we are not persuaded that, in the circumstances of this case, a consideration of US consumer preferences relating to the dolphin-safe status of tuna products should lead us to modify our conclusion with respect to the likeness of US and Mexican tuna products and tuna products originating in any other country.[36]

It is clear from the *US–Tuna II (Mexico)* ruling and other adjudications[37] that consumers' perception is an indispensable element in the analysis of 'likeness'. Products which are the same in any other aspects except for npr-PPMs can therefore still be distinguished. Therefore, there is a possibility that, where there is significant evidence showing consumers' perception and preference toward a carbon-light product, DSB may declare that carbon-light products and carbon-intensive products are not like products. However, the panel in *US–Tuna II (Mexico)* did not elaborate on how strong such evidence has to be in order to affect 'likeness'. We are of the opinion that a competitive relationship is the core issue in the analysis of 'likeness'. To judge whether two products compete, it helps to observe whether they can substitute for each other. From the competition

---

[36] Panel report, *US–Tuna II (Mexico)*, para. 7.249.

[37] In *EC – Asbestos*, the Appellate Body made it clear that is was inappropriate for the Panel to express a 'conclusion' after examining only one of the four criteria without examining the evidence relating to each of those four criteria, weighing all of that evidence and making an overall determination. See WT/DS135/AB/R, para. 109.

perspective, carbon 'content' does not affect the function of a product at all. It is therefore fair to conclude that a carbon-light product and a carbon-intensive product may substitute for each other, and are therefore highly likely to be deemed as 'like products'. The possibility of them being declared 'unlike' is slim.

Whether foreign carbon-intensive products are treated less favourably under carbon label measures. If foreign like products are treated less favourably, the measure is presumed to breach the non-discrimination principle. The 'less favourable treatment' issue is decided by a two-step examination. First, the DSB examines if the measure at issue modifies the conditions of competition to the detriment of products from the exporting country as compared to domestic products or like products originating in any other Member. Second, the DSB will review whether any detrimental impact reflects discrimination against the products or the exporting country.[38] It will also examine the causal link between the measure at issue and the detriment sustained by the exporting country, in order to find out if the detriment stems exclusively from the measure.

US–Tuna II (Mexico) shed light on how to carry out this analysis. In this case the measure prohibits any seller from including on the label of tuna products the term 'dolphin-safe' or any other terms with a similar message if the tuna is harvested by a vessel in a fishery other than as described by the law. The Appellate Body concluded that foreign products were 'not eligible for inclusion in a dolphin-safe product under the US dolphin-safe labelling provisions, while most tuna caught by US vessels is potentially eligible for the label', and 'the lack of access to the "dolphin-safe" label of tuna products containing tuna caught by setting on dolphins has a detrimental impact on the competitive opportunities of Mexican tuna products in the US market'.[39] Additionally:

> It is the measure at issue, rather than private actors, that denies most Mexican tuna products access to a "dolphin-safe" label in the US market. The fact that the detrimental impact on Mexican tuna products may involve some element of private choice does not, in our view, relieve the United States of responsibility under the TBT Agreement, where the measure it adopts modifies the conditions of competition to the detriment of Mexican tuna products. [40]

If the difference in labelling conditions is not "calibrated" to the risks to dolphins arising from different fishing methods in different areas of

---

38 Appellate Body Report, *US–Tuna II (Mexico)*, para. 231.
39 Appellate Body Report, *US–Tuna II (Mexico)*, paras 234–235.
40 Appellate Body Report, *US–Tuna II (Mexico)*, paras 234–235.

the ocean, the sustained detriment of foreign like products constitutes discrimination.[41]

As far as carbon labels are concerned, if a carbon label favours carbon-light products and works against carbon-intensive products, where most imported products are carbon-intensive products and most domestic products are carbon-light products, such technical regulation will undoubtedly modify the conditions of competition to the detriment of foreign products. However, whether such detriment constitutes discrimination largely depends on how the measure is designed, especially, whether such distinction calibrates at the risks of climate change. With limited information regarding the selected carbon labels, for example whether they are based on risk assessment, whether the distinction between carbon-light products and carbon-intensive products is 'calibrated at' climate change risk, we are not in a proper position to carry out a detailed analysis on this issue. However, it is still possible to make some recommendations which may enhance the legitimacy of carbon labels. Now that TBT Article 2.1 allows 'legitimate regulatory distinction', well-designed carbon labels that disfavour foreign carbon-intensive products may still amount to 'legitimate regulatory distinction' as long as they calibrate at the risk of climate change. To be qualified for such 'legitimate regulatory distinction', risk assessment to show the difference of risks posed by carbon-light products and carbon-intensive products should be carried out in advance of the label being introduced. Without this evidence, it will be hard to justify the unfavourable treatment of foreign carbon-intensive products. It is also very important that a carbon label measure must be even-handed and origin-neutral.

4.4 The Necessity Test and Legitimacy of Carbon Label Measures under TBT

The necessity test is another important constraint on domestic regulatory measures. The necessity test is established in both GATT (Article XX) and TBT (Article 2.2). The necessity test does not allow domestic regulatory measures to go beyond what is necessary to achieve the objective. In WTO jurisprudence, the necessity test under GATT has been more frequently applied and its analytical framework has evolved from 'least trade-restrictive' criteria to a more balanced and complicated three-tier criteria, that is (1) suitability, (2) necessity and (3) *stricto sensu* proportionality.[42]

---

41 Appellate Body Report, *US–Tuna II (Mexico)*, para. 297.
42 See *EC – Asbestos* and *Brazil–Retreaded Tyres*.

As regards the necessity test under the TBT, with the removal of tariff barriers and the flourishing of non-tariff-based trade barriers, one may expect that the necessity test will be used more often to regulate domestic regulatory measures such as environmental technical regulations. Under the TBT agreement, the necessity test is established by Article 2.2, which provides that:

> Members shall ensure that technical regulations are not prepared, adopted or applied with a view to or with the effect of creating unnecessary obstacles to international trade. For this purpose, technical regulations shall not be more trade-restrictive than necessary to fulfil a legitimate objective, taking account of the risks non-fulfilment would create. Such legitimate objectives are, inter alia: national security requirements; the prevention of deceptive practices; protection of human health or safety, animal or plant life or health, or the environment. In assessing such risks, relevant elements of consideration are, inter alia: available scientific and technical information, related processing technology or intended end-uses of products.

Compared with GATT Article XX, the necessity test under TBT Article 2.2 is more sophisticated. It is also worth mentioning that TBT Article 2.2 differs from GATT Article XX in its wording and the nature of the Article, as well as the structure of the treaty as a whole. These differences give the TBT necessity test several unique attributes:

(1) The burden of proof under the TBT Article 2.2 necessity test mainly falls on the complainant, who has to demonstrate that the measure creates unnecessary obstacles to international trade. By contrast, the necessity test under GATT Article XX is in the form of an exceptional clause, on which the defendant has to rely and demonstrate the necessity of the measure.
(2) The TBT necessity test has a risk assessment requirement to evaluate the nature and consequence of the risk.
(3) According to TBT Article 2.5, if a technical regulation is 'in accordance with relevant international standards, it is subject to the rebuttable presumption not to create an unnecessary obstacle to international trade'. No such rebuttal exists under GATT.

However, with very limited rulings made under the TBT, the analytical framework is far from clear. Since 2012, with the circulation of a few TBT case reports, namely *US–CLOVE*, *US–TUNA II (MEXICO)*, *US–COOL*, *EU – Seal products*, the TBT necessity test has begun to take shape. As revealed by DSB reports, the TBT necessity test has something in common with the necessity test under GATT, but it also has its own characteristics. The overall analytical framework of the TBT necessity test follows the GATT necessity test and includes (1) suitability analysis (whether there is a real link between the measure and its objective), (2) analysis of the necessity of the measure (evaluating its objective against its impact on trade), and (3) whether there are reasonable alternative measures which may contribute to the same degree to the objectives but are less trade-restrictive.[43]

4.5 Carbon Label Measures and the TBT Necessity Test

Now that TBT Article 2.5 provides a rebuttable presumption for compliance with the necessity test, if a carbon label measure is in accordance with relevant international standards, that is ISO 14067-1 and 14067-2, it is presumed not to create an unnecessary obstacle to international trade. Selected carbon labels are mostly based on PAS 2050, which is not an international standard; therefore, the presumption for TBT necessity test compliance does not exist. As a result, all selected carbon labels have to undertake the TBT necessity test.

In order to find out whether the selected carbon labels may pass the TBT necessity test, we examine their object as well as their impact on trade. It is worth mentioning that WTO members enjoy a substantial degree of discretion in setting their own public policy objectives – the greater the contribution of a measure to the objective, the greater the tolerance shown by the WTO to its stringency.

Carbon labels have as their objective to deliver accurate and relevant carbon emission information to consumers so as to promote GHG emission reductions and combat climate change. These are legitimate objectives recognized by the TBT. Each is considered in turn.

First, does the carbon label in question deliver authentic and meaningful carbon information? Carbon labels provide information to consumers to enable them to take informed decisions. Carbon labels thereby aim to influence consumer behaviour, which in turn may incentivise producers to reduce GHG emissions. In order to be able to generate GHG emission reductions, carbon labels must provide consumers with authentic GHG emission information in such a way that it is easily understood by consumers.

Carbon label measures must provide consumers with authentic GHG emission information in the sense that it must be correct and credible. Credible and correct GHG emission information is closely related to the accuracy of measuring and the verification and certification mechanism

---

[43] Appellate Body Report, *US–Tuna II (Mexico)*, para. 322.

envisaged under the particular carbon label. Self-verification measures (Casino) do not offer much credibility, while independent third-party verification combined with self-certification does offer some measure of credibility (Carbon Trust Footprint Label). The strongest form of authenticity is attained through independent third-party verification and certification (Climatop).

The issue of credibility and correctness is, however, not limited to the accuracy of the measurement and verification. It also extends to the underlying methodology of the carbon label. Carbon neutrality labels are facing severe criticism due to their lack of effectiveness in reducing GHG emission. Carbon Trade Watch, an independent research institute in the Netherlands, pointed out in its 2007 report that carbon neutrality takes a 'business-as-usual' approach that does not contribute to combating climate change. They argue that carbon neutrality distracts people from making efforts to reduce carbon emissions; it also provides companies the opportunity to green-wash their products. Carbon neutrality labels (Carbonfund) are therefore not free from such criticism.

In order to influence consumer behaviour, carbon labels must provide meaningful and transparent information that is readily understood by consumers. Hartikainen et al. show that even in Finland where consumers are environmentally-minded, consumers have significant misunderstandings about the meaning of carbon footprint labels.[44] A large-scale survey shows that even consumers who know about carbon footprints do not really understand what this means.[45] Only 7 per cent of the interviewees link it to GHG emission during production, and as few as 5 per cent connect it with climate change. Therefore, the effectiveness of communication by a carbon label is important. For example, the Carbon Trust label only reports a numeric value for GHG emissions and does not deliver any comparative information concerning the product's ranking. Consumers may find it difficult to interpret this numeric information, and as a result they are unable to make meaningful purchasing decisions. Carbon labels that provide comparative information (by means of a commentary or a rating) thus enable consumers to make better-informed decisions (Indice Carbone, Climatop) than those that merely produce numeric or technical information (Carbon Trust).

Second, how trade-restrictive is the carbon label measure? Research shows that labels will entail costs for exporters. Taking eco labels as an example, such costs range from fees for eco labels to production facility

---

44 Hartikainen et al. (2014).
45 Hartikainen et al. (2014).

transaction costs, as well as costs incurred in translating foreign laws and regulations. These could amount to 20,000–30,000 dollars or more.[46] Table 10.3 shows other elements of carbon label measures which may have an impact on trade.

This table gives a general indication of the trade-restrictiveness of carbon label measures. The real impact on trade requires much more detailed information on a specific carbon label. The underlying perception is that making being granted a label a precondition for market access will be more trade-restrictive, particularly if third-party certification – in contrast to self-declarations, for example – is required. Labels that are non-mandatory are less trade-restrictive, and even more so if third-party certification is not required.

All the labels we consider here are non-mandatory, which means that they have only a small effect on trade. Although the Carbon Trust, the Carbonfund and Climatop all require third-party certification, there are still some differences that can be identified by reference to the degree to which consumers can use the information provided by the labels to compare products. Carbon Trust labels only offer a single numeric value of carbon emissions, while Climatop labels are only granted to the top 20 per cent of the 'best' products. The latter may therefore have a stronger appeal to consumers. The strongest appeal to consumers could come from the Carbonfund label, which is based on carbon neutrality. The least effect on consumer behaviour and trade is expected to come from the Casino Index. Even though it offers some measure of comparison between different products, it is not based on independent certification.

Third, are there are alternative measures to carbon labels? The last, but not least, element of the necessity test relates to the availability of alternative measures that are less trade-restrictive. If such alternative measures may contribute equally to the objective, then the challenged carbon labels will be regarded as being more trade-restrictive than necessary.

There are two leading TBT cases (*US–TUNA II (MEXICO)* and *US–COOL*) which look into labelling measures. Analysis of alternative measures in these cases explores the possibility of using voluntary standards and a mandatory trace-back regime instead of labelling. They provide valuable guidance for the assessment of carbon labels. In *US–TUNA II (MEXICO)*, Mexico argues that the US may initiate a voluntary dolphin-safe measure, which will enable other dolphin-safe standards and labels to be recognized. The US argues that Agreement on

---

[46] Joshi (2004).

the International Dolphin Conservation Program (AIDCP) standards or labels are not feasible alternative measures because they cannot protect dolphins to the same degree. The Appellant Body agreed with the US and rejected Mexico's argument that a voluntary standard was a feasible alternative measure. This ruling reveals that even though voluntary carbon labels are potentially less trade-restrictive, their contribution to climate change risk reduction might be less, and therefore they may not be an effective alternative measure to a mandatory carbon label. Of course, one should not jump to the conclusion that voluntary carbon label measures will never be deemed suitable as an alternative measure to a mandatory carbon label. In fact the issue of the suitability of an alternative measure very much depends on the context of a specific measure. For example, if a WTO member were to set an extremely high GHG emission reduction objective, a voluntary carbon label might not be considered an alternative to a mandatory label because it is not able to contribute as much as the latter does.

In *US–COOL*, DSB discussed whether a trace-back regime can be considered as an alternative measure for a US mandatory label of origin. A trace-back regime requires the retailer to identify the origin of each piece of meat and pinpoint it accurately to the farm or even the processing facility. The US argues that this regime is more expensive than COOL because it would inflate the costs of the entire supply chain. It is a pity that the Appellant Body did not rule on this issue due to lack of detailed information about cost, price and demand. We are of the opinion that the likely costs incurred in the supply chain will make it unlikely that a trace-back regime will be a viable alternative to a carbon label measure, particularly for non-mandatory carbon label schemes.

Given the issues surrounding the specific context of the measure in question, it is hard to reach a conclusion as to whether a carbon label measure may pass the TBT Necessity test, because the test concerns not only the level of protection pursued by the objective, but also the availability of less trade-restrictive alternative measures. However, Tables 10.3 and 10.4 shed light on how a better-designed carbon label measure may enhance its TBT compliance.

Among all selected carbon labels, Climatop works the best to deliver credible and meaningful information to the customer. It lays down a solid foundation to enable customers to choose products that support GHG emission reduction. Now that carbon label measures are distinctive from other regulatory measures in the way they combat climate change – that is they are designed to affect consumers' behaviour – we believe that Climatop represents the model which should be followed, even though it is not the least trade-restrictive.

Table 10.4 *The TBT necessity test*

	Casino Index	Carbon Trust	Climatop	Carbonfund
Credible and correct information	+	++	+++	+/–
Meaningful information	+++	+	+++	++
Least trade-restrictive	+++	++	+	+
Overall	7	5	5	3

Note: The larger the number of plusses, the higher the evaluation of the labels.

5. COMPARATIVE AND CONCLUDING REMARKS

The analysis of carbon labels from a law and economics and a WTO law perspective reveals that the line of reasoning and the inherent incentive structures are quite different. Under WTO law rules the Casino Index and Climatop labels are evaluated positively, while the Carbonfund label is ranked lowest. From a law and economics perspective the situation is different. Here the Carbonfund label is evaluated positively, while Casino Index and Climatop labels are less well received. Economic considerations under WTO law mainly come to bear in the context of the necessity test and when the trade-restrictiveness of the measure is examined. Other efficiency considerations do not enter the legal analysis. It is therefore not surprising that the analysis points in different directions.

Given that the WTO legal framework is inherently intergovernmental, it is not surprising that it respects the sovereignty of its members. It therefore takes the policy objectives as granted and evaluates whether the proposed measures could be less trade-restrictive while still meeting the policy objective to the same degree. Using a law and economics approach, the measure itself is examined on the basis of additional efficiency criteria that are not considered under WTO rules. Consequently, less-trade-restrictive measures – but also more-trade-restrictive measures, provided they are more efficient – can be considered under a law and economics approach. It therefore appears that the WTO rules are as open to efficient measures as they are to less-efficient ones. There is thus no inherent guidance towards efficient measures present in the WTO rules as far as carbon labels are concerned.

Besides these insights, we also identified a few issues regarding the recent advances under WTO rules on labelling. We believe that carbon label measures are purporting to achieve objectives such as providing consumers with authentic and meaningful information, reducing GHG emissions and protecting the environment. All these objectives are recognized by the TBT Agreement. However, imperfect design of carbon label measures may negatively impact or even hinder fulfilment of the label's objectives. Based on the above observations, there are a number of recommendations which may significantly enhance the compatibility of carbon label measures with the TBT necessity test.

First, carbon label measures must calibrate to the objective of providing consumers with authentic and meaningful GHG emission information. To achieve this, commentary/rating information is preferred over numeric/technical information. Independent third-party verification and certification is also preferred because they may significantly enhance the authenticity and credibility of GHG emission information. In these aspects, the Climatop label sets a good example for carbon label measures.

Second, carbon label designers should avoid defects which may diminish the effectiveness of carbon label measures. The *US–COOL* ruling is helpful and informative in this respect. The measure in this case is a label of origin (COOL) for pork and beef. The Appellant Body ruled that COOL cannot deliver information to consumers effectively. Its unsuitability manifests itself, inter alia, in flexibility in enforcement, ambiguity in information communication and significant exemption at retail level. On one hand, the label incurred high costs for upstream producers who have to keep and transfer all origin-related information; on the other hand, the information delivered to the consumers is either oversimplified or ambiguous. The lesson we can draw from this case is that carbon label measures should avoid ambiguous information and sweeping exemptions.

Third, the fact that different carbon labels are not directly comparable means that carbon label measures still have a long way to go before they can promote GHG emission reduction in a powerful way.[47] In this regard, countries should sit down and discuss the harmonization of carbon footprint standards. If standard conflicts cannot be solved, the more carbon labels emerge, the more incomparable information will flood into the market. As a result, rather than leading consumers toward combating GHG emission, this flood of incomparable information will turn out to be a source of confusion.[48] Conflicting and incomparable information, accompanied by high expenses arising from verification and certification, will render carbon label

47 See Liu, Wang and Su (2016).
48 Hann (2013).

measures fragile when reviewed by the TBT necessity test, because the high cost cannot be justified by their contribution to the objectives.

REFERENCES

Akerlof, G. (1970) 'The Market for Lemons: Quality, Uncertainty and the Market Mechanism', *Quarterly Journal of Economics*, 85, 488–500.

Appellate Body Report, *Brazil – Measures Affecting Imports of Retreaded Tyres*, WT/DS332/AB/R, adopted 17 December 2007, DSR 2007:IV, p. 1527.

Appellate Body Report, *European Communities – Measures Affecting Asbestos and Asbestos-Containing Products*, WT/DS135/AB/R, adopted 5 April 2001, DSR 2001:VII, p. 3243.

Appellate Body Reports, *European Communities – Measures Prohibiting the Importation and Marketing of Seal Products*, WT/DS400/AB/R / WT/DS401/AB/R, adopted 18 June 2014, DSR 2014:I, p. 7.

Appellate Body Report, *European Communities – Trade Description of Sardines*, WT/DS231/AB/R, adopted 23 October 2002, DSR 2002:VIII, p. 3359.

Appellate Body Reports, *United States – Certain Country of Origin Labelling (COOL) Requirements*, WT/DS384/AB/R / WT/DS386/AB/R, adopted 23 July 2012, DSR 2012:V, p. 2449.

Appellate Body Report, *United States – Measures Affecting the Production and Sale of Clove Cigarettes*, WT/DS406/AB/R, adopted 24 April 2012, DSR 2012: XI, p. 5751.

Appellate Body Report, *United States – Measures Concerning the Importation, Marketing and Sale of Tuna and Tuna Products*, WT/DS381/AB/R, adopted 13 June 2012, DSR 2012:IV, p. 1837.

Averch, H. and Johnson, L.L. (1962) 'Behaviour of the Firm under Regulatory Constraints', *American Economic Review*, 52(5), 1052–69.

Baumol, W.J. and Oates, W.E. (1971) 'The Use of Standards and Prices for Protection of the Environment', *Swedish Journal of Economics*, 73(1), 42–54.

Bolwig, S. and Gibbon, P. (2009) Counting Carbon in the Marketplace: Part 1 – Overview Paper: Report for the OECD. Trade and Agriculture Directorate; Joint Working Party on Trade and Environment.

Charnovitz, S. (2002) 'The Law of Environmental "PPMs" in the WTO: Debunking the Myth of Illegality', *Yale Journal of International Law*, 27, 59–110.

Cooter, R. and Ulen, T. (2004) *Law & Economics*, fourth edition, Pearson, Addison Wesley, Boston, MA.

Cullis, J. and Jones, P. (1998) *Public Finance and Public Choice*, second edition, Oxford University Press, Oxford.

Dispute DS381, United States – Measures Concerning the Importation, Marketing and Sale of Tuna and Tuna Products, Case brief, see https://www.wto.org/english/tratop_e/dispu_e/cases_e/ds381_e.htm, last visit 18 April 2015.

Ernst and Young (2011) Product Carbon Footprinting – a Study on Methodologies and Initiatives, Final Report, available at http://www.saiplatform.org/uploads/Library/Ernst%20and%20Young%20Review.pdf.

Frank, R. (1997) *Microeconomics and Behaviour*, third edition, Irwin McGraw-Hill, Boston, MA.

Guenther, M., Saunders, C.M. and Tait, P.R. (2012) 'Carbon Labeling and

Consumer Attitudes', *Carbon Management*, 3(5), 445–55, DOI: 10.4155/cmt.12.50.
Hann, S. (2013) 'Eco Labelling Is Dead, Long Live the Eco Label', available at http://www.isonomia.co.uk/?p=1719, last visit 21 March 2017.
Hartikainen, H., Roininen, T., Katajajuuri, J.-M. and Pulkkinen, H. (2014) 'Finnish Consumer Perceptions of Carbon Footprints and Carbon Labelling of Food Products', *Journal of Cleaner Production*, 73, 285–93.
Holzer, K. (2014) *Carbon-Related Border Adjustment and WTO Law*, Edward Elgar, Cheltenham.
Hudec, R. (1998) 'GATT/WTO Constraints on National Regulation: Requiem for an "Aim and Effects" Test', available at www.worldtradelaw.net/articles/hudecrequiem.pdf, last visit 21 March 2017.
Joshi, M. (2004) 'Are Eco-Labels Consistent with World Trade Organization Agreements?' *Journal of World Trade*, 38(1), 69–92.
Kuik, O. and Hofkes, M. (2010) 'Border Adjustment for European Emissions Trading: Competitiveness and Carbon Leakage', Energy Policy, 38(4), 1741–8.
Liu, T., Wang, Q. and Su, B. (2016) 'A Review of Carbon Labeling: Standards, Implementation, and Impact', *Renewable and Sustainable Energy Reviews*, 53, 68–79.
Niskanen, W.A. (1968) 'The Peculiar Economics of Bureaucracy', *American Economic Review*, 57(1), 293–321.
Niskanen, W.A. (1971) *Bureaucracy and Representative Government*, Aldine-Atherton, New York.
Olson, M. Jr. (1975) *The Logic of Collective Action: Public Goods and the Theory of Groups*, Harvard University Press, Cambridge, MA.
Pelzman, S. (1976) 'Towards a More General Theory of Regulation', *Journal of Law and Economics*, 19, 211–40.
Philipsen, N. (2003) *Regulation of and by Pharmacists in the Netherlands and Belgium: An Economic Approach*, Intersentia, Antwerp.
Philipsen, N. (2007) 'The Law and Economics of Professional Regulation: What Does the Theory Teach China?', in Eger, T., Faure, M. and Naigen, Z. (eds), *Economic Analysis of Law in China*, Edward Elgar (online), 122–50.
Pigou, A.C. (1949) *A Study in Public Finance*, third (revised) edition (first published in 1928), Macmillan & Co., London.
Posner, R.A. (1975) 'The Social Costs of Monopoly and Regulation', *Journal of Political Economy*, 83(4), 807–27.
Schaefer, F. and Blanke, M. (2014) 'Opportunities and Challenges of Carbon Footprint, Climate or CO_2 Labelling for Horticultural Products', *Erwerbs-Obstbau*, 56, 73–80.
Stigler, G. (1971) 'The Theory of Economic Regulation', *Bell Journal of Economics and Management Science*, 3, 3–21.
Tollison, R.D. (1982) 'Rent Seeking: A Survey', *Kyklos*, 35(4), 575–602.
WT/DS135/AB/R European Communities – Measures Affecting Asbestos and Asbestos-Containing Products, 12 March 2001 (01-1157).

PART IV

Research agenda

11. Empirical analysis of regulation: the promise of field experiments in China

Jonathan Klick

1. INTRODUCTION

The "empirical revolution" has been the most exciting and important development in law and economics since the beginning of the twenty-first century. Law and economics went from being a field where theory and intuition dominated, to becoming a more mature social science where empirical testing is central in its scholarship. This approach to research holds the prospect of providing useful insights regarding the effects of policies and regulations. The combination of sophisticated legal and institutional knowledge with systematic empirical methods provides reliable guidance to policymakers.

The movement toward empirical work in law and economics was driven by improvements in research designs that allowed for more credible causal inferences to be made. These research designs rely primarily on so-called "natural experiments" to avoid the omitted variable bias problem that plagued earlier empirical work. Such methods, however, often require a stroke of luck as they exploit unplanned quasi-randomizations, leaving researchers with little to go on if proverbial lightning doesn't happen to strike in the policy domain where evaluations are needed. In these cases, we are back to theory, intuition, and poorly identified empirical work to provide policy advice that is often severely flawed.

Field experiments provide a promising alternative to the natural experiment approach, and China, with its large population, numerous jurisdictions, and active bureaucracy is well suited to implement systematic policy evaluations in the field. Such a program has the advantages of allowing for policy evaluations in real world settings without having to rely on the imperfect randomization that is studied in natural experiments. Additionally, field studies can be implemented on demand as opposed to relying on the serendipity that plays such a large role in quasi-experimental designs.

In this chapter I discuss the empirical revolution in law and economics, focusing on how it has made credible contributions to our understanding of the effects of regulations. I then discuss some of the shortcomings of the quasi-experimental approach that is at the core of modern empirical law and economics. Next I discuss how China could use field experiments to get an even more precise understanding of how regulations are likely to affect outcomes and behavior, providing a general roadmap of how such studies could be implemented.

2. THE EMPIRICAL REVOLUTION

While law and economics has been recognized as one of the most important innovations in legal scholarship during the second half of the twentieth century, for most of its history its tools were almost exclusively those of microeconomic theory. Posner's seminal *Economic Analysis of Law* had virtually no references to empirical work in its 1973 first edition; even today's eighth edition has a low ratio of empirical references relative to the theory works cited. The famous law and economics names – Coase, Posner, Calabresi, Shavell, Polinsky, Cooter, and so on – are all primarily theorists, and the standard textbooks in the field are basically silent regarding any data related to the topics discussed in each chapter. Relatively few law and economics scholars in US law schools prior to 2000 did empirical work. In discussing the roots of this absence of empiricists, Bill Landes (one of the few members of the older generation who does some empirical work) noted, "[M]ost law professors regard empirical work as a form of drudgery not worthy of first-class minds."[1]

Part of what motivated this institutional preference against empirical work was almost surely the fact that much empirical work that was being done was simply not very good. The practice of the time was to attempt to isolate causal relationships between laws and behavior or regulations and outcomes by trying to control for as many confounding factors as was convenient. This so-called control function approach, in principle, is perfectly reasonable. If it is literally the case that a researcher controls for every factor involved in generating an outcome in the regression, then all estimated coefficients can be interpreted causally. However, in practice this approach is doomed to fail. First, no researcher can know all of the factors that influence an outcome. Second, even if he did, many of those factors will be difficult, if not impossible, to quantify. Lastly,

1 Landes (2003).

even if the factors are known and quantifiable, data availability problems would often impede the researcher from being able to carry out this ideal regression.

Although everyone was aware of these problems, most empirical research was carried out with the implicit belief that effort was enough to overcome these problems. A good empirical paper was one that simply controlled for more stuff than the last paper written on the topic. While correlation wasn't causation, correlation conditional on a subset of the most important covariates (which was defined, roughly, as whatever data the researcher could find) was close enough for academic work. In such an environment, empirical papers were written, but it was wise not to believe their results. Recognizing this, Ed Leamer pleaded for increased transparency and humility, calling the standard practice a "con."[2] But since not much credence was given to the work anyway, con doesn't seem to be the right word. Perhaps more accurately (if metaphorically), empirical work was like masturbation: after a little work, and a little mess, you could see an outcome, even if it wasn't all that fulfilling – and it was probably better kept private. Given that, maybe it's not too surprising that law schools were not enamored with empirical work.

The situation began to change in the mid to late 1990s, riding the wave of what Josh Angrist has dubbed the "credibility revolution,"[3] empirical law and economics scholars started exploiting "natural" or "quasi" experiments to identify the causal effects of laws and regulations on behavioral outcomes. In addition to yielding more credible outcomes, this new approach is more intuitively accessible, combining to make the work and the scholars doing it more attractive to law school faculties.[4]

The fundamental problem of empirical studies using observational (that is, non-experimental) data is that they will contain some variety of the omitted variable bias.[5] This problem goes by many names – endogeneity, simultaneity, self-selection, reverse causality, and so on – but it all boils down to leaving out important variables that confound the estimation of the causal effect of interest (e.g., the effect of regulation x on behavioral outcome y). Formally, this problem arises when the research leaves out some variable (or variables) that helps determine the outcome (after all the effects of all of the included variables are controlled for) and the left-out

2 Leamer (1983).
3 Angrist and Pischke (2010).
4 For more on this aspect, see Klick (2011).
5 For a more detailed discussion of these issues, see Gelbach and Klick (2014).

variable (or variables) is correlated with the policy variable of interest (after controlling for the effects of all of the included variables).

This deceptively simple problem is ubiquitous. For virtually all outcomes, it is not clear a priori to the researcher which variables determine the outcome of interest, and it is equally unlikely that the researcher knows what subset of those variables is correlated with the policy of interest. Further, even if such knowledge existed, many of the relevant variables would be unquantifiable, or at least the researcher would not have data for all of the variables.

In the old approach, after controlling for whatever variables were at hand, researchers would suggest that because more could not be done, the estimated results were as good as it gets, and in any case, since the current approach controls for more stuff than the last paper on the topic, it is better. Unfortunately, there is an empirical analog to the theory of the second best.[6] If some but not all of the omitted variables leading to an omitted variable bias are controlled for, including more of those omitted variables can move the parameter estimate closer to or further away from the unbiased value of the parameter relative to the estimate that arises when fewer of the omitted variables are controlled for. What's worse, it is not possible to know whether the estimate has gotten better or worse.

Others in the old approach would begrudgingly admit the bias in their estimates, but then would provide some intuition for the direction, and perhaps even the magnitude, of the bias so as to be able to give a rough correction of the estimate. This too was largely folly, since any such correction requires knowledge of the conditional correlations between the omitted variables and the policy of interest, as well as the conditional correlations with the outcome being studied. Essentially this is question-begging, since, by and large, the entire reason the omitted variable bias arose in the first place was because the researcher did not have the relevant data. Thus, making claims about conditional correlations of non-existent data would seem to be simply making things up.

The newer, more credible[7] approach exploits a natural or quasi-randomizing shock which affects the treatment status (i.e., whether some entity is affected by a policy-relevant variable) of individuals (or firms, jurisdictions, etc.) and examines how some behavioral outcome changes

---

6 Lipsey and Lancaster (1956).

7 For an excellent and wide-ranging discussion of how much more credible the new work actually is, see the symposium "Con Out of Economics" in the Spring 2010 issue of the *Journal of Economics Perspectives*, which, in addition to the Angrist and Pischke piece, has important critiques from Ed Leamer and a number of others.

for those affected after the shock relative to their behavior prior to the shock. Further, to net out any background trend, the same before and after comparison is made for similar entities that are not affected by the shock. This comparison group is the analog to the "control" group in a true randomized experiment. Because there is no true randomization, special care must be taken to ensure that the chosen comparison group is indeed comparable.[8]

When the examined shock occurs just once, the study is often referred to as a differences-in-differences study. If various shocks occur over time, the general approach is referred to as a fixed effects model (which can be thought of as estimating the policy coefficient of interest as averaging over a series of differences-in-differences comparisons).

If the shock is plausibly random (relative to the behavioral outcome of interest) and if the comparison groups are plausibly comparable, the estimated treatment effect is plausible (or credible) as well. From a communication standpoint, this methodological approach is much more easily explained to a non-expert audience than discussing the control function approach. From the perspective of reliability, this approach relies on seemingly more plausible assumptions than the control function approach, or at least more transparent assumptions, as it is fairly simple for an audience to consider the assertion that the shock is random and that the comparison groups are sufficiently similar.

This approach has led to successes in a number of literatures that have, in turn, improved actual public policy. One such literature is the work on police and crime. While the old work in this topic generated crazy results that were widely dismissed,[9] the quasi-experimental work[10] has been very well received.

3. THE VALUE OF REAL EXPERIMENTS

However, despite the successes of the natural or quasi-experimental approach, there are at least two drawbacks. First, as discussed above,

---

[8] This is easier said than done. The necessary comparability applies both to observable and unobservable characteristics. In an actual randomized experiment, the randomization ensures this. In a natural or quasi-experimental design, this is necessarily an assumption, since comparability on unobservable characteristics cannot be verified.

[9] For a survey of the older work, see Cameron (1988).

[10] See, for example, Klick and Tabarrok (2005), MacDonald, Klick and Grunwald (2016) and Evans and Owens (2007).

the assumptions that the shock is truly conditionally random and that the comparison groups are sufficiently similar are untestable. While it is true that every research design relies on some assumptions, this surely limits confidence in this approach. Second, this approach relies on lucky happenstance in terms of finding a usable shock that is related to the research question. There will be some questions that simply do not benefit from the required shock, but need to be addressed anyway.

Actual experiments have the potential to address these shortcomings. In a truly randomized experiment, the first concern goes away since the policy treatment is randomized. Further, since the researcher himself is running the experiment, there is no longer the need to wait for lightning to strike – instead, the researcher throws the bolt down himself, and he can craft the shock to match whatever policy needs to be studied. The shortcoming of this kind of experiment, however, is one of external validity. How do we know that people in the lab act like people in the real world? The setting itself might make a difference. Further, if the people studied in the lab are different than the people to whom the policy will actually be applied, there is another concern about the relevance of the experimental results for guiding policy.

Field experiments have the potential to mitigate both of these external validity concerns. By randomizing the policy implementation (i.e., randomly choosing jurisdictions to serve as the treatment units and using the other jurisdictions as the comparison units) in the real world setting, one can get the best of both worlds – the internal validity (or reliability) of experiments and the external validity (or relevance) of the observational studies. John List has written extensively on the promise of field experiments and their implementation.[11] More generally, the value of learning from this kind of approach is highlighted by Abramowicz, Ayres, and Listokin, who advocate "randomizing law."[12]

China, in many ways, is uniquely suited to engage in systematic testing of regulations and policies. Its large population and numerous jurisdictional units make statistical power a foregone conclusion. Further, its well-functioning bureaucracy expedites implementation of and adherence to experimental designs. Taking such an approach to regulatory development could put China in a position where it can not only improve its own policies but also teach other countries about what works and what doesn't when it comes to policy design.

---

11 See http://home.uchicago.edu/~jlist/research2/methodology.html.

12 Abramowicz, Ayres and Listokin (2011).

4. CONCLUSION

Empirical policy analysis has improved substantially since the beginning of the twenty-first century. The use of natural or quasi-experimental research designs has improved the credibility and, therefore, usefulness of law and economics scholarship. However, these approaches are somewhat limited in that they rely on shocks that are outside of the researcher's control. This means that sometimes it is just not possible to study a particular policy of interest. Field experiments have the potential to remedy this shortcoming, and China may be uniquely suited to leverage field experiments to provide important insights for policymakers.

REFERENCES

Abramowicz, Michael, Ian Ayres and Yair Listokin (2011), "Randomizing Law," *University of Pennsylvania Law Review*, 159(4), 929–1005.

Angrist, Joshua D. and Jörn-Steffen Pischke (2010), "The Credibility Revolution in Empirical Economics: How Better Research Design Is Taking the Con out of Econometrics," *Journal of Economic Perspectives*, 24(2), 3–30.

Cameron, Samuel (1988), "The Economics of Crime Deterrence: A Survey of Theory and Evidence," *Kyklos*, 41(2), 301–23.

Evans, William N. and Emily G. Owens (2007), "COPS and Crime," *Journal of Public Economics*, 91, 181–201.

Gelbach, Jonah B. and Jonathan Klick (2014), "Empirical Law and Economics" in Francesco Parisi (ed.), *Oxford Handbook of Law and Economics*, available at http://ssrn.com/abstract=2507324.

Klick, Jonathan (2011), *The Empirical Revolution in Law and Economics*, Inaugural Lecture for Erasmus Chair in Empirical Legal Studies (Erasmus Law Lectures), Eleven International Publishing.

Klick, Jonathan and Alexander Tabarrok (2005), "Using Terror Alert Levels to Estimate the Effect of Police on Crime," *Journal of Law & Economics*, 48(1), 267–79.

Landes, William M. (2003), "The Empirical Side of Law & Economics," *University of Chicago Law Review*, 70(1), 167–80.

Leamer, Edward E. (1983), "Let's Take the Con out of Econometrics," *American Economic Review*, 73(1), 31–43.

Lipsey, R.G. and Kelvin Lancaster (1956), "The General Theory of Second Best," *Review of Economic Studies*, 24(1), 11–32.

MacDonald, John M., Jonathan Klick and Ben Grunwald (2016), "The Effect of Private Police on Crime: Evidence from a Geographic Regression Discontinuity Design," *Journal of the Royal Statistical Society: Series A (Statistics in Society)*, 179(3), 831–46.

12. Regulatory reform in China and the EU: comparative and concluding remarks

Niels Philipsen, Stefan E. Weishaar and Wenming Xu

1. BACKGROUND

In the introductory chapter we explained that this book is the result of a conference that was held in May 2015 in Beijing, organized by the School of Law and Economics (SLE) at the China University of Political Science and Law. That conference constituted a follow-up to three earlier conferences held in Beijing in 2012, 2013 and 2014, on economics and regulation in China, the role of law and regulation in sustaining financial markets, and market integration and implications for regulatory reform, respectively. The 2015 conference also marked the 10-year anniversary of SLE.

This book contains several contributions that examine how the regulatory state and regulatory reform could help to unleash the economic forces of China to foster more sustainable economic growth and prosperity[1] and to set out a reform agenda in selected legal areas. These areas include financial, administrative and environmental law and regulation, as well as regulation of contracts. This is particularly important considering that the Chinese government recently launched a national project to comprehensively deepen its regulatory reform that only sets out general principles.[2]

Several contributors take a comparative perspective and have selected the European Union or the United States as a reference point. In some cases this foreign experience suggests what Chinese legislators may wish to

[1] See the introduction to this book for an elaboration.

[2] See Decision of the Central Committee of the Communist Party of China on Some Major Issues Concerning Comprehensively Deepening the Reform (Zhonggong Zhongyang Guanyu Quanmian Shenhua Gaige Ruogan Zhongda Wenti de Jueding), adopted at the Third Plenary Session of the 18th Central Committee of the Communist Party of China, 12 November 2013 (PRC).

consider for China, while in others it can be insightful for Chinese legislators in pointing to pitfalls and problems that they may wish to avoid.

The predominant methodology relied upon by the authors to examine law and regulation and their effect on developments in China is law and economics. In addition, disciplines such as comparative law and financial economics were used, paying tribute to the fact that law and (economic) regulation are embedded in institutional environments that are influenced by a multitude of factors. Some authors went beyond positive analysis by providing carefully defined policy suggestions.

In this concluding chapter we seek to distil some central lessons from the analysis made in the previous chapters regarding regulation in China. The regulatory state is characterized by independent regulatory agencies which oversee specific areas of the economy. This entails that rule making and public enforcement attain a central role, but there may also be room for private enforcement when striving for optimal strategies for controlling businesses.

These lessons will therefore be grouped around the following overarching issues:

- Regulatory governance
- Actors: public, private, and self-enforcement
- Relevance of interdisciplinary research
- Reform agenda and recommendations.

We would like to point out that several of the more 'general' lessons presented below (and in the conclusions of the various chapters in this book) may also be relevant for regulators in other jurisdictions. This is more particularly the case where they follow from an application of the economic theory of regulation and the 'regulatory state' literature, both of which were briefly introduced in Chapter 1.

2. REGULATORY GOVERNANCE

Several chapters assessed issues of regulatory governance that are either executed by the state directly or by regulatory authorities. Tao Xi points out that the Law of Commercial Banks is only a subset of the financial regulatory system, which is embedded into a wider regulatory framework that impacts diverse socio-economic actors. Hence, one of the most important points in any regulatory endeavour is the recognition that the regulated area is not 'an island entire of itself', but that it forms part of a larger legal and economic system. This has implications for the (optimal) design of regulatory intervention.

In the economic literature explaining the so-called 'private interest approach to regulation', issues of regulatory capture, rent-seeking by private interest groups and public servants, and opportunities for corruption created by inefficient regulation are frequently discussed. It is therefore not surprising that these topics are also thematized by the authors who have contributed to this book when assessing how an active government could be combined with market competition. Niels Philipsen (in the context of State aid), as well as Stefan Weishaar and Ruohong Chen (in the context of environmental labels), warn of regulatory capture of institutions and rent-seeking behaviour by the regulator. Their findings are consistent with the public choice theory. In that respect, Niels Philipsen, when assessing State aid rules that are – inter alia – directed at curing market failures and avoiding wasteful government spending, reminds us that it is particularly difficult to maintain consistency with past decisions in the field of State aid law if there is a shift in the underlying policy goals. This is an assertion that can hold true equally for other policy areas.

Some authors are critical about specific practices of government organs or regulatory authorities. For example, Binwei Gui, Michael Faure and Guangdong Xu question the quality of official data and argue that at times data is manipulated to attain policy goals. The authors refer to this when examining the applicability of the environmental Kuznets curve hypothesis to China and the role of institutions in shaping the relationship between income and pollution. They find the counterintuitive result that pollution abatement measures increase rather than decrease pollution, that is that a greater number of pollution abatement measures leads to higher pollution levels, and suggest that poor data quality or data manipulation could be an explanation for this.

Regulatory governance also posits the question of accountability of the regulator. Tianshu Zhou and Wenjing Li point out that regulatory bodies can be extremely powerful. When examining insider trading, which has long been identified as a problematic issue in China's capital markets, they vividly show that there is little legal power that can be used against the regulatory authority: nearly all review cases are unsuccessful, implying that the regulatory body in essence is not subject to outside checks and balances. Accountability is particularly important in circumstances where corruption or the neutrality of the regulator is in doubt – as the authors show in the case of the China Securities Regulatory Commission. Such practices undermine the authority's credibility and hence the strength of the incentives that are being created by the regulation in place.

An essential part of any form of regulatory governance is of course enforcement of rules (which is discussed in section 3 below). Without enforcement there is no incentive to adhere to the rules, at least from a law and economics perspective. Binwei Gui, Michael Faure and Guangdong Xu find that that without a sound institutional framework, investments in pollution control will have no real effect on pollution abatement, which emphasizes the importance of effective implementation and enforcement mechanisms. The authors convincingly argue that the way institutional quality impacts the environment is different from that predicted by conventional theory. They show that institutional indicators affect pollution levels via the operational outcome of pollution abatement measures, rather than by affecting structural transformation or the volume of pollution abatement facilities.

3. ACTORS: PUBLIC, PRIVATE AND SELF-ENFORCEMENT

When seeking to reconcile an active government with market competition, the enforcement of legal rules becomes important. There is an array of different actors that can be instrumental in supporting regulation, and they mainly fall in three broad categories: public, private and self-enforcement.

Public enforcement is a central feature of regulatory agencies. Tianshu Zhou and Wenjing Li reveal the randomness in the (vague) legal standards employed by the China Security Regulatory Commission, calling into question the neutrality of the regulatory body in applying the law. They also point out that the scarcity of resources of the regulatory body impedes its enforcement capacities. Tao Xi, in his in-depth analysis of the Law of Commercial Banks in China, also posits that supervision of financial markets should be designed in line with the development of those markets.

Assessing offshore carbon capture and storage, Roy Partain and Michael Faure suggest that China could efficiently implement CCS regulations that rely on both public and private enforcement. Private enforcement via liability rules is identified as an important complement to regulation where the latter has become outdated or has fallen prey to regulatory capture.

Private enforcement is not only impeded by sometimes high burdens of legal proof but also by formal requirements and limited incentives to undertake legal action. Jiajia Dai, Shiting Feng and Wenming Xu look at the Chinese stock market, which is about to establish a registration system for initial public offerings. However, the private enforcement regime is restricted, because The Supreme People's Court of the People's Republic of China's 2002 Notice Regarding Accepting Tort Cases Arising from Stock Market False Disclosure requires that private action is only permitted following administrative or criminal sanctions. The authors show that private enforcement is ineffective if benefits to investors are too small to overcome the collective action problem; this is frequently the case for retail investors. Institutional investors by contrast value enforcement rights and are more likely to litigate. Institutional investors are also shown to be willing to pay a premium for litigating in jurisdictions where the court system operates with a high rate of efficiency.

4. RELEVANCE OF INTERDISCIPLINARY RESEARCH

Qi Zhou critically reflects upon the unjustifiable underrating of legal research in the mainstream law and economics literature. Qi convincingly shows that legal research has an important guiding and correcting function to play for law and economics research. He equally shows that more collaboration in the development of a Civil Law Code in China could help to unleash the economic forces to foster more sustainable economic growth and prosperity and to set out a reform agenda. Equally, Qi Zhou laments that few law and economics insights have found their way into Civil Law Code proposals and calls for more consideration to be made of law and economics insights. Taken together, this shows that more interdisciplinary research and a more holistic approach are needed to establish efficient regulatory reforms.

In this respect some of the points made by Niels Philipsen, in his application of the economic theory of federalism, can be highlighted and extrapolated. Namely, where there is a clear tension between efficiency and other, non-economic policy goals, a balancing of these interests would ideally require insights from both economics and law, as well as other disciplines such as sociology and anthropology. In addition, where conflicts between efficiency and other social values arise at the international level, one should be very careful in shifting regulation and enforcement to a higher regulatory level.

5. REFORM AGENDA AND RECOMMENDATIONS

Several authors expressly identify societal challenges and set a reform agenda for China. Looking at global warming and the domestic Chinese policy objectives, Roy Partain and Michael Faure posit that China should develop a regulatory framework to address carbon capture and storage and provide concrete suggestions for this purpose.

Analysing the importance of institutional investors in stabilizing capital markets, Jiye Hu and Yang Chen recommend the further strengthening of such investors and point out that the Chinese legislation is well on its way. They specifically stress the importance of internal control systems of investment management to safeguard pension funds and that insurance companies should not necessarily be bailed out in the event that they experience problems.

Johnathan Klick highlights the great possibilities for China to overcome methodological deficiencies of law and economics research by drawing upon its well-functioning bureaucracy, large population and numerous jurisdictional units. By basing its regulatory reform on randomized field experiments, China is uniquely suited to systematically test its regulations and policies, and this would provide important and robust lessons for other countries and jurisdictional units.

Niels Philipsen highlights that rules for avoiding wasteful spending of funds that distorts competition between undertakings do not exist in China, and that it might be worthwhile for the Chinese legislator to examine if such a system might not be valuable for fostering more competition.

Index